# STATES OF IRELAND

Conor Cruise O'Brien

# States of Ireland

**PANTHEON BOOKS**
A Division of Random House, New York

FIRST AMERICAN EDITION

*Library of Congress Cataloging in Publication Data*

O'Brien, Conor Cruise, 1917-
  States of Ireland.

  Includes bibliographical references.
  1. Ireland—History—20th century.   2. Northern Ireland—History.   I. Title
  DA959.019  1973      941.59      72-3415
  ISBN 0-394-47117-2

# Contents

To the Derry women who demanded peace, and especially to those women, bereaved by violence, who refused to allow their loss to be exploited for the perpetuation of violence.

# Acknowledgments

I am particularly grateful to Jack Dowling, Owen Dudley Edwards, and Michael and Nancy McInerney for having read this book over in proof and given me the benefit of their comments—based on long and perceptive study of Irish life and history, both North and South—thus helping me to revise the text significantly.

I myself remain solely responsible for any subsisting errors of fact, interpretation or emphasis.

More generally I should like to thank both the Northern and Southern members of the Movement for Peace in Ireland who, in many discussions, helped me and others to begin to realize how much there is that the main sections of the population of Ireland do not understand about one another.

There are many other friends—several of them named in the text—whom I would wish to thank for the light they have cast on various aspects of Irish life. The list would be long however and, as the interpretation in these pages is both highly personal and necessarily to some extent controversial, I felt I might well not be doing my friends a service by inserting a roll-call of their names at this point.

I should like, however, to make exceptions in the cases of Miss Norah Corringham and Mrs. Joan McMullen—for their unfailing helpfulness and patient care in typing from a difficult and crabbed manuscript—and Miss Frances McGuinness for help with research.

I thank also the authors and publishers of various works on which I have drawn, notably Bernadette Devlin, *The Price of My Soul*; Owen Dudley Edwards, *Sins of Our Fathers*; R. J. Lawrence, *The Government of Northern Ireland*; Liam de

Paor, *Divided Ulster*; Richard Rose, *Governing Without Consensus*; James Whyte, *Church and State in Modern Ireland*; and the *Sunday Times* 'Insight' group's *Ulster*.

Finally I want to thank my wife, not only for her valuable criticisms, suggestions and help in the preparation of the book itself but for her wise advice and good company during the controversies touched on in the concluding chapters.

# Foreword

This is not a book about Ireland. If it were, it would be a pleasanter book. I live in Ireland by choice, after experience of living in many other places, and I am happy here. Our neighbours are friendly, our view is beautiful, my political friends are fine upstanding people, my political enemies fascinating in their own way. I don't mind the gossip any more than the rain. The censors are no longer eating writers in the street. We are not as bad as we are painted, especially by ourselves. In fact I love Ireland, as most Irish people do, with only an occasional fit of the shudders.

Unfortunately the subject of this book—the relations between Catholics and Protestants, and between the two political entities created by those relations—is one peculiarly conducive to shudders. When one has to write about that aspect of Ireland one has to take leave of almost everything that is lovable in Ireland: the affection, the peace, the mutual concern, the courtesy which exist in abundance—if they cannot always be said to prevail—*inside* each community. Instead we must discuss the conditions of a multiple frontier: not just the territorial border, but a very old psychological frontier area, full of suspicion, reserve, fear, boasting, resentment, Messianic illusions, bad history, rancorous commemorations, and—today more than ever—murderous violence. This is not Ireland, and it is not peculiar to Ireland: such frontiers, of tribe, colour, religion, language, culture, scar a great part of the surface of the globe, and have cost millions of lives even in this decade (Israel, Biafra, Bangladesh, etc.). Our frontier is exceptionally old—over three-and-a-half centuries—and now so disturbed that many of us fear we may be approaching the brink of full-scale civil war.

I lived in New York from 1965 to 1969. During that period, Northern Ireland and its peculiar institutions were already becoming, for the first time in many years, matters of front-page news and editorial comment in the American and world press. Students questioned me about it:

'Why do the Irish Catholics and the Protestants hate one another so much?'
    'It's not really a religious problem, is it?'
    'Is it a colonial problem?'
    'Is it a racial problem?'
    'Why does England keep Ireland divided?'
    'When is Ireland going to be united?'
    'Don't you *want* Ireland to be united?'
    'What is the solution?'

I had no simple answers to any of these questions. Rather, they started other questions going in my own mind. For example:

What do the terms, 'Catholic' and 'Protestant' in Ireland mean?

Do they mean the same in the North, and in the South?

What relative importance have class, tribal, religious, and colonial elements in the conflict?

What do my own background and experience, as distinct from theoretical analysis, tell me about Catholics and Protestants in Ireland?

In the early summer of 1969, I resigned my chair at New York University and returned to Ireland to run as a Labour candidate in the General Election. I was elected for the mainly working-class constituency of Dublin North-East: it was a four-seat constituency, and I finished second. The candidate who finished first was Mr. Charles Haughey, then Minister for Finance in the Fianna Fáil government, and later acquitted on charges of complicity in the running of guns into Ireland (see Chapter 9).

After I took my seat as a member of a minority Opposition party, I became fairly closely concerned with the situation in the North (as indeed I had been ten years before as a civil servant in the Department of External Affairs) and especially now with the far-reaching effects of that situation on politics in the South. (See Chapters 9 to 12.)

When I was asked to write 'a book about the North',[1] I found that I could not write about the North *in isolation* partly because others, both participants and journalists present in Northern Ireland through long months of crisis, are better qualified to do so, and some of them have in fact done so; but also because it seemed to me that the political entity called Northern Ireland should not be viewed only in isolation, since this entity is only part of a not entirely successful historical answer to continuing problems: those of the relations between Catholics and Protestants in the island of Ireland, and of the relations between these communities, and their territories to Great Britain.

Specifically: The population of Northern Ireland consists of about two-thirds Protestants to one-third Catholics. But Protestant fear and suspicion of Catholics in Northern Ireland do not correspond to these proportions, but to the proportions between Catholic and Protestant in *the entire island of Ireland,* in which Protestants are outnumbered by Catholics by more than three to one. And Catholics in Northern Ireland are also strongly conscious of this proportion, and of rights which they believe it to imply.

Also: The manner in which the island is divided—with the 'Protestant' area of Northern Ireland including cities, towns and counties with Catholic majorities, while the 'Catholic' republic includes no city, town or county with a Protestant majority—does not reflect a 'natural' balance between the communities that make up the population of Ireland; it reflects the different historical relations between these communities and the people of Great Britain. The British Government of 1920 did not create—nor does the British Government today artificially preserve—the relations between the two communities in Ireland which resulted in the partition of the island, but when partition became

[1] The terms 'North' and 'South' are used here for convenience and are without geographical precision. The most northerly part of the island of Ireland, Donegal, is in what is here referred to as 'the South': the twenty-six-county territory of the Republic of Ireland.

inevitable, the British Government of 1920 ensured that the
benefits of all doubts went to one community: the Protestant
community descended from settlers from Britain.

Thus, both communities in Northern Ireland have looked
for support from outside the area. Catholics have looked to
the Republic, with its Catholic majority, and also to the
descendants of Irish Catholics in the United States, Canada
and Australasia, as in the past they looked to European
powers. Protestants have looked to Britain and—to a much
lesser extent—to areas like the American Bible Belt or, in
the past, to some of the Protestant princes of Europe.

Today, conflict in Northern Ireland is waged with, on
both sides, an appeal to the outside world, and a hope of
influencing outside decisions—especially but not exclusively,
decisions in London.

I am convinced that the distinct communities indicated
by the terms 'Catholic' and 'Protestant' are the prime
realities of the situation. This is not the same as saying that
religion is the main factor. Religious affiliation, in Ireland,
is the rule of thumb by which one can distinguish between
the people of native, Gaelic stock (Catholic) and those of
settler stock from Scotland and England (Protestant).

The area now known as Northern Ireland is the only part
of Ireland where sizable populations of both stocks have
long existed, and now exist, together. And in Northern
Ireland they have functioned, and function, not just as
religious groupings but as political groupings too. Protestant
almost always means Unionist: favouring union that is, not
with the rest of Ireland, but with Britain. Catholic almost
always means anti-unionist, and implies support for some
kind of united Ireland; this is not always conceived as
incorporation in the present Republic, but the distinction is
negligible, from a Protestant point of view.

In Northern Ireland, especially in conditions of tension,
but also in normal times, the basic social information which
people look for, in relation to any unfamiliar person or group,
is 'religion'. The same person who may tell you that 'religion'
is not important, or that its importance is exaggerated, will
talk freely, or not freely, with a friend in a taxi, depending

on whether or not he knows that the religion of the taxi driver is the same as that of the group to which he himself adheres.[2] In troubled times he may not take a taxi at all, unless he knows the driver personally, and can assess his reliability for a given drive, under given conditions of socio-religious stress. A well-known Catholic politician might take a Protestant taxi, even in conditions of tension, if he knew the driver and thought him safe. But if that driver took an unexpected turn into a Protestant street, the passenger would at least become tense, and not just about the fare. And both the driver and the passenger would be conscious, throughout the journey, of whether they were travelling along a Catholic or a Protestant street. And in no circumstances would either of them in the presence of the other allude to this situation, or to any subject bordering on politics or religion.

This state of Protestant-Catholic relations—the social electricity present in the air of Belfast and Derry even in time of peace—is almost as uncomfortable for people who write about Northern Ireland (and Ireland generally) as it is for those who live there.

Writers favourable to Northern Ireland, as a political entity, have had obvious reasons, in modern conditions, to 'play down' the tensions between the communities: or rather the alternations of latent and overt hostility between them. The founders and early leaders of the state were, it is true, not mealy-mouthed about the situation. Lord Craigavon, first Prime Minister of Northern Ireland, spoke of 'a Protestant parliament for a Protestant people' implying that the Catholic people of Northern Ireland, about one-third of the total, were to be governed by the parliament of a people to which they did not belong; which was true in substance. But in more recent times, most educated Protestants and Unionists found this kind of language both distasteful and unrewarding. Realities inside Northern Ireland, in terms of Protestant-Catholic relations, did not change very much since

[2] Not necessarily his own religious belief. In Northern Ireland a person who adheres to the politics of the other religion—a Protestant Nationalist, or Catholic Unionist—is for most practical purposes deemed, by the group he left, to have gone over to the other religion: which of course is worse than having been born in it.

Lord Craigavon's day until very recently indeed (see Chapters 7 and 8). But realities outside changed. Britain has changed internally, and in its relations to the rest of the world. In Lord Craigavon's day, Protestant feelings were still a great political force in Britain, and so was the idea of loyalty to the Crown and Empire. Lord Craigavon 'spoke the language' of many, probably of most, ordinary English people. Today, Britain is a secular society, and the Empire is gone; the Crown is still there, but no longer evokes quite the old feelings. Furthermore, people who emphasize their loyalty to the Crown and the Union Jack, while being seen to push Roman Catholics around, are an embarrassment and a nuisance to contemporary Britain. There are after all a great many Roman Catholics, including Roman Catholics of Irish descent, in the United States, and relations with the United States are considerably more important than they appeared to be in Lord Craigavon's day. (The Catholics of the Common Market, not being conscious of any Irish origin, are somewhat less relevant.)

Thus Lord Craigavon's successors had adequate reasons for not talking Lord Craigavon's language. They had sought to present Northern Ireland as essentially *modern,* a progressive corner of the United Kingdom. In this picture the actual state of relations between the two communities needed to be glossed over, and received this treatment.

In Britain itself for somewhat different reasons (and in addition to the 'American' factor) word of Catholic and Protestant relations in Ireland was unwelcome and boring. Ireland had bedevilled British politics for generations: people in Britain wanted to think that *that* problem at least was solved. On the very eve of the Civil Rights explosion, Professor A. J. P. Taylor wrote that 'Lloyd George solved the Irish question in 1921', and few people in Britain would have seen, or would have wanted to see, much reason to doubt this historical assessment. The Irish of the Republic had got what they wanted and gone; the Irish of Northern Ireland had got what they wanted and stayed, and that was that. This was a rough approximation to the truth. Attention to the state of Catholic-Protestant relations in the North, and relations between Catholics on both sides of the border, showed where the rough approximation broke down. Such attention was, therefore, not lavished. On the contrary there was a strong disposition to assume that Northern Ireland was a part of the United Kingdom, like any other, and that Protestant-Catholic relations there, tedious though they might be, were of no more significance than similar conditions in, say, Liverpool.

The official propaganda of the Republic (see Chapters 6 and 7) also glossed over these relations, using a green gloss. It stressed the responsibility of London for 'the artificial partition of the country', and in concentrating on this factor presented the Protestant-Catholic relationship as a side-issue or diversion. Furthermore it presented this relationship in terms of a purely *political* controversy. The Republic's propaganda quite legitimately sought to expose that system of gerrymandering and discrimination in jobs and housing which made the minority in Northern Ireland second-class citizens (see Chapter 7). But in exposing this, Dublin publications simply translated the religious descriptions of the Census returns ('Roman Catholic'; 'Church of Ireland'; 'Presbyterian', etc.) into political terms: 'Unionists' and 'Nationalists'. The equation in itself is accurate enough, but the substitution of the political for the religious term is subtly misleading, turning cultural separateness into a mere difference of opinion on a constitutional issue. In fact *either* the religious or the political description, by itself, is incomplete: what is significant is the fact that either set of descriptions can be used equally efficiently to identify the communities for day-to-day practical purposes.

The Catholic-Protestant relationship and the relation of both communities to Britain have also been distorted or analysed out of existence, by various 'Marxist' or post-Marxist interpretations adopted by some left-wing activists, mainly from the Catholic community, and diffused by journalists and others in contact with those activists. These interpretations vary rather widely, but a common feature is the effort to trace the evils of Northern Ireland and the Republic, to a source in British imperialism, apprehended as being as active a force now as at any time in the past, intensely concerned with keeping its grip on Ireland, and able to control the policies and actions of British governments, whether Tory or Labour. The grip of British imperialism is to be broken by revolution, for which the way will be prepared by various forms of activity (there is disagreement as to what forms) as a result of which the consciousness of the masses will be raised to a level at present attained only by a few people, the authors of the interpretations in question.

These people are not merely non-sectarian, but sincerely and militantly *anti*-sectarian, in their conscious outlook. Their intention has been to raise the level of consciousness of the masses, in terms of class interest, up out of the sectarian bog. The effect of their efforts, gestures and language, however, has been to raise the level of *sectarian* consciousness. They have encouraged the Catholics, and helped them to win important and long-overdue reforms (Chapter 8). They have frightened and angered Protestants, and if their efforts could be continued on the same lines, and with the same kind of success, they would bring to the people of the province, and the island, not class-revolution but sectarian civil war. And in fact, even at present, language and gestures which are subjectively revolutionary, but have appeal only within one sectarian community, are objectively language and gestures of sectarian civil war. (See Chapters 8 to 11.)

Granted the existence and influence of what seemed to me dangerously distorted green and orange, left and right, versions of the situation in and around Northern Ireland, I thought it might be of use to try to re-examine that situation, both in its historical and actual context, with reference always to the two communities, the Catholics and Protestants of Ireland, their interactions and their external relations.

Most history is *tribal* history: written that is to say in terms generated by, and acceptable to, a given tribe or nation,[3] or a group within such a tribe or nation. If you know

---

[3] That Marxist history is only an apparent exception to this is shown by Marx's correspondence, and the development of Marxism itself, and therefore of Marxist history, into a number of national schools.

the language, etc.,[4] in which any 'standard' history of the
origins of the First World War is written you will be able to
make predictions, with a small margin of error, about its
selection of data, conclusions on controversial points, and
general emphasis. It would *not* be true to say that if you
know the religion of an Irish historian you could make
similarly accurate predictions. But it would not be true,
either, to say that the choice of history text books in use in the
Republic and in Northern Ireland, and in schools of the
different denominations within each entity, has been unaffected by the sectarian context. Nor would it be true to say
that the composition and production of schools of history in
the various universities of Ireland are altogether unaffected
by the sectarian context within which these schools have
historically developed, and in which they now exist. Historians, like other people, tend to identify with a community—
not necessarily the one into which they were born—and in the
case of modern historians this identification is likely to affect,
and interact with, the character of their work, their career,
their geographical location, and their public. Normally they
write within a convention which suggests that these conditioning factors do not exist, or can be ignored. Marxist
historians, indeed, emphasize such factors, but only as
limitations on bourgeois historians.

This book is not a history, but an enquiry in the form of a
discursive essay; an enquiry into certain aspects of Irish
history, consciousness and society, as part of an effort to
understand what has been happening in the two parts of
Ireland in recent years.

The *historian* may claim—though we may be sceptical
about the claim—that the scientific rigour of his work, and
the accepted standards by which it will be judged, dispense
him from any need to identify his own point of view, or the
factors which may have conditioned it. The writer of an
essay like the present, containing so much commentary and
interpretation in proportion to fact, can claim no such
dispensation.

[4] It is sometimes necessary to distinguish dialects, notably 'American' from
'English'.

This essay is concerned directly and throughout with the Catholic and Protestant communities in Ireland, and it is therefore relevant that the reader should know where the writer stands in relation to these communities. This is not essentially a matter of theology: a Protestant writer may identify with the Catholic community, and several have done so; the reverse identification seems much rarer, perhaps for the reason that when it occurs it tends to take the person concerned out of Ireland altogether, and certainly away from any preoccupation with Irish history—which is, in general, the concern of a Catholic more than of a Protestant public.

My own connection with the two communities is somewhat complex, which is perhaps in part why I am drawn to discuss the relation between them. My roots are entirely in one community: my formal education has been almost entirely in schools of the other community. These communities have traditionally very different attitudes to Britain. But in the community within which I was born there have also been very significant political differences, concerning the relationship with Britain, and with the other community in Ireland itself. My family was a political one, and the activities of its members, since the eighteen-seventies, traversed at different times most of the range of what seemed politically, culturally and socially possible and desirable within their community. My own attitude to these past activities, and to present-day alignments, is undoubtedly affected by family influences, as well as by my later education. In order that the reader may understand, as far as possible, the historical standpoint from which the enquiry begins, I have thought it well to include, along with the general history, a thread of family history.

There are no privileged observers, as Sartre remarked. My own background, education and capacities have provided me with blind spots as well as, I hope, some possibilities of insight. I have tried, in this essay, to develop these last possibilities, where I think I am aware of them, without trying to impart much information on subjects which I am conscious of understanding imperfectly myself. Thus, I have more to say about the literary movement than about econo- mic history, not because I am saying that the first is more

important than the second, but because I think I have something of relevance and interest to say about the first, which
has not been said before, whereas I can have no such
pretension in relation to the second. Such value as this essay
may possess, as well as its obvious limitations, derives from
its character as a personal enquiry. Let me end this foreword,
therefore, with a few words of autobiography.

My own family background is entirely Southern Roman
Catholic. I was born in Dublin in November 1917; my
mother's family came from Limerick and Tipperary, my
father's from Clare. We were on the lower fringes of the
educated middle class. My father was a journalist—a leader-
writer on the (Catholic) *Freeman's Journal*. My mother was
a vocational school-teacher. I was an only child.

The family politics (speaking of our relations generally)
were Irish Nationalist, as was normal for Irish Catholics, but
both the span and the intensity of our politics—within the
general spectrum of Irish nationalism—were somewhat unusual. Our politics tended to affect our religion, and our
relations with Protestants, in rather curious ways.

My maternal grandfather, David Sheehy, had been a
Nationalist Member of Parliament, first for South Galway,
later for Meath, from 1885 to 1918, at Westminster. He had
been a seminarian student at the Irish College, Paris, had
left it and had made a runaway match with my grandmother,
who eloped with him from the convent where she was at
school. He had been active in his early youth, in the revolutionary movement of the Irish Republican Brotherhood
(often referred to as 'Fenians') (see Chapter 2). His brother,
Father Eugene Sheehy, also of Fenian sympathies, was
imprisoned in 1881, and later, as parish priest of Bruree,
Co. Limerick, exercised a crucial influence over a young
parishioner, Eamon de Valera. I have in my possession a
yellowed photograph of my great-uncle which President
de Valera gave me with the words, '*Eisean a mhúin an tír-ghrá
dhom*'. 'He taught me patriotism'. (A political enemy of Dev's
commented sourly to me that if my great-uncle taught de
Valera patriotism, he had a lot to answer for.)

Both these Sheehy brothers had been active in the radical

agrarian movement of the Land League, whose successful
activities in the eighties, under Davitt and Parnell, gave the
word 'boycott' to the languages of the world. My great-uncle
had been known as 'the Land League priest': the article
was significant: there was only one such priest at the time
the Land League was founded, in 1879, and Father Eugene
long remained the most active priest in the League. Many
Catholic bishops were at this time hostile to the Land
League, considered 'Garibaldian' and 'Communistic'. The
Pope specifically condemned boycotting and the Plan of
Campaign. Neither David nor Eugene was much impressed
by this. There is a family tradition of a sermon preached
by my great-uncle, whose Bishop required him to take up a
collection for 'the Prisoner of the Vatican'. Father Eugene's
sermon began:

Beloved brethren: I know what the words 'the Prisoner of the
Vatican' must convey to you. When you hear them you must
think of the prisoners you know, in Kilmainham or Tullamore
jail: men who, if they refuse to wear the prison clothes, are left
naked in winter, in unheated cells, on bread and water. [These
were the conditions of imprisonment of Eugene's brother, David,
in Tullamore Jail in 1887.] When you think of that, and you hear
the words 'the Prisoner of the Vatican' it must conjure up a terrible picture in your minds. Fortunately, I am in a position to
relieve some of your anxieties. I have been to Rome, and I have
had the privilege of an audience with Our Holy Father. His
Palace . . .

The description that followed raised sixpence in all for
the Prisoner of the Vatican. The sermon seems to have been
a reprisal for the Pope's action in permitting the faithful
(and loyal) to eat meat on a Friday in Queen Victoria's
Jubilee.

Against this background, it might seem rather surprising
that in the great split of 1891, following the Parnell divorce
case, David Sheehy should have taken what is regarded in
retrospect as the Catholic and clericalist position, against
the 'Protestant adulterer' Parnell: that he should have been,
in the words of Mr. Casey in *A Portrait of the Artist as a Young
Man*—among the 'priests' pawns' who 'broke Parnell's heart'.

I remember as a boy being troubled by this. It would have been much more romantic and distinguished to have had a grandfather who had 'stood by Parnell'. Also I was puzzled. My mother's family had their faults, but they were not like pawns and they prided themselves—including Father Eugene —on opposing clerical influence in politics. This surely should have made them Parnellites, not anti-Parnellites. But anti-Parnellites they were, except for Tom Kettle, my Aunt Mary's husband, and he hardly counted since (as well as being only a courtesy uncle) he had not been there to vote for or against Parnell. My grandfather had been there in Committee Room 15 in the House of Commons, and he had voted *against*. Why?

The Parnell split occurred twenty-seven years before I was born, and it must have been about forty years in the past by the time I became involved in it. In between, there had been the Rising of 1916, the Black-and-Tans, the Civil War of 1922, the coming of independence (or was it independence?) and the partition of the country. There had also been the First World War, but that seemed a side issue, in terms of the only history that really counted. And in that history, as far as it affected my imagination, the great primal and puzzling event was the fall of Parnell.

*Postscript:* The degree and kind of Catholic–Protestant tension described in this Foreword were those prevailing *before* the Provisional I.R.A.'s offensive opened in 1971. (See Chapters 8 to 12.)

I

# The Fall of Parnell

'The modern literature of Ireland, and indeed all that stir of thought which prepared for the Anglo-Irish war began when Parnell fell from power in 1891.[1] A disillusioned and embittered Ireland turned from parliamentary politics and the race began, as I think, to be troubled by that event's long gestation.'

W. B. YEATS, *Address to the Swedish Academy on accepting the Nobel Prize for Literature in 1925.*

The event was one thing, the way the event was imagined another thing, and more powerful. And there were men and women who lived through the event, *and* through the imagining of the event. Their lives, marked by this double experience, marked mine. And both the event and its imagining, and the consequences of the way in which it was imagined, helped powerfully to shape what happened in Ireland in the early twentieth century, and what is happening now.

Charles Stewart Parnell, in the summer of 1890, was at the height of his power and reputation. He was the Protestant leader of a Catholic people. The religious-political cleavage was already quite clear. The then still novel techniques of mass democracy, universal suffrage and the secret ballot showed a clear pattern. Every constituency in the country in which Catholics were in a clear majority returned Parnellite candidates: that is to say, candidates pledged to work for

---

[1] I don't know whether this is a mistake or not. Parnell ceased to be leader, in the eyes of a majority of his party, after a vote taken on 6th December 1890. Parnell, however, never acknowledged the validity of this vote. I suppose that on a strict Parnellite interpretation—and Yeats was a Parnellite—Parnell did did not fall from power until he died, on 6th October 1891.

Home Rule, under the iron discipline of Parnell's party. Home Rule meant self-government: how much self-government it meant depended on how much Britain could be induced to concede. The Catholic voters were prepared to leave to Parnell's judgment the question of how much could be won. He had earned their trust. They credited him with the great reforms in the land system which the agrarian movement had won. They credited him also with having converted Gladstone and the Liberal Party to Home Rule. At the time of that 'conversion', five years before, Parnell's party had held the balance of power in the House of Commons, and Gladstone's Liberal Government, which introduced the First Home Rule Bill in 1886, depended at the time on the block of votes which Parnell controlled. True, Gladstone had been defeated in 1886—through the defection of some of his Liberal following—but by 1890 most observers correctly assumed that he would soon be back in office, supported by a Liberal party fully committed to Home Rule. They also assumed that Parnell would then still be in command of a united Irish party, and that the alliance of Parnell and Gladstone would prove irresistible. In the event, by the time Gladstone did return to office, in 1892, Parnell was dead—having bitterly denounced Gladstone—and his party was split.

Even had he lived and remained on good terms with Gladstone, Home Rule for Ireland would certainly not have been won, in the 1890's, anything like as easily or as bloodlessly as Irish nationalists and English Liberal Home Rulers were assuming. For the figures, which showed so clearly the overwhelming support of Irish Catholics for Home Rule, also showed that Irish Protestants were overwhelmingly *against* Home Rule. Every constituency with a comfortable Protestant majority returned a Unionist candidate—that is, a candidate pledged to uphold the Union of the Kingdom of Great Britain and Ireland. A block of such candidates was returned—and has continued ever since to be returned —for Eastern Ulster, the area centring on the Belfast region which is now the core of the present Northern Ireland.

This condition—the sharp religious-political division of

the Irish population—had been known to realistic observers for a long time. Unrealistic observers, who were more numerous, had been able to pretend that the division was not really there, or was 'grossly exaggerated'. English public opinion wanted to think that most Irish Catholics were basically loyal enough, at least when they were not misled by 'a handful of village ruffians' or American agitators. Irish majority (i.e. Catholic) public opinion wanted to think that 'many Protestants' favoured their cause. They made much, on public occasions, of the few living Protestants who actually did, and they were genuinely devoted to the memory of Protestant patriot-martyrs of the past, especially Robert Emmet and Theobald Wolfe Tone. And to Parnell.

The results of the arrival of political mass democracy, in the last third of the nineteenth century, made it hard to keep up the pretence that the division had been exaggerated.[2] But on the whole, these results were naturally more encouraging to Catholics (nationalists) than to Protestants (unionists). The Catholics were, after all, in a large majority in the whole island when they voted *en bloc*, as they were now doing. And a majority was what mass democracy was about. Ireland had been a distinct unit—in both the British and the Irish traditions—for many centuries. If, then, a majority of the inhabitants of this island wanted Home Rule—and they had voted for it four to one—then on democratic principles home rule is what the island should have. The minority had the right to vote against, but after that it should do like other minorities and accept the majority decision. That is what the majority of Irishmen (a Catholic majority) believed, and still believes, substituting only independence for home rule. And that is what about half of the English people found itself committed to when Gladstone declared for home rule for Ireland. The difference was that whereas most Irishmen (Catholics) took majority rule for all Ireland to be something self-evident, in terms of democratic principle, few Englishmen felt about it in this way. For Englishmen—with a few exceptions, which included Gladstone—it was never a

---

[2] 'A chasm opened between North and South in the 1880's'—Richard Rose, *Governing without Consensus* (London, 1971).

question of democratic right, but of what concessions it might be prudent, in the interests of England and the Empire, to grant to the exceedingly tiresome inhabitants of the neighbouring island. The answer to this question would fluctuate with changing political situations both in Britain and Ireland, the Liberals being dubiously committed to home rule, the Tories fiercely committed against it, from 1886 on. And the Tories saw, in those election returns from eastern Ulster, their opportunity. Lord Randolph Churchill decided that the Orange Card was the one to play, and played it in Belfast in   86. The sectarian riots of the home rule bill summer were the worst Belfast had ever had. It was clear that resistance to home rule, in eastern Ulster, would not be verbal only. On 13th May 1886, during the home rule debates a significant advertisement appeared in the [Protestant and Unionist] *Belfast News-Letter:*

Wanted a few men thoroughly competent in military drill . . . Apply . . . Loyalist.

The idea of partitioning Ireland was already mooted—by Joseph Chamberlain—in the course of the home rule debate, but only casually: the Unionists had as yet no reason to give up hope of holding the whole island. Parnell, for his part, insisted on the inclusion of all Ulster. 'We cannot give up a single Irishman.' He thought that the inclusion of Ulster would lessen, not increase, the danger of religious discrimination. With Ulster in, there would be no risk of the Catholic hierarchy using its power unfairly. There were 'many liberal nationalists that do not share the views of the Roman Catholic hierarchy on education'. This was a note that no elected leader of the majority of the Irish people, since Parnell, has been in a position to strike. Certainly since 1921 no head of a Government in Dublin, in arguing the case for unifying Ireland, has made the point that the inclusion of so many Protestants would stop the Catholic Bishops from abusing their power.

Yet it would be a mistake to think that these Bishops, resenting their inability to control Parnell, jumped at the divorce case as their opportunity to destroy him, and regain full control of Catholic Ireland. This became the 'black legend' of this particular affair. The reality was different.

On 17th November 1890, a verdict was given in the divorce court in London in favour of Captain W. H. O'Shea and against his wife Katharine, and Parnell.

On 20th November, at a public meeting in Dublin, all the leading figures in Parnell's party reaffirmed confidence in Parnell and upheld his leadership. At this point no major voice was lifted up from the nationalist right—where the Irish Bishops were generally to be found—against Parnell. The first influential Irishman to come out against him was the founder of the Land League, Michael Davitt, in the *Labour World* on 20th November. Davitt, who favoured land-nationalization, was regarded by Parnell as much too far to the left, and the two men had been estranged since 1882. Indeed, Parnell, to counteract Davitt's influence, and other extremist influence, had deliberately brought the Catholic clergy, *ex officio,* into the grass-roots organization of his party, the National League, where they played an important part in the screening of candidates.

At this point, the key figures in the Catholic hierarchy felt there was nothing they could do. Archbishop Walsh so informed Michael Davitt, who was pressing him to act. The Archbishop threw out Parnell's bust 'which for some time past has held a prominent place in my hall'. The fact that the Archbishop had possessed a bust of Parnell and displayed it prominently is at least as significant as the fact that he threw it out after the Divorce Court verdict.

On 27th November, Davitt not only repeated his call for Parnell's departure, but complained of the Catholic hierarchy's silence on 'the moral issue'. The Catholic hierarchy was also attacked on the same grounds by the Protestant and Unionist press in the North. But the really effective 'Parnell must go' call came not from Ireland, but from England. The English non-conformists made it clear to Gladstone that they would not tolerate any further co-operation by the Liberals with a party led by Parnell. This forced Gladstone to come out against Parnell. The Irish party re-elected Parnell as

Chairman on 25th November. Gladstone's letter saying he could no longer work with Parnell was published on 26th November. Immediately a special meeting of the Irish party was convened to consider the situation. It was only *after* all this that the Irish Catholic hierarchy decided to act. On 28th November, a special meeting of the standing committee of the hierarchy was summoned, for 3rd December. By the time they did meet, almost all the leading figures in the party had declared against Parnell, because of Gladstone's letter. The hierarchy's call, on 3rd December, to the Catholic people of Ireland to repudiate Parnell was not the eager stab at the Protestant leader which it has been represented as being. It was, rather, a necessary piece of face-saving for the hierarchy itself. Once the matter had become one of con-troversy among Irish politicians, the Bishops could hardly, after all, afford to appear less sensitive on the issues of adul-tery, divorce, and morality in public life, than were the English non-conformists, the Belfast Protestants and the editor of the *Labour World*. Of course, *after* the hierarchy had spoken out, the maintenance of its authority required the total political destruction of the man whom it had denounced. On 6th December—after a long and emotional debate which hinged mainly on Gladstone's letter, and attempts at com-promise with Gladstone, the majority of Parnell's party repudiated his leadership. After this point, when Parnell tried, in three frightful by-elections, to appeal to the country against the party majority, the weight of the hierarchy was thrown against him, sometimes brutally, and with complete success, as far as the adults were concerned whose votes alone counted. Parnell died on 6th October 1891, less than a year after the divorce verdict.

David Sheehy was among the thirty-one members who took the decisive act in the divorce crises, by signing, on 26th November 1890, the requisition calling for a resumed meeting of the party, after Gladstone's letter. It was a decision heavy with consequences, not only for Parnell, but for people then unborn. *For this was the decision that discredited constitutional democratic politics, and began the revival of enthusiasm among the young for the idea of armed revolution.* When Parnell died, the Gaelic Athletic Association in Cork elected as their patron in his place, not any constitutional politician—even among those who had stood by Parnell—but James Stephens, the founder of the Irish Republican Brotherhood. And it was the Irish Republican Brotherhood which was to decide, and time, the Rising of Easter Week 1916. As Parnell's most vindictive enemy, Tim Healy, had said: 'We have the voters, but Parnell has their sons'.

The point about the fatal decision of 26th November 1890 turned out to be, not that the party was changing its leader, but that it was doing so *at the bidding of an Englishman.* They threw their leader—in Parnell's own words—'to English wolves now howling for my destruction'. Until the Englishman spoke, they had stood by Parnell, in full knowledge of the divorce court verdict; they had unanimously re-elected him to office as chairman of the party. Then, on the day after his re-election, they had dropped him, by the Englishman's command.

To them, of course, it looked quite different, and in logic they had a good case. In their eyes, the important thing was, not what happened in the Divorce Court, or loyalty to a personality, or the opinions of individuals. The important thing was to win Home Rule. The only way of winning Home Rule was through alliance with an English party. The only party available for such an alliance was the Liberal Party. The Liberal alliance had been Parnell's great achievement, and Parnell himself had taught them to subordinate everything to that alliance. (He discountenanced, for example, the agrarian agitation of the late eighties, in which men like Sheehy had been engaged, because it might upset British public opinion.) They had re-elected Parnell, because they assumed he could maintain the Liberal alliance, or he would have stepped down. However, if Gladstone refused to co-operate with him, the Liberal alliance would be unworkable, and Home Rule unattainable in their generation. Therefore they voted against Parnell, not 'at the bidding of an Englishman', but solely in order to win home rule. It was because they were loyal to Parnell's policy—which Parnell himself, for personal and selfish reasons, had ceased to follow—that they had to jettison Parnell.

Logical enough, but it was not a logic that could work alone at the hustings against the magic of Parnell, and the emotions evoked by his 'English wolves'. The thing that could smash Parnell was the blunt instrument of the moral issue— 'convicted adulterer'—and the *only* people who could use that effectively were first the clergy and, secondly, the village yahoo, with 'Kitty O'Shea's petticoat' on a pole. A few of Parnell's opponents—notably Tim Healy—were ruthless enough to encourage this sort of thing, and robust enough to enjoy it. Most were sickened by it, and by their own relation to it. They were fighting the campaign openly by high-minded and logical argument, but they were winning it off-stage by arguments that they could not defend publicly. For they had re-elected Parnell in full knowledge of the circumstances which, in the hierarchy's view, constituted. 'a scandalous pre-eminence in guilt and shame'. The dirt and the dishonesty of the Parnell split were long to contaminate Irish life, and are not fully shaken off yet. Not that dirt and dishonesty are not pandemic, in politics and otherwise, but there is a special form of holy calumny which has reached a high degree of sophistication in Irish politics, since 1891. Our present Taoiseach, Mr. Jack Lynch, is a master in the game. (See Chapters 9 to 11.)

Looking back, across nearly a century, and out of some recent experience of Irish politics, I try to enter into the mind of my grandfather, on that morning of 26th November 1890, reading Gladstone's terrible letter in *The Times*.

The first sensation must have been that of the ground giving way under him, slabs of Galway rock sliding away. So far, he and his friends had been able to say: 'This is a *political* issue, you must leave it to us. You want Home Rule? Then you cannot afford to drop Parnell.' But the leader of the Liberal Party—the indispensable ally—is now telling us all: 'You want Home Rule? Then you *must* drop Parnell'.

Could he, David Sheehy, go back to South Galway and tell his constituents that, whatever Mr. Gladstone might think—and Mr. Gladstone's picture was on the walls of many homes in his constituency—he, David Sheehy, thought they should stick by a convicted adulterer, even if it meant the total disruption of the policy for which he, David Sheehy, had been advising them, the people of South Galway, to sacrifice all else?

And if he did that, what would his wife, Bessie, say? It was not so much that Bessie would think he had been corrupted by all these months in London; Bessie knew him far too well for that. No, she would say that Parnell had made a fool of him. She would tell him that if he, David Sheehy, thought he understood politics better than Mr. Gladstone he might well be mistaken. She would ask him whether he really thought the people of Ireland—and especially the women of Ireland—were prepared to give up home rule, or indeed anything, for the sake of Mrs. O'Shea? And she would urge him to think of the children. He, David Sheehy, had earned a respected place in Irish life—he had been losing his hearing in that cold cell in Tullamore jail while Parnell was in Brighton with that woman. It was up to him, David Sheehy, now to keep that respected place, for his family's sake, and for the country. (Bessie *might* put it the other way round, perhaps.) He couldn't keep it if he ignored Gladstone's letter. Parnell was finished.

David Sheehy talked with his colleagues who had been reading the letter with corresponding thoughts. The most experienced leaders of the party were away in America. There must have been panic in the air. Nobody seems even to have considered telling Gladstone that, as the party had just elected its chairman for the session, no change was possible until the next session—the only policy, as it seems in retrospect, that might have given the party time to save its unity and its face. But panic prevailed, and it is not surprising that it did. The posture maintained up to this point by so many respectable, Victorian Catholic fathers of families, supporting the leadership of the 'convicted adulterer', was far too unaccustomed for most of them to be able to resist a sudden, new great strain on it.

Family tradition—an unreliable medium in such a case as this—says that my grandfather became disillusioned because Parnell had deceived him. David Sheehy with other rank-and-file M.P.s called on Parnell, after O'Shea had issued his

Writ, to ask what the truth was. Parnell, leaning against the mantelpiece and with his arm stretched out along it, looked coldly at the group and asked: 'Gentlemen, could you believe that of me?' They accepted this as a denial, and themselves denounced the divorce charges as another English plot against Parnell, on the same lines as *The Times* Pigott forgeries, which had just been exposed.

David Sheehy had been engaged in such a denunciation in his constituency when a news-boy came by with the stop-press: 'Divorce Suit Undefended'. Sheehy was then attacked by some of his audience—pig-buyers from Limerick—and had to have six stitches in his head.

Whatever the degree of literal truth in this, it is certain that Parnell had equivocated with his followers and others —with Michael Davitt and William O'Brien among others —giving them to understand that his honour was stainless. He meant that he had not deceived Captain O'Shea: They took him to mean that he had not committed adultery. The landlord and the peasants failed to understand one another's codes, in every sense. So what the 'pig-buyer' story says is: 'We did not break faith with our leader. He broke faith with us.' It was a plea, and one not without merit. But it was incapable of reaching the younger generation. There were too many swinging croziers and English wolves in the way. The version that reached the young put David Sheehy and his friends into unenviable company, as appears from the ballad Yeats made of that version years afterwards:

> *The Bishops and the Party*
> *That tragic story made*
> *A husband that had sold his wife*
> *And after that betrayed.*

After Parnell's death, Irish affairs seemed to recede in importance. The second home rule bill, in 1893, seemed an anti-climax. It passed the Commons, the Lords threw it out, Gladstone retired and there were bonfires in Belfast. That seemed to be that. The Tories were soon back in power, and it seemed to many, when Gladstone died in 1895, that the idea of a self-governing Ireland died with him. The British

Empire was the theme of the day: ideas like Home Rule for Ireland seemed petty and retrogressive even to the Liberals, embarrassed by their Gladstone heritage.

In Ireland, one basic pattern remained unchanged and remains so to this day. The electoral returns continued to show that Catholics were Nationalists and Protestants Unionists. The noisy fight between Parnellite and anti-Parncllite was a faction-fight *among Catholics*: Protestant Ulster[3] was interested in this struggle only by *schadenfreude*, as a horrible example of the inability of Papists to run their own affairs. For Belfast, the storm of the eighties had blown over. Yet the Unionist leaders knew—and had an interest in spreading the knowledge—that their Ulster was still in danger. The Catholics were divided, but only on trivial questions connected with leadership: they remained united—as Ulster Protestants saw it—in wanting to get an independent Ireland in which Protestants, not Catholics, would be the underlings. And the Catholics could always count on between eighty and ninety representatives[4] in the Commons, as against the dozen or so from Protestant Ulster. As long as there was a Tory majority in the Commons, Ulster was safe. Even a Liberal government, with a safe majority of its own, would leave Ireland and Ulster alone. But a day was almost sure to come when the Liberals would need the Irish nationalist bloc in order to hold office. On that day the Liberal leader, whoever he might be, would blow the dust off Gladstone's speeches. Ulster had to be prepared against that day. Siege operations had been suspended, but it was clear that they would be resumed. Protestant Ulster was well prepared for such a contingency. The siege-mentality had been its heritage from its beginnings in the seventeenth century, when the conquerors had followed with imperfect success a counsel of Machiavelli's.

[3] Then as now, Protestants made up only about half the population of the historic province of Ulster (nine counties). 'Protestant Ulster' is used here to refer to that Protestant population, in Ulster, which liked, and likes, to think of itself as 'Ulster'.

[4] Curiously, Ireland was *over*-represented in the Parliament of the United Kingdom. Its representation had not been adjusted to meet the decline in the population.

# Machiavelli in Ulster

'But when states are acquired in a province differing in language, in customs and in institutions, then difficulties arise: and to hold them one must be very fortunate and very assiduous: One of the best, most effective expedients would be for the conqueror to go to live there in person. . . . The other and better expedient is to establish settlements in one or two places; these will, as it were, fetter the state to you. Settlements do not cost much, and the prince can found them and maintain them at little or no personal expense. He injures only those from whom he takes land and houses to give to the new inhabitants, and these victims form a tiny minority, and can never do any harm since they remain poor and scattered. All the others are left undisturbed, and so should stay quiet, and as well as this they are frightened to do wrong lest what happened to the dispossessed should happen to them. To sum up, settlements are economical and more faithful, and do less harm; and those who are injured cannot hurt you because, as I said, they are scattered and poor. And here it has to be noted that men must be either pampered or crushed, because they can get revenge for small injuries but not for fatal ones. So any injury a prince does a man should be of such a kind that there is no fear of revenge'.

MACHIAVELLI, *The Prince,*
Chapter III, 'Composite Principalities'.

The Elizabethan and Jacobean conquerors and rulers of Ireland knew their Machiavelli: Edmund Spenser, himself a settler in Ireland, and an enthusiastic advocate of a solution by 'settlements', quotes Machiavelli in his *View of the State of*

*Ireland* (1590). The plantation of Ulster by grants and sales of land to immigrants from Scotland and England seemed just such a settlement as Machiavelli recommended. The Ireland of the seventeenth century did indeed differ from England 'in language, in customs and in institutions'. Its language was Gaelic, a Celtic language and about as remote from English as one Indo-European language can be from another; its customs and laws were so unknown to the English that the author of *The Faerie Queene*, a relatively assiduous enquirer, supposed them to be unwritten; its 'institutions', notably its system of land-tenure, were pre-feudal. And its religion was different, and by its difference a political danger to the Crown of England. When the English monarchy became Protestant the native people of Ireland overwhelmingly followed the Counter-Reformation. This made them automatically rebels since, on Counter-Reformation principles, subjects owed no allegiance to a schismatic prince. The existence of this disaffected realm was a standing invitation—more than once accepted—for intervention by foreign princes. The English monarchy had therefore a strong motive not merely for a settlement—to 'fetter the state'—but specifically for a *Protestant* settlement.

From the very beginning, religion, politics and economic status were firmly linked together. The Protestants held the land and were loyal to the Crown. The Catholics were dispossessed and loyal to the Pope. Applying the opinion that each section had of the other, the entire population was made up of heretics and traitors.

Since those distant days, the outlines of the problem have shifted many times, but the seventeenth century settlement was so massive and vital a fact that its original character continues to dominate every aspect of the life of the region affected, and to permeate the politics of the whole island.

Curiously, the conquerors carried Machiavelli's advice both too far and not far enough. If the whole island had been settled as North-Eastern Ulster was settled, there would be no 'religious' or native-and-settler problem today. Alternatively, if Eastern Ulster had been settled, and native proprietors elsewhere left warned but undisturbed, this might

conceivably have had the effects which Machiavelli predicts.
But in fact the result of the long and tortuous seventeenth
century conflicts was that real settlement, of farmers working
the land, took root in Ulster only, while in the rest of the
country, the native proprietors were dislodged and replaced
by English proprietors, but the land continued to be worked
by the natives. Thus those who were injured, although poor
and often scattered, were not 'a tiny minority'. In the event
the policy of the British rulers of Ireland failed by Machiavelli's basic test, since the injuries inflicted by the various
princes proved not to be 'of such a kind that there is no fear
of revenge'.

That fear was there from the beginning. At different
times it has faded away, only to return; it is there now.

The early colonists were conscious of the dispossessed
natives as enemies biding their time. The farmer in his tidy
holding in the valley had to keep an eye out for the Gaelic
Catholic outlaws in the hills, and for signs of treachery
among his Gaelic Catholic servants if he had them. The
position of the seventeenth century Ulster Protestant was
like that of his puritan contemporaries in New England, and
his Dutch Calvinist contemporaries in South Africa. His
descendants have grown more like Afrikaners in spirit than
like New Englanders. The reason for this is that in Ulster,
Ireland, as in South Africa, the natives are still there too.

Yet the relation has not always been one of unmitigated
settler-native hostility. That was the spirit of the entire
seventeenth century, of which the events which left the
greatest marks in Ireland were a massacre of Protestants by
Catholics in 1641, massacres of Catholics by Cromwell at
Drogheda and elsewhere in 1649; the siege of Protestant
Derry by the Catholic forces and its relief by the Protestant
forces in 1689, the final victory of the Protestant cause at the
Boyne in 1690,[1] and the enactment by the victorious Protestants of the Penal Laws, codifying the underling status of
the Catholics for most of the eighteenth century (and, in

[1] The real 'final victory', if there was one, came at Limerick in the following
year, but the Boyne, with the flight of the Catholic king, makes a more satisfactory ending for the mighty purposes of folk-history.

mitigated form, well into the nineteenth century with social consequences that reach into our own time).

The victory was so complete that the old siege-mentality relaxed, and almost seemed to disappear. By the second half of the eighteenth century, with the great growth in the power and prosperity of England, the defeated and demoralized—'poor and scattered'—Irish Catholics could hardly be thought of as a threat. There were more pressing problems. The descendants of those who had welcomed their Glorious Deliverance in 1691 soon felt themselves oppressed by their English deliverers. The monopoly laws of the English parliament were felt by the settlers in Ireland in much the same way as the settlers in America felt them, and there were ties of sympathy and of blood between the two groups of settlers. This factor tended to *reduce* Irish Catholic sympathy with the American revolution. In so far as that revolution was a revolution of Protestants, Irish Catholics could not, and did not, respond to it warmly. Yet Irish Catholics could hardly fail to note with interest the fact of a successful revolution against the power of England. If America was free, then there was more hope that Ireland would be free. And they meant of course *their* Ireland, the home of their ancestors from beyond recorded history, the land in which they remained the despised majority, dispossessed of everything. Basically their feelings were more like those of the Red Indians than like those of the American colonists.[2]

At the time of the American Revolution, the Protestants of Ireland, including Ulster, were not very conscious of this way of thinking. They knew that Catholic traders, for example, supported their economic demands, and that Catholics generally supported the demand for an Irish parliament, with greater powers, even though these powers would be exclusively in Protestant hands. Most Protestants thought of local Protestant control of an Irish parliament as essentially permanent: Catholics thought of it as a stage on the way to freedom. The armed movement of the Irish

[2] There were, of course, Irish Catholic colonists in America before the Revolution, but they were relatively few, and not conspicuous to Catholics in Ireland itself.

Volunteers was Protestant and landlord-led, but it was popular with Catholics, because of its anti-English tendency. The so-called 'Grattan's parliament' (1782–1800) remained exclusive—a Protestant body, representative of the Protestant landlord interest (and eventually liquidated by the same, partly for cash).

Catholic-Protestant *rapprochement* continued in somewhat different forms, under the influence of French revolutionary ideas. A curious feature here is the partial crumbling of the criterion by which persons of 'native' and 'settler' stock were identified. In regions like America and Africa, where the settlers were marked off from the natives by visible differences in pigmentation and other physical characteristics, the criterion presented no problem: a good light was all that was required. But in Ireland there were no surely distinguishable physical differences between the native and the settlers. Genetically they were of the same mixed stock. The criteria had been theological: settlers were Protestants, natives Catholics. In the consciousness of each group, its religion had been the most important thing about it, and constituted its essential and literally salutary difference from the other group.

By the late eighteenth century, many, though not a majority, of the settlers could no longer feel like that. Minds affected by the Enlightenment, professed 'the religion of sensible men', and regarded the whole Catholic-against-Protestant antagonism as a relic of the barbarous past. The Catholics, as the principal victims of the past in question, excited some sympathy, and the penal laws against them were hard to defend, within a liberal system of ideas. Yet there was also a sense in which the eighteenth century Protestant of deist tendencies—as many Presbyterians, in particular, were—found himself farther away from Catholics even than his pious ancestors were. Catholicism, after all, remained the great reservoir of 'fanaticism' and superstition. One could deplore the laws against Catholics and yet find the Catholic mind, when one came in contact with it, repulsively alien and medieval. Nor did the sufferings of the Catholics make them any more agreeable. The Protestant

United Irishman, William Drennan, thought he saw 'as far into the Catholic mind as others. I do not like it. It is a churlish soil, but it is the soil of Ireland, and must be cultivated, or we must emigrate.'

There were those, however, who—while experiencing such reactions—saw in the feelings of oppressed Catholics the best hope of revolution, and in revolution the best hope of freeing the minds of the oppressed from Catholic superstition. One of these was the United Irish leader, Theobald Wolfe Tone, whose grave at Bodenstown is central to the cult of modern Catholic Republicanism (chapters 9 to 12). Here, I am concerned with the place of his movement in the history of the Ulster Protestant siege-mentality: first as apparently breaking down that mentality: and then as re-establishing it.

The first centenary of the Glorious Deliverance was a quiet affair compared with what the second centenary was to be—not to speak of what the third may be. In 1790, the big event to be commemorated fell, not on the twelfth but on the fourteenth: the first anniversary of the fall of the Bastille. That was in the euphoric period when most people in Britain—with Edmund Burke as one of the few exceptions—regarded the French Revolution with complacent approval. But even four years later, when respectable people in England were horrified by the progress of the Revolution, Belfast illuminated to celebrate a great event: the execution of Louis XIV.

It is worth noting, and not just as a historical curiosity or paradox, that the enthusiasm of Dissenters generally for the French Revolution—an enthusiasm expressed in the sermon that aroused Burke to write *Reflections on the Revolution in France*—was anti-Catholic in character (overthrow of superstition). Thus there was an inherent tension in the United Irish movement which sought to bring Dissenter and Catholic together on French Revolutionary principles. The Catholic who would accept these principles as Dissenters understood them would have had to cease to be a Catholic—at least in the sense in which the word Catholic was understood by Irish Catholics generally.

The movement of the United Irishmen preached Liberty,

Equality and Fraternity, and under the head of Fraternity, proposed the substitution of 'the common name of Irishman' for the denominations of Catholic, Protestant and Dissenter. The movement had both Catholic and Protestant members and supporters, but never really succeeded in welding them into one. It was, in a sense, the same story, as with the American revolution. Protestant and Catholic United Irishmen both looked to France, but it was a different France. For the Protestant artisan, strong farmer or professional man, France was the preferred home of ideas which he shared: ideas which included war against superstition, as well as against feudal privileges, great landowners and the Crown. For the poor Catholic peasantry, France was England's enemy: in so far as they looked to France it was in in spite of rather than because of the philosophy of the revolution. The only 'French Revolutionary' idea that 'travelled' to them in an assimilable form was that of war against landlords. The trouble with that was that the landlords were almost all Protestants. There are conditions in which it is hard to tell class war from religious or tribal war, and hard even for those involved to be sure which it is they are at.

Even at the height of the partial *rapprochement* between some Protestants and some Catholics in the United Irish movement, the old seventeenth century spirit continued to animate much of the countryside, particularly in areas where Protestant and Catholic members were fairly even, and there was keen competition over land between Catholic and Protestant secret societies. The most famous Protestant society, the Orange Order, was founded in Co. Armagh in 1795. Orangeism, originally a peasant movement, attracted landlord support, as a reaction against the United Irishmen —from 1796—Orangemen, and people of similar outlook, were used by the Government in the brutally conducted arms searches which were aimed to prevent, and partly provoked, the United Irish rising of 1798.

There were in reality three risings: a Catholic one in the South, mainly in Wexford, followed by a mainly Protestant one in the North, in Antrim and Down, followed by a final Catholic rising in the West, after the belated and misplaced

landing of the French. All three risings were put down. The
Wexford rebels put up the best fight. They also massacred a
number of Protestants; some were piked to death on Wexford bridge, others burned in a barn at a place called Sculla-
bogue. It wasn't religious war in conscious intent. Where the
rebels were convinced that a Protestant was a United Irishman, they welcomed him with delight: one such Protestant,
Bagenal Harvey, became their altogether nominal leader.
Nor did the priests encourage outbursts of 'fanaticism': they
seem invariably to have tried to save the lives of Protestant
prisoners. But the rebels were out for the lives of Orangemen
and Orange sympathizers, and they simply assumed that
Protestants were Orangemen, until the contrary could be
proved.

The dismal news from Wexford was not offset by any
effective record of Protestant Catholic comradeship-in-arms
in the United Irish rising in Ulster. The Catholic support on
which the Protestant United Irish leaders in Ulster had counted
was only half-heartedly forthcoming, and soon melted away.

The rising of 1798 was not only a failure, in terms of the
noble and humane ideals of many of the United Irishmen,
including their leaders. It did more than any other single set
of events to *divide* Irishmen, and to re-establish among
Protestants the old siege-mentality of the seventeenth century.
The best summary of the development of effects of the Rising
is provided by the historian of Orangeism, Hereward Senior:

... The rebellion of 1798 had as much the character of a civil war
as a war of independence. It had its beginning in an attempt by
Belfast radicals to challenge the authority of the Castle, but as the
traditional alignment in Irish disputes had been the English
government with the Protestant gentry and Ulster Protestants on
one side, and the Catholic peasantry and any foreign allies it
could find forming the other, whenever politics took a violent
turn, this pattern reasserted itself. Ulster radicalism, like the
liberalism of the gentry, had matured when the Catholic peasantry was politically dormant. When the peasantry awakened in
1798, this radical sentiment died and Orangeism took its place.
Henceforth Irish nationalism was to be based almost exclusively
on the Catholic population.[3]

[3] Senior, *Orangeism in Ireland and Britain* (London and Toronto, 1966).

In 1803, just after Robert Emmet's rebellion—a brief, tragic postscript to the great rebellion of 1798—William Drennan's sister, Mrs. McTier, who had been, like him, an ardent believer in United Irish ideas, was frightened by 'a singing procession of Catholics'. 'I begin to fear these people', she wrote, 'and think, like the Jews, they will regain their native land.'

In the course of the nineteenth century, Belfast grew into a great industrial city, the only one of its kind in Ireland. It attracted immigrants: Protestants from Great Britain, Catholics as well as Protestants from rural Ireland. The relations between the two groups increased sectarian antagonism. O'Connell's Catholic mass movement and its success in winning Catholic emancipation in 1829 increased Protestant fears. These fears were exploited and exacerbated by the Tory landlords, and by Tory politicians and divines. They were not, however, created by these groups.

In the Young Ireland movement of the forties, a few Protestant intellectuals, notably Thomas Davis and John Mitchel (an Ulster Unitarian), continued the 1798 tradition. Their writings, especially the stirring martial verses of Davis, kindled national pride, among Catholics, in that and later generations. They evoked little or no response in Ulster. There, the radical Presbyterian tradition of the late eighteenth century gave way everywhere to a kind of seventeenth century revival, militantly anti-Catholic in character. The great controversies of the period, within the Presbyterian Church, were theological in form, but political and social as well as theological in content. Henry Montgomery, taking his stand upon the Bible alone, lost to Henry Cooke, insisting on a test—The Westminster Confession—which identified the Pope with Antichrist. Cooke, encouraged by the nobility and gentry, led Presbyterians in their thousands into the Orange Order. The radical Presbyterian tradition did not entirely disappear with the defeat of Montgomery: it continued as the intellectual heritage of a few families. Most Presbyterians however became, and remain, more conservative and anti-Catholic—more *verkrampte*, in South African terms—than members of other Protestant denominations.

At the end of the forties, Ireland was stricken by the

greatest disaster in its history: the Great Famine of 1845-9, in which a million died, and another million emigrated, mainly to America. Those directly hit were almost all Catholics, subsistence farmers, dependent on the potato as almost their sole diet, and reduced to starvation by the potato blight. Among the survivors and their descendants, both in Ireland and in America, the famine left a heritage of increased hatred against English rule: the government's relief measures were so miserably inadequate that the Catholic Irish believed that the clearance of the land by famine was a fact welcomed by their English rulers.[4] In some parts of the country, and among emigrants from some parts, there was also a heritage of increased ill-feeling towards Protestants. Some Protestant missions had dispensed soup, on condition of the abandonment of 'superstitious practices'. In other parts, Protestant groups—the Quakers in particular, but also some of the Church of Ireland clergy—did much more to save lives than the government did, and without conditions.

An attempted rising in 1848, in the wake of the Famine, collapsed miserably. Protestant Ulster seemed now to have little to fear, its besiegers dispersed by hunger. Its militant divines could see in the famine, a vindication of the Protestant traditions of thrift and good husbandry, and a judgement of God on Popish fecklessness. Catholic Ireland seemed a hopeless, ruinous failure, more to be pitied—or despised— —than feared, while Great Britain was now at the height of its unexampled commercial success, with Protestant Ulster sharing in that success.

By a strange reversal it was as a result of the famine that the Catholic Irish themselves began—initially in a most modest way—to share in another great success: that of America. It was from America that the materials came for the renewal of revolt: renewal, from Protestant Ulster's point of view, of the siege.

[4] The usual defence of the British Government's inertia is that it was applying the economic *lassez-faire* doctrines then held paramount. Some of the official correspondence shows a state of mind quite similar to that of Edmund Spenser writing about a sixteenth century famine in Munster: 'They died of famine they themselves had wrought.'

The children of the famine emigrants grew up in America hating England; they had chosen the U.S.A. rather than the nearer Canada. Their hatred grew out of Gaelic tradition (and their family experience), and—together with the 'boss' politics learned from O'Connell—was the element in that tradition that prepared them to be Americans. The same people who had oppressed America were still oppressing Ireland. So an Irishman could be a patriotic American: perhaps a more patriotic American than many other Americans. Immigrant children of other stocks might hear about the American revolution without much emotion. But to an Irish boy, in the mid-nineteenth century, the American revolution, 'freeing the country from the British', genuinely sounded good. Many a successful political career must have grown from the seed of that first sincere, spontaneous identification.[5]

In the American forcing-house, many Irish-Americans became more anti-English than were many Irishmen who remained in Ireland. There is a wider divergence here than is commonly recognized. Most—certainly not all—of the post-famine emigration to America came from the desperately poor and at that time overcrowded regions of Western Ireland. There people were still mainly Gaelic-speaking: some of them spoke only Gaelic, most of them were only faintly touched by anglicization. The population of their descendants had a significantly different balance from the population remaining in Ireland, of which the preponderant elements are in the relatively long-anglicized eastern counties. And even the Irish living in the now thinly populated western counties are today much more anglicized than were the common ancestors of themselves and their American cousins in the mid-nineteenth century.

In fact, what happened as a result of the famine is that the original Gaelic stock of Ireland split into two branches, one of which learned English and the other American. They could still communicate with one another, and did. And those who

[5] I once heard a small boy, on a sidewalk in Manhattan, answering another small boy's questions about the difference between Republicans and Democrats: 'The Republicans are up for the British. The Democrats are up for the Americans.' I have no doubts about the ethnic origin of that definition.

stayed at home were encouraged to rebel by those who had left. The beginnings of the Irish revolution—that is, the revolution of the Catholic Irish—are as much in America as in Ireland.

The revolutionary secret society, which was founded in 1858, and which organized the Rising of 1916, developed as a combination between revolutionary elements in both main bodies of the native Irish people. It was called the Irish Republican Brotherhood in Ireland but—perhaps significantly—it is through the name it took in America— the Fenians—that it is best remembered. The military operations planned by the Fenians were uniformly unsuc- cessful: in the sixties, a quickly crushed insurrection in Ireland, and several bungled raids on Canada. The move- ment was, none the less, a school of brave, determined and imaginative revolutionaries. The most imaginative of these, John Devoy in America and Michael Davitt in Ireland, broke away from the original Fenian emphasis on direct military action, and helped create a socio-political movement of astonishing effectiveness: the New Departure, launched in the late seventies. The New Departure brought together revolutionaries of Fenian formation, and constitutional par- liamentary politicians, into a great radical agrarian and political movement. The mass organization of this movement was the Land League. Its leader, at first in name and later in fact, was Charles Stewart Parnell.

The significance of the New Departure movement was accurately stated by Joseph Chamberlain's biographer, J. L. Garvin: 'Nothing less than the strongest native revolt for over two hundred years, it sought to disrupt the bases of the Cromwellian settlement and of British Rule.'

The British Home Secretary of the day, Sir William Harcourt, stated with equal accuracy the reason why this native revolt could not be crushed:

In former Irish rebellions the Irish were *in Ireland*. We could reach their forces, cut off their reserves in men and money and then to subjugate was comparatively easy. Now there is an Irish nation in the United States, equally hostile, with plenty of money, absolutely beyond our reach and yet within ten days sail of our shores . . .

In Machiavelli's terms the 'injured' who had been 'scattered' were neither a 'tiny minority' nor all, any longer, poor. Some of them had found refuge with another Prince. They had been neither 'pampered' nor 'crushed'. Their injuries, though not small, were much less than 'fatal'. There were therefore grounds to fear 'revenge'. And these grounds were strongest in the area of the primal 'injury', the 'settlement' of Protestant Ulster.

For Protestant Ulster, the eighteen-eighties constituted the renewal of the siege, in a more dangerous form than at any time since the seventeenth century. Under the pressure of the Land League, using the weapon of the boycott, the landlord power—which was also the Protestant ascendancy—was decisively weakened throughout the Catholic-majority area. In terms of the siege, the outposts of Protestant Ulster were driven in. And out of the most effective mass movement in the history of Catholic Ireland, the representation of that Ireland in parliament had emerged for the first time as an effective organized force. Its leader was a Protestant, but in the eyes of Ulster Protestants—and most other Protestants at the time—he was the leader of the Catholics. And now this leader, Parnell, had brought about what seemed to Ulster Protestants an unthinkable event: the conversion of a Prime Minister of England to the idea of self-government for Ireland: self-government after Catholic emancipation and universal suffrage: implying domination of Protestants by Catholics, Drennan's sister's nightmare.

The Orange Order had long commemorated the Boyne, but it is in 1886 that this became the great mass demonstration that it is today. Even today, the style of the Belfast procession is Victorian. One of the banners still proudly carried shows the Great Queen handing the Bible to a kneeling black. The caption is: the Secret of England's Greatness. It carries a neat and cryptic point. There are natives whose distinguishing native characteristic it is to reject the Bible, and be disrespectful to the Monarch. They are thus below the poor black, who at least tries to share the Secret.

I have myself seen a Ghanaian Orangeman, a clergyman, whom I had known in Accra, on the platform of the dignitaries of the Order at Finaghy on 12th July, when this banner was carried through the field. I don't know whether he saw it or not, but a picture of him with the banner would not have looked as well in Accra as in Belfast.

My aunt Mary, David Sheehy's daughter, remembered as a child hearing of the Parnell divorce court verdict from Protestant children next door. They were laughing. So was Protestant Ulster. The fall of Parnell came as a welcome and appropriate present at the end of the bicentenary year of the defeat of James II.

The besiegers had been driven back. But they were still around.

# 3

# Songs of the Irish Race

*Droch-chríoch ort, Éire, is a ndintear d'amhráin ort.*
*'Bad end to you, Ireland, and the songs that they make for you.'*

MONSIGNOR PÁDRAIG DE BRÚN

The besiegers, most of them, were not thinking about the siege at all. Few, outside Ulster, gave much thought to Ulster. Most people in Ireland, when they thought in political cultural or 'national' terms, thought in terms of 'Ireland' as one, coherent entity and 'England' as another. The axis of their preoccupations ran east and west, not north and south. And the theme which preoccupied many of the most active minds among them in the period between the fall of Parnell and 1916 was not the unity of Ireland—which was strangely taken for granted—but the recovery of national identity, in cultural as well as political terms. Both Protestants and Catholics engaged in this quest, but their paths tended to diverge. The story of the Irish literary revival in one of its aspects is one of Protestant and Catholic consciousness in intermittent contact, often leading to increasing mutual distrust.

'The race,' as Yeats wrote, 'began, as I think, to be troubled by that event's long gestation.' The term 'the Irish race' was much used in the last decades of the nineteenth century and the first decades of this one; there were periodical 'Irish race conventions' in the United States—the most successful one, perhaps, being that of 1919 in Philadelphia—and frequent toasts to 'the Irish race at home and abroad'. The popularity of the term 'race' came, I think, partly from the Zeitgeiast but mainly from the need to include the Irish-Americans, whose jealously guarded Americanism would have been prejudiced by inclusion in 'the Irish nation'. An 'Irish Race' on the other hand could be claimed to be a desirable ethnic contribution to America, as well as justifying a claim to separate European nationality in Europe.

The term was ambiguous, but it possessed a fairly stable core of meaning. Only very few of those who used 'the Irish race'—or the older 'the Irish nation'—used it with close restriction, to include only those of native, Gaelic ancestry and Catholic religion. Yeats himself being wholly of Protestant, settler stock, could not have used it in this way. But most Catholics who used it did not quite mean it in this way either. Theobald Wolfe Tone and Robert Emmet were among the great heroes and martyrs of the Irish race, or nation:[1] its favourite poetry was that of Thomas Davis, its favourite prose that of John Mitchel. Protestant Patriots all. It is important to notice that this is not just a matter (among Catholics) of jingling together the names of prominent Protestant patriots—though this does happen on certain official occasions—but often a tie of real love and veneration. I have seen tears in the eyes of an Ulster Catholic Republican when he tried to express what he felt about Wolfe Tone.

Was 'the Irish race' then felt to include all those who were born in Ireland, whatever their religion, ancestry, political opinion or allegiance? And also, by extension, the American-born descendants of people in Ireland, whatever, *etc*?

This was the maximum definition, never wholly believed in and never wholly abandoned. 'We cannot give up a single Irishman,' said Parnell, claiming with the whole territory of Ulster, all the Ulster Protestants. Thomas Davis after describing the sufferings of the Gaelic-Irish at the hands of the English had added the words:

> *But start not, Irish-born man*
> *If you're to Ireland true—*

[1] I am using the term here to cover all those who thought of themselves as belonging to the Irish race, or nation. Most of these were, and are, Catholics. For Protestants the idea of being 'Irish' tends to combine with the feeling that this is essentially a regional description, or any rate not incompatible with being British. Since the second world war, however, most 'Southern' Protestants who have elected to remain and work in the Republic regard their nationality as being Irish. Ulster Protestants do not agree with them.

This implies, I think, that the 'Irish-born man' who refuses to be 'to Ireland true'—on the poet's terms, or the terms of whoever quotes the poet—is not a true Irishman and would do well to 'start'. Davis was of Protestant, settler stock. A later poet, of native, Catholic stock, added a harder, more explicit emphasis. Thomas MacDonagh, one of the signatories to the Proclamation of the Republic, wrote in his *Literature in Ireland: Studies Irish and Anglo-Irish*, published in the year of his execution, 1916:

Anglo-Irish literature is distinctly a new literature, the first expression of the life and ways of thought of a new people, hither-to without literary expression, differing from English literature of all the periods, not with the difference of age, but with the difference of race and nationality. That race is the Irish race, now mainly English-speaking.

MacDonagh adds that this race is filled with memories of the old Gaelic literature, 'moving to the rhythm of Irish music', etc.—a clear implication that by 'the Irish race' he means here those of native, Gaelic stock. He goes on:

... The term Anglo-Irish literature is applied very rarely to the meagre writings of the planters: it is worth having as a term only to apply to the literature produced by the English-speaking Irish, and by these in general only when writing in Ireland and for the Irish people.

In a variant of Yeats's 'long gestation' MacDonagh says that 'The revival of nationalism among the Irish subject majority following the days of the Irish Volunteers, the United Irishmen, the Independent Parliament: this national-ism, strengthened by O'Connell with Catholic Emancipation and the franchise; this nationalism, hardened by the austere independence of Parnell, by the land war and its victorious close, this brought to full manhood by the renewed 'struggle for legislative freedom, and the certainty of triumph and responsibility; this, free from alien hope and fear, craving no ease, hearing always the supreme song of victory on the dying lips of martyrs, this produced the unrest, the mysteri-ous intrepid adventure that shouts the song of joy for the sad things and for the glad things of life'.

Anglo-Irish literature, he concluded, 'could come only, when English had become the language of the Irish people mainly of Gaelic stock'. What MacDonagh writes about literature implies a view of what 'the Irish race' was, and I think McDonagh is fairly representative of those who used the term, or who use corresponding terms today. By 'the Irish race' is meant, as far as Ireland is concerned:

Primarily, people of native Irish stock, descended from Gaelic speakers, professing the Catholic religion, and holding some form of the general political opinions held by most people of this origin and religion;

Secondarily, people of settler stock in Ireland, and Protestant religion: to the extent that these cast in their lot with people in the first category, culturally or politically, or preferably both.[2]

It is people belonging to these categories, and these only, who would have been welcomed at an Irish Race Convention in America, or in any similar gathering. Furthermore, persons belonging to the second category would be welcomed only in so far as they emphasized those characteristics which linked them to the first. Sir Samuel Ferguson, for example, would have been warmly welcomed had he spoken on Gaelic literature—that is to say the ancestral literature of people in the first category—but would have been at best coldly received had he dwelt on his political opinions, which were those shared by most of his own community: the Unionist opinions common to most, though not all, of the descendants of Protestant settlers. He would have been welcomed, in short, as a member of the Irish race, precisely to the extent that he was unrepresentative of his own community.[3]

Sir Samuel Ferguson, well aware of this, would not have

[2] 'The Irish nation' was and is used in exactly this way. In the standard Fianna Fail history, *The Irish Republic,* the late Dorothy MacArdle repeatedly says that 'the whole nation' rejoiced or grieved at various tidings which were received in the reverse way by Ulster Protestants. Miss MacArdle was herself a Protestant in a way—she had been born a Catholic but changed her religion during the Civil War, when the Catholic Church excommunicated Republicans.

[3] Compare the welcome given in Protestant Ulster to speakers and writers like M. J. F. McCarthy, who were Southern Catholics *but* determined to expose the role of the priest, etc., and so became honorary 'Ulstermen'. There are differences: a Protestant who attacked the Protestant clergy or customs would not then have been well received at an Irish Race Convention anywhere.

been seen dead at any such gathering. Indeed he suppressed some of his later writings of Gaelic inspiration for fear, precisely, of contributing to the kind of national-cultural-political ferment that Yeats and later MacDonagh described. This was the act of 'an honest man' according to Gerard Manley Hopkins, who as an English patriot feared the separatist nationalism that pervades Irish Catholicism.

Ferguson was an Ulster Protestant. The leading figures of the Irish Literary Movement and Irish language revival, which became forces after the fall of Parnell, were Protestants, but Southern Protestants.[4] Yeats, Synge, Lady Gregory, Douglas Hyde. The distinction is much more than geographical. Southern Protestants are, and even then were, a very small and scattered minority, almost all middle class, or landed. Their relations with Catholics, though not always easy, are far more frequent, subtle and varied than is generally possible in the Ulster siege conditions. A Samuel Ferguson, in Ulster, could interest himself in Ancient Ireland, but not too much in the degenerate descendants of a great Celtic past: the feelings of such a man about ancient Rome and contemporary Romans (dirt, superstition, cruelty to animals) would have been rather closely comparable. But some Southern Protestants excited by the wealth of the old Gaelic literature now open to them in translation, and having a significantly more open relation to the Catholic—and recently Gaelic—world around them began to explore the living traditions; the possibilities of an English permeated by Gaelic; the idea of a literature growing from these traditions, and this kind of English: the possibilities of the revival of the Gaelic language itself, as still spoken in the remoter parts of the West; cultutral nationalism.

As Yeats and Hyde explored these things in the eighties and nineties they met, and came to work with, Catholics who were also interested in them. By no means all Catholics were, or are. Most were too poor to concern themselves consciously with such things. Many of those who were better off felt that they had 'left all that behind them'. Gaelic—

---

[4] The leading exception was George Russell (AE) an Ulster Protestant by birth, but a Southerner by residence, and member of the Irish race as above defined.

spoken by most of the population up to the Great Famine of the 1840's—was backward, associated with poverty and defeat, English was the language of reality and progress— even the language of effective struggle against England. You could be 'for' English while being 'against' England. English was what they spoke in America. The Irish in America, who hated England more than the Irish at home did, had little use for the Irish language. Nor had the Catholic clergy in general much use for it, or for the pagan myths and legends of the Celtic past, or for young Protestants who were drawn to such things. The Irish race was now a scattered race; what it was scattered through was the English-speaking world. It might perhaps be the destiny of the Irish race to convert the English-speaking world, or at least to influence that world in a Catholic direction. In any case English was the language now needed for the care of Irish souls, as well as for the material welfare of Irish people.

There were, however, some Catholics, including some Catholic priests, who felt differently, and set store by Irish traditions, by the concept of Irish culture, by Irish patriotic writings in English, and by the idea of acquiring some knowledge of Irish. These people met in various local Irish literary or cultural groups, in Ireland and Britain, drawing most of their inspiration from Thomas Davis and from the Young Ireland movement of the 1840's. Such societies were widespread among the Irish in Britain, for whom they served as meeting places, and also as centres for the preservation of national identity—clearly threatened with Anglicization in Britain even more closely than in Ireland itself. What proved to be the most important of these societies, the Southwark Irish Literary Club, was formed in January 1883 out of a Junior Club for teaching children, and probably other societies had a similar origin. The objects of the Southwark society were 'the cultivation of Irish history, art and literature and the providing of a medium of social and intellectual intercourse for Irish people of both sexes'.[5] The

[5] W. P. Ryan. *The Irish Literary Revival*, London 1894. This is an important document for the early history of this movement. Quotations in this part of the text about the movement are from Ryan, unless otherwise stated.

Catholic clergy had a general pastoral interest in all this—
as tending for example to promote Catholic rather than
'mixed' marriages—but this of course did not rule out a more
spontaneous and specific interest in Irish history and culture
on the part of some priests. Nominally, these societies were
not Catholic, in England at least, though in Scotland they
sometimes were: either explicitly in name (like the Dundee
Catholic Literary Society and the Glasgow and West of
Scotland Literary Associations) or in substance, like the
Sunderland Irish Literary Society, headed by 'two types of
the Soggarth aroon'.[6] The equivalent society in Belfast was
the Belfast Young Ireland Society, founded about 1883: 'a
virile Celtic centre', according to Ryan, with 'an essentially
missionary career'. Ryan also claimed that the Belfast Young
Ireland Society 'united all creeds and classes'. Perhaps he
obtained this information from the then secretary of the
Belfast Society, whom he names: Joe Devlin. Joe Devlin
was the most dynamic and able Catholic leader in Ulster, a
pillar of the Ancient Order of Hibernians (the Catholic
answer to the Orange Order) and later boss of Belfast's
Catholic ghetto.

These societies were in fact drawn from 'the Irish race',
as defined above. As far as the Northern tier—Scotland and
Ulster—was concerned, the participation of the second
category of the Irish race was negligible.[7] For the Southern
tier however—including London and Dublin—the interaction of the two categories was to have important results.
Yeats used the Southwark Literary Society as the nucleus for
the Irish Literary Society, London, founded in 1891. As he
recalled years afterwards in *The Trembling of the Veil*:

There was a little Irish Society of young people, clerks, shop-boys,
and shop-girls, called 'The Southwark Irish Literary Society', and
it had ceased to meet because the girls got the giggles when any
member of the Committee got up to speak. Every member of it
had said all he had to say many times over. I had given them a

[6] Soggarth aroon: 'darling priest' (in pidgin Gaelic).
[7] Some at least of the Scottish Societies with 'Catholic' in their titles were
founded after the Parnell split, and may imply a clerical defensive measure
against Parnellite cultural infiltration.

lecture about the falling asunder of the human mind as an opening flower falls asunder, and all had professed admiration because I had made such a long speech without quotation or narrative; and now I invited the Committee to my father's house at Bedford Park and there proposed a new organization: 'The Irish Literary Society'.

W. P. Ryan, a member of that unfortunate Committee, gives the date of the meeting at the Yeats' house as 28th December 1891—not quite three months after Parnell's death. He also remembers Yeats coming to the Southwark Literary Society, and even the date on which he came first: March 1888. He remembers him as having given a talk about 'fairies'—probably the talk to which Yeats refers, about 'the falling asunder of the human mind'—and remembers people having felt there was too much about Co. Sligo fairies: inter-County rivalry was always a marked feature of Irish societies overseas. 'Gradually', as Ryan remembers it, 'he [Yeats] became one of ourselves'.

For Yeats, in retrospect, this was 'the baptism of the gutter', about which he wrote to Lady Gregory; he was also to remember telling his acquaintances from 'the prosperous educated classes' whose support he attracted for his literary movement: 'Now you must be baptized of the gutter'.

The most obvious features of the situation are those of social class: cultivated upper-middle-class among raw lower-middle-class. Yeats, like the girls, must sometimes have found it hard not to giggle at members of the Committee—if for example Ryan spoke, as he wrote in his book, of Oscar Wilde as 'the head centre of asceticism'. What drew them together, however, was not an attribute of class, but the concept of the Irish nation, or race. London strengthened this bond—on the same principle as London by failing to differentiate between Africans of different tribes helped to create African nationalism—but the bond existed also in Ireland, where Yeats established the National Literary Society in 1892. (It is true that this was in a Dublin exceedingly conscious of London's consciousness of Ireland.) But also the two groups had something to offer one another, which had little to do with class. The Catholic natives were pleased by the idea that *their*

culture—the language and achievements of *their* ancestors—
was prized at its just and high worth by a Protestant, because
the Protestant's judgment had to be accepted as impartial,
since he was, after all, an outsider, in the sense that these
were not *his* ancestors.[8] The Protestant—Southern Protestant
—for his part gained, for a time, a somewhat deceptive
sensation of being accepted as fully Irish, not an uncertain
marginality between Ireland and England. There was a
misunderstanding here, but a fruitful one.

There were also questions of revolutionary politics involved,
interacting in curious ways with the 'religious', caste and
class factors. Ryan recalls that 'the first workers in the literary
movement' were 'of that cultured and studious force in the
Land League, who saw in the agitation at first a real national
upheaval . . . but who as time went on were somewhat
disillusioned'. This is interesting because—to the extent we
accept it—it would make the beginning of the great ferment,
not Parnell's fall, but Parnell's swing to the right—what
might today be called his 'sell-out', eight years earlier, in
1882. Up to that point, a revolutionary section—known as
the 'ribbon-fenians'—had supported the movement headed
by Parnell and Davitt, because they hoped it would prepare
the way for armed revolution. But by the 'Kilmainham
Treaty', with Gladstone, in May 1882, Parnell committed
the movement to the use of purely constitutional means,
accepted the partial estrangement of Davitt, and some of the
'ribbon-fenians', and enlisted on his side the conservative
force of the Catholic clergy, enrolled into the organization of
the National League. This settlement he maintained
until 1890, when, under pressure of necessity, he tried to
liquidate the Kilmainham Treaty. As the old Fenian,
John O'Leary told Yeats: 'In this country a man must have
on his side the Church or the Fenians.' Parnell chose the
Church in 1882: in 1890 he had to choose the Fenians.

There is no need to split hairs about exactly when the

[8] Similarly Africans are pleased by the interest of Africanists, and people in
the Aran Islands were pleased by the interest of German philologists and
American anthropologists. In all these situations there seems to be a curious
delight in the feeling that the stranger knows far more than oneself and yet—
being a stranger—understands nothing.

movement started. What is certain is that Yeats, after the fall and death of Parnell, used—for the creation of what became known to history as the Irish literary movement— a society which was founded in 1883, in the wake of the Kilmainham Treaty, and that in both phases, Fenian revolutionaries, opposed to the political influence of the Church, played an important part in the society; as they also did in the shaping of the Parnell movement, in its original form, before 1882, and in supporting Parnell's final defiance in 1890-91.

The Fenians—more properly, Republicans—were interested in the literary movement primarily as a means of restoring national pride; Yeats remembered how often his Fenian mentor, John O'Leary, who introduced Yeats into the brotherhood in 1887, used the term *morale*. It is also clear that they used the literary societies as recruiting grounds, or sounding boards, or as what would later have been called 'fronts'. The comparison is not a forced one. The Irish Republican Brotherhood, a secret oath-bound society founded in 1868, and operating both in Ireland and North America, was one of those disciplined revolutionary societies which drew its inspiration from continental models, in France and Italy: the same models which inspired the Russian Social Revolutionaries from whom the Bolsheviks derived methods, organization and discipline, though not doctrine. There was some contact between the Fenian movement and contemporary Marxism. James Stephens, founder and original 'head centre' of the Brotherhood, joined Marx's International Working Men's Society in New York: Marx seems to have feared that his joining might damage the reputation and standing of the First International. As for Stephens, he was not a Marxist, but a singleminded Irish national separatist revolutionary. He seems to have been interested in making use of the International, like other things, for purposes of Irish propaganda—using the Communists as a front.

The Catholic Church in Ireland was opposed to the Fenians, because they were a secret oath-bound society, which was forbidden; because they resembled organizations in Europe which were hostile to the Pope and condemned by him—especially Mazzini's movement—and because, in 1865 and 1867, they had fomented revolutionary uprisings which were hopeless, and as such immoral, according to Catholic doctrine, and, more generally, because Fenians were headstrong, refractory Catholics, some of whom had in the past led others into social revolution, and acts of terrorism, or both.

The Fenians, for their part, did their best to treat Church condemnation as irrelevant, a result of the political manipulation of individual Bishops in Ireland, and of the Vatican itself, by the long arm of the British Government. Such manipulation existed, marginally; it was tactically convenient to exaggerate it. In any case there were many priests, especially younger priests, who were personally sympathetic to the Fenians, and who felt that there was something in what they said about certain Bishops, and even about the Vatican. Orangemen believed that the Catholic Bishops condemned the Fenians for reasons of expediency only, and that they too were Fenians at heart. In Orange Ulster, 'Fenian' or 'Fenian bastard' remain generic terms for Catholics. The Catholic Bishop who said that 'hell is not hot enough nor eternity long enough' to punish the Fenian leaders was himself a Fenian, according to Belfast usage.

Inside the literary societies, relations between clergy and Fenians seem normally to have been not unfriendly. But conditions at the time when the Irish Literary Society was founded, just after Parnell's death, were far from normal. These were conditions propitious for the Fenians rather than for the clergy, because the kind of young people who made up these societies—and the Gaelic Athletic Association and later the Gaelic League—were mostly Parnellites, being almost by definition people who believed that an Irish leader should not be dropped at the bidding of an Englishman.

For a time, this made the going easier for a Yeats who was—if only nominally—a Fenian himself, and was a strong Parnellite. Social clubs conducted by the Catholic clergy, as the Scottish 'Irish literary societies' obviously were, and as the societies in England had also been to a more limited extent, would not easily have lent themselves to a 'Protestant' initiative. But to Parnellites and Fenians—overlapping groups at the end of 1891—a *Protestant* Parnellite (and Fenian) was especially welcome. As for the Catholic clergy, who were accused of having murdered Parnell, they would have been ill-advised at this point to challenge the credentials of a Protestant Parnellite.

The second category of the Irish race was never again in as good a position to lay down terms to the first category as it was in the early 1890's, when Yeats founded the Irish Literary Society in London, and the National Literary Society in Dublin, and George Moore thought: 'So Ireland is awakening at last out of the great sleep of Catholicism.'

By the end of the century, however, the first category was reasserting its national claim to preponderance.[9] The Parnell struggle had spent most of its fury. In 1900 the Irish parliamentary party was re-united. Old anti-Parnellites like David Sheehy accepted the leadership of an old Parnellite, John Redmond. The Catholic and nationalist society was knitting together again. The social influence of the clergy was restored to normal: Yeats felt uncomfortable: it is from this period that his first reference to 'the baptism of the gutter' comes. He increasingly felt that Maud Gonne, and himself, were wasting their lives on a quixotic enterprise. His play *The Countess Cathleen*, which reflects this feeling through a pastoral allegory, was the cause of the first major literary controversy, with overtone of Catholic versus Protestant, landlord versus peasant, when it was first produced, in 1899. The plot of the play was simple. In famine time, demon-merchants buy the souls of peasants; Countess Cathleen gives away all she has, and finally sells her own soul, to save the peasants;[10] she is, however, saved through the goodness of her motives.

Formally, the main attack on the play seemed to be theo-

[9] I am not here concerned with the history of the Irish literary movement in itself: only with what we can learn from it about 'the Irish race' and its two categories.

[10] There may or may not be an indirect echo of this transaction in the title of Miss Bernadette Devlin's autobiography: *The Price of my Soul*.

logical: against the heresy that one could sell one's soul to demons and still save it. Cardinal Logue, who had neither seen nor read the play, recommended others to do likewise. George Moore understandably thought it all nonsense: 'The play of course shocks nobody's feelings but it gives people an opportunity to think their feelings have been shocked, and it gives other people an opportunity of making a noise.'

Moore was probably right as far as the theological point was concerned. Indeed, Cardinal Logue's provisional condemnation possibly 'saved' Yeats, as far as his Fenian friends were concerned. If the Cardinal condemned the play, without seeing or reading it, then a good Fenian would defend it, without seeing or reading it either. But Moore was wrong in supposing that the play 'shocks nobody's feelings'. It did shock people who saw it; it shocked not for theological, but for social and tribal reasons. To begin with, it explicitly depicts 'peasants', a word so long used contemptuously in generalization about Irish peasants, as to be virtually taboo among the new Catholic middle class of peasant origin: the audience for Irish theatre of this kind. Then these peasants are 'bad' and 'good'. The bad peasants are the first to appear, Sheamus and Teig.[11] They say things like this:

SHEAMUS: My curse upon the rich.
TEIG: They're coming here.
SHEAMUS: Then down upon that stool, down girl, I say
And call up a whey face and a whining voice
and let your head be bowed upon your knees.

The only landowner who appears is the fantastically noble and generous Countess Cathleen, and the *good* peasants recognize her intrinsic superiority:

OONA: O, that so many pitchers of rough clay
Should prosper and the porcelain break in two!
(*she kisses the hands of Cathleen*).

[11] 'Teig' was unfortunate: 'Teig' or Teigue [Gaelic Tadhg] as a name is one of the terms of contempt used by Protestants about Catholics, still heard in Northern Ireland. I heard, at Finaghy in 1967, one Orangeman tell another, with disgust, of Captain O'Neill's alleged desire for social fraternization with Catholics: 'He wants to meet Mick, he wants to meet Teig'.

It must have puzzled as much as it shocked. It is presented in a language based though rather remotely on the language of 'the people'—Gaelic idioms, Catholic blessings and curses: 'The Scene is laid in Ireland and in old times'. Yet its myth of famine is based not on a tradition alive among the people, but on one acceptable to the Ascendancy. In the people's tradition the good—not peasants, but people—kept their Faith, through their own sufferings, not through alms. The bad, or the most unfortunate, sold their souls, or their Faith, but not to the 'Eastern', rather Jewish-seeming merchants of the play, but to the establishment of the English Protestant evangelical societies who dispensed soup, conditionally, in the great famine of the 1840's. *The Countess Cathleen* is so alien to the living traditions of those on whose lives it claims to be ultimately based that it must have embarrassed as well as shocked. It was a reminder of how far apart, in their vision of Ireland, the two categories of the Irish race could actually be.

The students of the new Royal University—founded to make University education available to Catholics[12]—protested against *The Countess Cathleen*:

We feel it our duty, in the name and for the honour of Dublin Catholic students of the Royal University to protest against an art, even a dispassionate art, which offers as a type of our people a loathesome breed of apostates.

Only one Dublin Catholic student at the Royal University refused to sign this manifesto. That was James Joyce. Among those who signed were Richard Sheehy, David Sheehy's son; Francis Skeffington, who later married Hanna Sheehy, and took the name Sheehy-Skeffington, and Tom Kettle, who later married Mary Sheehy, with whom James Joyce was at this time in love.[13] Skeffington and Kettle were among the student leaders at the time, and probably helped to draft the manifesto.

[12] Some Catholics went to Trinity College, but the Catholic hierarchy was hostile to it. The hierarchy's ban on Trinity was not lifted until 1970.
[13] See Richard Ellman, *James Joyce* (1959). Professor Ellman, in a rare factual error, describes Mary as the youngest Sheehy daughter. She was the second youngest; the youngest was Kathleen, mother of the present writer.

As Catholic Dublin went, round the turn of the century, the Sheehy family seemed prosperous. There was little money—David Sheehy was wholly dependent on his stipend as an M.P.—but Dublin, unlike Belfast, is a city designed for keeping up a high proportion of state ('pretence') in proportion to income. The family—David, his wife Bessie, two sons, Richard and Eugene, and four daughters, Hanna, Margaret, Mary and Kathleen—lived in a fine Georgian house at 2 Belvedere Place, and most observers were struck with how very pleased with themselves they all seemed to be. The children went, not to the grandest Catholic schools—Clongowes Wood (for boys) and Mount Anville (for girls)—but to the next best: the best *day* schools: Belvedere College (Jesuit) for the boys, the Dominican Convent, Eccles Street, for girls. Exhibitions—substantial money prizes—were then available at three levels of secondary education, and Bessie systematically encouraged the children to go out and get these, which they did: they were an important element in the Belvedere Place economy. Bessie discouraged any idea that woman's place was in the home; servants were cheap and winning exhibitions made more economic sense than doing the housework. The girls did not look on the thing in quite the same light. Finding that they could beat boys in competitive examinations but that men, however stupid, remained in control, they all became ardent feminists and women's suffragists (not suffra-*gettes*: a frivolous and derogatory term).

Bessie did not know words like 'upward social mobility' and 'rising national bourgeoisie', but she had the idea. The brightest students from the Royal used to come to Belvedere Place on Sundays; we have James Joyce's word for it that Frank Skeffington was the second cleverest man at the Royal, Joyce himself being the cleverest: most people of the time would have rated Tom Kettle the cleverest of the three: all three were there. The Sheehy girls were so conditioned that they could have no use for stupid boys. Bessie was to find that this was not as unmixed an advantage as she supposed.

My grandmother intended, quite consciously I believe, to preside over the birth of a new ruling class: those who would run the country when Home Rule was won. It was not a fanciful ambition. The Parnell split was over, the Irish party united once again. This unity was soon symbolized by a family event: Mary's marriage to Tom Kettle, whose father Andrew Kettle had been one of 'Parnell's faithful few', Parnellite candidate in one of the ghastly by-elections of 1891. (Parnell, whose oratory was understandably not at its best that year, introduced his candidate to one meeting with the words: 'The name Kettle is a household word in Ireland.') Tom Kettle himself joined the parliamentary party, when he was elected for one of the 'evenly balanced' areas of Northern Ireland. He was also Professor of National Economics at the Royal University. To some, and certainly to his mother-in-law, he looked a likely future Prime Minister in a home rule government.

They were all conscious—as Unionist Ulster in its own way was conscious—of the day that must come when the Liberals would hold office depending on Irish support, and would introduce the Third Home Rule Bill. For the first Home Rule Bill, the Liberals had been split; for the second, the Irish party had been split; for the third, the two parties united would put the thing through. The Lords would put up a struggle but could not, in a democratic age, hold out indefinitely.

It seemed reasonable, around 1900, to base policy on such an expectation: to most people it seemed far more realistic than the policy of Arthur Griffith's Sinn Féin: withdrawal from Westminster, and organizing mass demonstrations in favour of a dual monarchy. In fact, it now seems as if both policies would have led to essentially the same result, through different channels and at different prices. For both policies, and the policy of the Irish Republican Brotherhood also, were firmly rooted in the soil of Catholic Ireland, which they identified with Ireland; not formally, but in reality.

Number 2 Belvedere Place was a Catholic household; all the children were at Catholic schools and the Catholic university, so all the children's friends were Catholics, and all my grandmother's subtle match-making and her ambitions pre-supposed Catholic dynasties. 'Home Rule means Rome Rule', said the Ulster Protestant slogan. Not at all. When

Rome had opposed the social and economic interests of 'our people'—the people of rural Ireland, practising the Catholic religion—then Rome had been told, in effect, to mind its own business. John Dillon, David Sheehy's leader, had spoken, in the land war time, in a manner that, according to a Protestant newspaper, 'would have gladdened the heart of poor old Luther', and David Sheehy had followed him without hesitation. The aspiring middle class of Belvedere Place still identified with the tenant-farmers of the Land War, from which it sprang, and what 'the Dublin Catholic students' resented in *The Countess Cathleen* was not an abstract blasphemy against the Faith, but a concrete insult to 'our people'. It was 'our people', neither Rome nor the Protestant ascendancy, who should rule in Ireland. 'Our people', through an *élite,* sprung from it, trained for its service, justified through success in the democratic process (first generation) and in open competitive examinations (second generation), as well as through an honourable history of sturdy resistance to oppression. The Jesuits were helping to train such an *élite.* So was my grandmother. James Joyce in *Ulysses* records the tone of a meeting between the two forces, towards the turn of the century:

[Father John Conmee, S.J.] walked up the avenue of sunnywinking leaves and towards him came the wife of Mr. David Sheehy M.P.
 —Very well, indeed, father. And you, father?
 Father Conmee was wonderfully well indeed. He would go to Buxton probably for the waters. And her boys, were they getting on well at Belvedere?[14] Was that so? Father Conmee was very glad indeed to hear that. And Mr Sheehy himself. Still in London. The house was still sitting, to be sure it was. Beautiful weather it was, delightful indeed. Yes, it was very probable that Father Bernard Vaughan would come again to preach. O, yes: a very great success. A wonderful man really.
 Father Conmee was very glad to see the wife of Mr. David Sheehy, M.P. looking so well and he begged to be remembered to Mr. David Sheehy, M.P. Yes, he would certainly call.
 —Good afternoon, Mrs. Sheehy.
 Father Conmee doffed his silk hat, as he took leave, at the jet beads of her mantilla glistening in the sun.

[14] They had left Belvedere long before 1904. The literalness of that date is sometimes exaggerated.

# 4

# Colonists and Colonized

*Au mensonge de la situation coloniale, le colonisé répond par un mensonge égal.*

FRANTZ FANON, *Les damnés de la terre*

i

The Boer War encouraged 'physical force' ideas in Ireland. Almost all Irish nationalist opinion—that is, almost all Irish Catholics, plus category two—sympathized with the Boers, who were seen simply as a small nation rightly struggling to be free. The idea that a better parallel might be with the aboriginal natives of the country in question did not occur to most people, and was generally rejected by those to whom it did occur. John Mitchel, years before, had indignantly rejected any analogy between the position of the Irish and that of the black slaves of America and Arthur Griffith—who, as the founder of Sein Féin was now beginning to be the most influential mind among militant Irish nationalists and had worked in South Africa—was in the Mitchel tradition and ridiculed any suggestion that the Irish had much in common with non-white subject peoples of the Empire. The Irish were an ancient, civilized *European* people, and any comparison with non-whites was an insult to them. Michael Davitt thought somewhat differently, but Davitt also was a pro-Boer. The tone of the chorus of British 'jingoism' at this time was such as to make it impossible for an Irish nationalist to be anything other than pro-Boer.

At the time of the American revolution, Belfast more than Dublin, Protestant more than Catholic, had sympathized with the rebels. By the time of the Boer War, however, Protestant Ulster was one of the most jingo parts of the Empire, noisily hostile to a people, the Afrikaners, which was in fact very like itself: dourly Protestant, thoroughly besieged, sure of its God-given superiority, slow, suspicious, determined and tough. Today these similarities do not go altogether unmarked: Some Protestant Unionists favour the cause of the whites of Southern Africa, and the white backlash generally: the *Protestant Telegraph* has carried communiqués from Ian Smith's Rhodesian Front, and members of his movement denounced the boycott by the Irish Trade Unions of the South African Rugby Team on its visit to Ireland at the beginning of 1970.

But in the Boer war time there were decisive reasons for being against the Boers. The Empire was at war, and a sense of the might of the Empire had become important to the morale of Protestant Ulster. Also, as the Catholics rejoiced over every British humiliation, the Protestants were once more reminded of the reality of the siege, the ineradicable hostility and—in Protestant eyes—disloyalty of people who, in quiet times, might be taken for peaceable neighbours. At the same time, the poor performance of the British Army was a disquieting intimation of how fragile the great Empire might really be, and of the need for Ulster to be vigilant. Finally, there was good material here for Ulster and Tory propaganda: the disloyalty of Catholic Ireland during the Boer War showed what kind of people these were to whom the Liberals wanted to hand over control of a part of Her, and later His, Majesty's Realms. It was an effective argument, especially with officers in the British Army: a critically important section of opinion, as events were to show.

It was in fact an argument that tended towards the rehabilitation of violence, both North and South. From the Ulster Protestant point of view, since Catholic disloyalty to the English was now an obvious proven fact, the Liberal theory that a Home Rule Ireland would be a loyal self-governing part of the Empire was untenable. Home Rule was, therefore, a poorly disguised treasonable enterprise, which it would be right to resist by force if necessary. Such ideas had been in the air since Home Rule had first been seriously mooted. They were greatly strengthened by the Boer War.

As far as Catholic and nationalist Ireland was concerned, the general enthusiasm for the Boers worked specifically against the constitutional Irish Parliamentary Party, and in favour of the militant and physical force groups. The Irish party were caught in a dilemma quite like that of the Northern Ireland Unionist Governments of Captain O'Neill and Major Chichester-Clark in our own time. They had, that is to say, to give some satisfaction to a local Irish public, and to a British public, in conditions in which these two publics had strongly conflicting feelings and opinions. The Irish party's only hope of winning Home Rule was by working the Liberal alliance, and this meant convincing the British that a Home Rule Ireland would be friendly to Britain. For this reason, the Irish Party had to play down the spontaneously anti-British reactions of its constituents—and of its own members—to news of British victories and defeats. And this muted style tended to reduce the appeal, particularly to the young, of the reunited Irish Party, and to favour the influence of more uninhibited groups like Sinn Fein.

To speak of 'spontaneously anti-British reactions' might be misleading. Simple hate for the English was a common emotion, for quite adequate reasons, among the Catholic Irish from the sixteenth century into the first half of the nineteenth. But by the end of the nineteenth century, the Catholic Irish, having lost their native language, had become, if they remained in Ireland, to a great extent Anglicized. This did not entirely eliminate the old hate, but turned it into one element in a more complex system. So far as hate survived, it had now to include self-hate and self-contempt: quite important components in the psychology of some Irishmen, as of other 'colonized peoples'. But it was also possible for Irishmen to identify, in part, with a section of the English, as the Irish Party did with the Liberals, and, for a time, successfully encouraged its supporters to do; the Englishman Gladstone attained a fame and popularity in Ireland, from 1886 to 1891, unequalled by any Irishmen of the nineteenth century, except O'Connell and Parnell, and excepting also the posthumous popularity of martyrs. On the left, ideology and a common language produced the idea of the identity of interest and the solidarity of the English and Irish working class. Among the educated, a knowledge of English literature—and generally an ignorance of Irish and other literature—developed a special spiritual bond, cutting across history and religion. It must be very difficult really and thoroughly to hate a people on whose language and literature one is brought up.[1] Certainly the only educated Irishman I ever knew whose anti-English feeling seemed to me unquestioning and without flaw was a man whose first language was French.

This complexity of feeling affected not only the Catholic Irish, but 'the Irish race' in its full extension. Yeats expounded it in his old age:

The 'Irishry' [he wrote in *A General Introduction for my Work* (1937)] have preserved their ancient 'deposit' through wars which, during the sixteenth and seventeenth centuries, became wars of extermination; no people, Lecky said at the opening of his *Ireland in the Eighteenth Century*, have undergone greater persecution, nor did that persecution altogether cease up to our own day. No people hate as we do in whom that past is always alive, there are moments when hatred poisons my life and I accuse myself of effeminacy because I have not given it adequate expression. It is not enough to have put it into the mouth of a rambling peasant poet. Then I remind myself that though mine is the first English marriage I know of in the direct line, all my family names are English and that I owe my soul to Shakespeare, to Spenser and to Blake, perhaps to William Morris, and to the English language in which I think, speak and write, that everything I love has come to me through English; my hatred tortures me with love, my love with hate. I am like the Tibetan monk who dreams at his initiation that he is eaten by a wild beast and learns on waking that he himself is eater and eaten. This is Irish hatred and solitude, the hatred of human life that made Swift write *Gulliver* and the epitaph upon his tomb, that can still make us wag between the extremes and doubt our sanity.

But however complex the feelings of the Irish race about the English people, their language and their culture might

[1] Consider James Baldwin's losing struggle to hate Shakespeare.

be, their feelings about the Crown, and about British power, were generally simple enough. There was a sizeable minority that served the Crown—in the police, the Army and the civil service—and among these and their families there were indeed notable tensions and complexities of loyalty. But for those not connected, or only distantly connected, with that service, dislike of British power was automatic: it was indeed the mainspring of the Home Rule vote. And this dislike was fanned to a more active hostility by the spectacle of British power being used to crush a small people, and by the spectacle of the small people's resistance. The question became more insistent: if the Boers can do it, why not the Irish?

Some Irishmen went to South Africa to fight on the Boer side. One of them was Major John MacBride.

## ii

It was at this time of nationalist and martial excitement that the literary movement made its most significant contribution to revolutionary feeling. Yeats wrote, and Maud Gonne played, *Cathleen ni Houlihan* in 1902.

*Countess Cathleen* had reflected Yeats's feelings about Maud Gonne's sacrifices, and his own, to the popular patriotic cause:

> *She pity-crazed had given her soul away.*

In a sense the tone of that play, and the way in which the peasants were depicted represented a sort of defection by a member of the second category of the Irish race from voluntary servitude to the first, defection through glorification of the pathos of condescension. The defection had been sensed and rebuked. *Cathleen ni Houlihan* represents a temporary reversal of the mood of *Countess Cathleen*: a glorification of Maud Gonne's romantic idea of Irish nationalism: a rejoining of the Irish race. The play is set apparently in 1798. Cathleen ni Houlihan—a traditional allegorical personification of Ireland—appears, in the guise of an old woman, to summon to the rebellion a young man who is about to be married. She insists on the need to sacrifice all for Ireland, and that those who die in this cause 'shall be remembered for ever'. At the end she is transformed into her true likeness.

—Did you see an old woman going down the path.
—I saw no old woman but a young girl and she had the walk of a queen.

Long afterwards, and long after the Rising of 1916, Yeats as he lay dying asked himself the question:

> *Did that play of mine send out*
> *Certain men the English shot?*

A question of this kind had been asked at the time *Cathleen ni Houlihan* was first produced. 'The effect of *Cathleen ni Houlihan* on me', said Stephen Gwynn, 'was that I went home asking myself if such plays should be produced unless one was prepared for people to go out to shoot and be shot. Miss Gonne's impersonation had stirred the audience as I have never seen another audience stirred.' Gwynn was a Protestant constitutional nationalist, a supporter of the Irish Party. More militant nationalists experienced something like religious ecstasy from *Cathleen ni Houlihan*. For the Republican revolutionary, P. S. O'Hegarty, it was a 'sort of sacrament'. Constance Markievicz, sentenced to death for her part in the 1916 Rising, recalled in prison that, for her, *Cathleen ni Houlihan* had been 'a sort of gospel'. There is a distinct touch of Yeats's *Cathleen ni Houlihan* about the personified Ireland of the 1916 Proclamation of the Republic who summoned her children to her flag. The personification itself was a very old Gaelic literary tradition, but it was undoubtedly Yeats who made it come alive for those who lived in the first decades of the twentieth century.

Yeats himself almost immediately recoiled from *Cathleen ni Houlihan*. The being he had created continued to beckon others, but left her creator cold. The literary and political movements, which had been so close together since Parnell's death, now diverged. Maud Gonne, in 1903, married the Boer War hero, Major John MacBride. Yeats's point of view, now strongly influenced by Nietzsche, became more distinctly aristocratic: the mood of *Countess Cathleen* clarified and hardened. His theatre would be a theatre of art, not of propaganda: the uneasy alliance of art and national propaganda which had in fact existed in the earlier phase of the literary movement—and of which *Cathleen ni Houlihan* remained the most potent example—was now dissolved. Synge's plays, *The Shadow of the Glen* (1903) and *The Playboy of the Western World* (1907), offended nationalist opinion for essentially the same reasons as *Countess Cathleen* had done: they showed the Catholic people of the country—'peasants'—in what their urbanized children considered to be an unfavourable light. In fact, it was not the peasants, but their urbanized descendants, whom Yeats, Synge and Lady Gregory disliked. In *The Cutting of an Agate*, which appeared in the same year as *The Playboy*, Yeats referred to:

. . . Men who had risen above the traditions of the countryman, without learning those of cultivated life, or even educating themselves and who because of their poverty, their ignorance, their superstitious piety, are much subject to all kinds of fear.

Synge wrote to Stephen McKenna at the time of the *Playboy* controversy:

The scurrility and ignorance and treachery of some of the attacks upon me have rather disgusted me with the middle-class Irish Catholics. As you know I have the wildest admiration for the Irish Peasants and for Irishmen of known or unknown genius—do you bow?—but between the two there's an ungodly ruck of fat-faced sweaty-headed swine'.

Yeats and Synge—especially Synge—were writing under considerable provocation; also there was much truth in what they said. It is a truth which the colonist is likely to see, and in whose contemplation he may indulge himself to excess. The unspoiled Bedouin is more attractive than the literate, politicized Arab of the towns:[2] also he is less of a danger to the colonist. The root-relation between Protestant and

[2] A Belgian gangster in the Congo once explained to me how he preferred to recruit his native hired assassins from among those 'unpolluted by town life'.

Catholic in Ireland is one between settler and native. Yet
the vegetation sprung from these roots is complex and intertwined. Frantz Fanon's stark, dramatic Manichean contrasts
between *le colon* and *le colonisé*, though suggestive, are too
simple for the situation, and for most others. In the *Playboy*
situation, for example, it is relevant to distinguish not just
two groups but six:

First, the actual people (peasants) of the West whose life
Synge depicts in a vein of heroic pastoral comedy. The
interesting thing about these people, in this context, is that
they are neither *colons* nor *colonisés*: they are essentially *pre-
colonial*. In the world at large there are far more people than
Fanon seems to have suspected whose lives have been barely
touched by the colonial experience, and even in Ireland after
centuries of foreign occupation and partial Anglicization of
most of the people, there were still some such lives—in the
Irish-speaking Aran islands for example.

Second, the country people of other areas, who were in
fact profoundly affected by modernization and Anglicization
(*colonisés*). These entered into the situation, mainly as a
result of confusion on the part of members of the third
group.

Third, the children of people in the second group, who
had become urbanized, middle- and lower middle-class, and
from whom the Abbey Theatre audiences were drawn. These
were indeed quite close to Fanon's *colonisés*, in that they
were quite heavily Anglicized themselves, and increasingly
conscious of their Anglicization as something alien which
they felt required to get rid of if they could. They had a
double reason for resenting something like *The Playboy*. It
was a calumny against 'our people'. Respectable farmers'
daughters from Limerick or Tipperary—like Richard
Sheehy's aunts—simply could not be imagined using an
indelicate expression in the presence of a man, so the
audience, as Lady Gregory reported in a famous cable to
Yeats—'broke up in disorder at the word *shift*'. But the
audience resented also, in a slightly different way, the
presentation of a *comedy* about *Irish-speaking* people. They
resented it for the same reasons as black Americans would

COLONISTS AND COLONIZED 73

be likely to resent a comedy about black Africa. Not only were 'our people' being ridiculed, but they were being ridiculed in that which constituted the essence of 'us': 'us' as we were before the foreigner came and changed us. The foreigner liked to say that we were savages, *The Playboy of the Western World* seemed to say that the foreigner was right. So Richard Sheehy and Frank Skeffington protested against the *Playboy* as they had against *Countess Cathleen*.[3]

The fourth group is that of alienated descendants of the settlers: people of Protestant stock who refused to share the Unionist feelings and opinions general among people of that stock. This was a small group—though much larger proportionately in the South than in the North—but it was important, for it was from it that the writers and organizers of the literary revival were mainly drawn. Contrary to what Fanon suggests, these particular *colons* tended to resent the *colonisés* precisely to the extent that they were *colonisés*: To the extent, that is, of their Anglicization. The natives they idealized were those who had remained most thoroughly native: and unfortunately they idealized these in ways that did not appear to the Catholic *colonisés* to be ideal. It is important to notice that, in terms of Fanon's system, these particular Protestant *colons* felt *themselves* to be *colonisés*: felt, that is, that an alien culture had been imposed on them: Yeats often writes (as in part of the 'Tibetan monk' passage) in the persona of a man of Gaelic ancestry, and Synge cursed the English language 'that a man can't swear in without being vulgar'. From this point of view they resented the Catholic *colonisés* as being a vulgar caricature of that part of themselves which they wished to reject: The Catholics, in this perspective, were not merely imitation Englishmen, but imitation *lower middle-class* Englishmen. Furthermore, even the Catholic attempt to reject this imitation could be seen as a vulgar caricature of the Protestant and upper-class mode of rejection: the

[3] Joyce in Zurich, fascinated by the *Playboy* situation, and irritated by both sides, wrote that Sheehy and Skeffington 'seem to have just been taking a walk round themselves since October '04'. He could have said 'since 1899'. Joyce also said that Yeats in trying to quell the riots said: 'The author of *Countess Cathleen* addresses you.' What he actually said was 'The author of *Cathleen ni Houlihan*.' The slip is interesting.

crude demands of the political demagogue, in substitution
for a genuinely distinct cultural growth.

The fifth group is less complicated: descendants of settlers
holding the settler ideology of Unionism. These appeared in
the form of what might be called the *pro-Playboy* rioters:
young gentlemen from Trinity College who came to the
Abbey to wave Union Jacks and sing God save the King.
Some of these, I am sure, were of Ulster origin. The exact
point of their demonstration remains a little obscure: that it
was a counter-demonstration to the native one is clear. Presumably they agreed with the natives that the play represented the
natives as savages, but denied that the natives had a right to object to such a representation, since savages was what the natives
were. Politically, the natives were unfit for self-government, and
the play, and the natives' reaction to the play, both proved it.

The sixth group consists of the English, of whom the three
preceding groups were strongly aware. The English were
not really very interested, and for those who were interested,
the literary revival had done more than anything else to
raise Ireland's hitherto low reputation in England. The
revivalists were conscious of this and it was among the effects
that they desired. But the early Abbey audiences, in their
often raw and insecure Anglicization, were tortured by the
thought of English ridicule, and were easily led to feel that
Ireland was being 'let down', by conscious or unconscious
treachery on the part of the writers. Protestant writers. The
two categories of the Irish race, drawn closer together by
the literary revival after the death of Parnell, were further
estranged again by the development of the revival after 1903.

### iii

The Irish language movement, stemming from the same
source as the Anglo-Irish literary movement—in the quest
for identity—took a different course. Douglas Hyde, who
founded the Gaelic League in 1893, was a Protestant of
landed stock in the West of Ireland: the Hydes of Frenchpark,
Co. Roscommon. Unlike the young Yeats he was not politically inclined and he was not even in theory a revolutionary.

Indeed although he later became President of an independent and putatively Republican Ireland, such politics as he himself had were possibly Unionist. Hyde insisted that the organization he founded should be non-political and it remained so, in form at least, until the demand that it should align itself politically forced his resignation, in 1915. Until then, a Unionist could join it, and although few did, its 'non-political' character probably made it a little easier for sons and daughters of Unionist families to join it than would have been the case if it had been avowedly 'rebel'. The fact that the Catholic Church looked askance at the language movement, and that therefore those Catholics who joined it could be considered 'not bigoted' probably helped also. The Gaelic League became in fact more 'mixed' in terms of religion than most other bodies at the time, and it is also clear that Catholics and Protestants worked in it together with more unaffected ease than they were able to do in other contexts. It could perhaps be argued that the fact that both groups were struggling with a medium of communication which they had imperfectly mastered deprived them of resources, copiously available in the English language, for getting on one another's nerves. It is simpler to say that when young people meet to learn something they have all chosen to learn, sympathy easily springs up between them. The situation of the Abbey audiences, *passive* spectator-victims of a usually invisible dramatist whose mind was moving away from them, was altogether different.

Ernest Blythe, one of the Protestant Gaelic enthusiasts of the time, and later Minister for Finance in the first government of the Irish Free State, has argued that the restoration of the Irish language presents the best hope of uniting Ireland. There are Irish-speaking Orangemen, and a banner with an Irish-language device is carried in the 12th of July parade.[4] Certainly the Irish language movement, if it could possibly have kept non-political as Hyde wished, could be thought of as a possible unifying cultural force. But in fact most, though

---

[4] Official notice taken of this in the Bulletin of the Department of External Affairs in Dublin in the Summer of 1970 led to a correspondence that showed that Irish unity was still remote.

by no means all, of those who took up the study of the language were those whose lost ancestral language it was: the Irish Catholics. And those Irish Catholics who were interested in such a thing as a lost ancestral language were invariably Irish nationalists, and often Irish nationalists of the most militant kind: Republican separatists. The Gaelic League, quite contrary to its founder's intention—but in line with the predictions of his Unionist critics—became a revolutionary organization. And once it did so, it not only lost any considerable capacity it might have had to unite the two communities, but it made the Irish language itself, and enthusiasm for it, suspect among that community which, in overwhelming majority, rejected the revolution in question: the Protestant community. This, however, did not become fully apparent until the political crisis which opened in 1911. For the first decade of the twentieth century the cultural seems to have predominated over the political element in the Gaelic League, and the League's ecumenical possibilities seemed promising.

The same could hardly be said of the other 'Gaelic' movement of the day: the Gaelic Athletic Association. Unlike the literary movement and the language movement, the athletic association, founded in the 1880's, soon became a mass movement. It was like the others in that it aimed at an assertion of national identity—replacing foreign games by native games—and in that it was penetrated by Fenian and Parnellite influences. G.A.A. members armed with hurleys formed Parnell's bodyguard during the by-elections of 1891. But unlike the other movements it was created by Catholics and its membership remained overwhelmingly Catholic. The operation of 'the ban' determined this: no-one could remain a member of the G.A.A. and play or watch a foreign game. Rugby, soccer, hockey. The social effects of this were interesting. G.A.A games—hurling and Gaelic football —became the games of the Catholic country people. Soccer remained the game of the urban working class Catholic in Dublin, Catholic and Protestant in Belfast, and Rugby the game of the middle classes, both Catholic and Protestant, throughout the island. There was nothing anti-Protestant in the purpose of this ban, but it did have the effect of shutting out most Protestants, as well as many Catholics, from something presented as 'national' and it tended to reinforce the idea that Gaelic meant 'Catholic, but more extreme'.

Some of the journalism of the period had a similar effect. D. P. Moran, of *The Leader,* was a brilliant journalist with a policy of using ridicule to discourage Anglicization, and assert the claims of 'Irish Ireland'. His main targets were the Catholic upper middle class (*shoneens*) and its ambitions to attend Vice-regal receptions, but Protestant loyalists—that is to say, most Protestants—also came inevitably under attack, usually as *West Britons,* but sometimes also as *sourfaces*: a term presumably reflecting the tendency of the Protestant ethic to favour the appearance of the sterner virtues as against the claims of affability. There was nothing especially affable about Moran's own style, but he spoke for a people— the Irish Catholics—who have sometimes carried good manners to lengths which seemed extravagant to their neighbours: hence the term *blarney. Sourface* was both a reprisal for *blarney,* and a hint that blarney would not be much in use in the new, free Ireland that was coming.

All in all, by the time the great home rule crisis opened in 1912, it was apparent that Catholic Ireland had rallied in a remarkable way from the demoralization that had seemed to follow the fall of Parnell. Protestants like Yeats and Hyde had been important in the early phases of this revival, but their influence had waned. The years of Tory government had not, as Unionists had hoped they would, turned back the Catholic and nationalist tide. The Tory policy of 'killing home rule by kindness' had actually strengthened the forces working for self-government. The Tory democratization of local government in Ireland in 1898 meant that there were now Catholic majorities on all local bodies outside the core of Protestant Ulster, and these bodies were ready to pass 'disloyal' resolutions on any topical subject whether it was technically within their competence or not. In Ulster itself many Protestants, outside the area of densest Protestant settlement east of the Bann, experienced a sort of foretaste of 'Catholic rule' through this democratization of local government. It was, from an Ulster Protestant point of view, another turn of the screw: a constriction of the siege.

Economically and socially also the position of the Irish farmers—overwhelmingly Catholic—had improved. The Wyndham Land Act of 1903—advancing the tenants money to buy their holdings—resulted in the virtual euthanasia of the landlord class in Ireland, outside Protestant Ulster. In Protestant Ulster, the landlords working large estates for themselves, and enjoying relations with their Protestant tenantry of a character significantly distinct from landlord-tenant relations in the rest of the country, retained their power and influence. With their strong military tradition—resembling in some ways that of the Junkers of eastern Germany—they were the natural leaders of a people who felt besieged. They exploited this state of affairs for their own advantage, but they did not create it.

As far as Catholic Ireland was concerned, Tory strategists, like George Wyndham and the Balfours, were to be disappointed, at least in their short-term hopes. The idea that concessions to the peasantry would weaken the demand for home rule was not realized. On the nationalist side, it had long been feared that this strategy might work. Parnell had been questioned about his policy of accepting any economic concessions that could be wrung from British government, and whether these might weaken the political movement. He had replied: 'If the people wax fat, then they will kick.' The events of the twenty years following the Land Act of 1903 seemed to show that Parnell was right. Yet in another sense—in too long a term to be of use to them—the Tory strategists were right too. The farmers who became owners of their holdings continued to support the idea of political independence, but they became on the whole a socially conservative class, and made that Ireland, which asserted and won political independence, a socially conservative country.

Protestant Ulster was conscious of the changes taking place in Catholic Ireland: the operation of the new system of local government, and changes in the demeanour of Ulster Catholics, were enough to assure that. But Catholic Ireland, up to 1912, was in general barely conscious of the

existence of an Ulster problem at all. The practising politicians of the Irish Party, knowing the realities of the Ulster
voting pattern, and the ferocities of electioneering in constituencies where the religious balance was almost even,
were necessarily aware of a problem. But it was a problem
which they had a very strong political interest in minimizing.
Any recognition of it, any warning, would be used by their
enemies, from the Unionists round to 'Irish Ireland', passing
through the bitter and eloquent little factions of estranged
members of the party itself.

Good liberals speak of 'the cleansing power of debate' and
it is true that a debate which actually takes place can have
such an effect, among others. But there is also a blinding
power possessed by a debate which you have reason to fear,
and ability to avoid. The Irish Party, before the crisis broke
them, generally could avoid such a debate. Unionists on the
whole—for reasons similar to those which affected the Irish
Party—generally preferred to seem to regard home rule for
Ireland as a closed chapter, not a question of the twentieth
century. As for the Irish Irelanders and the splinter groups
they were not likely to see an obstacle to Irish independence
in a quarter where 'even the corrupt and effete Irish Parliamentary Party' apparently could not see one.

Silence and ignorance have their own dynamics. Most of
the people of Catholic Ireland, outside Ulster itself, knew
little or nothing about the real situation in Ulster. Their
political leaders, who did know, did not tell them; for the
reasons noted. The longer the existence of the problem was
suppressed, the harder it became to break the news. The
conviction of the Catholic people, that there was no Ulster
problem—or at most a spurious 'artificially created' problem
—became part of the environment of every nationalist
politician. It has remained so, though in modified forms,
into our own day.

iv

Mrs. David Sheehy, at the end of the first decade of the
century, had probably no idea that Ulster could interfere

with her dynastic projects. I say 'probably', for she was a shrewd woman and must have detected something hollow in David's public references to 'staunch Ulster Presbyterians' and the unity of all creeds and classes in the new Ireland. In any case the new Ireland was one thing, her own drawing-room another: there the range of creeds and classes was quite narrow. Whatever she may have thought about Ulster—and I have no evidence that she thought about it at all—she was conscious of danger coming from the general direction of 'Irish Ireland': that is to say the generation that was becoming dissatisfied with the Irish Party, not just for not being active enough, but for not being *Irish* enough, of all things. That really puzzled grandmother.

Not that the Sheehy children and the in-laws, generally speaking, were 'Irish-Ireland-minded' in the new sense. All good nationalists, of course, but that was different. The Skeffingtons, Frank and Hanna, were radical certainly. . . . *Causes*: women's suffrage, pacifism, socialism, English sort of things, really, Grandmother thought. Frank had given up his job as Registrar in the new University, on some issue of principle. Heaven alone knew what the issue was. And it was a nice job. At the same time, there was something about a man who would give up a job for a principle. Like old times, under the Plan of Campaign, when David had refused to wear the prison clothes. Eighteen months. David might not be the cleverest member of the party, but not one of the others had served as long a jail sentence. That showed what the English thought of him anyway. These were things that made a family respected. Money wasn't everything.

They said Frank had given up going to Mass. Hanna too? That would be principle again. Better not to talk about it. You couldn't to Hanna, anyway. In any case, Frank neither smoked nor drank.

You couldn't say the same about Tom Kettle. But a wonderful man. Big and handsome and lovely manners. Clongowes Wood. Always very respectful to David, though of course. A fine Catholic, and not in a country sort of way either. Not an Irish-Irelander sort of man at all, at all. A good European they said he was, and a writer. Beginning to have an international reputation, Mary said he was. She had a right to be proud of him.

Pity Frank wouldn't start going to Mass and Tom stop drinking. But they were fine boys all the same.

Dear Margaret was all right too. No politics, just the stage. Pity her husband and his family gave themselves such airs. They were only in trade really. But wholesale of course. Feathers. Good Catholics, but went on about it too much. A private chapel. Well! Still, everybody thought it was very suitable, and dear Margaret seemed to be very devoted, and very pious. Maybe a bit too pious. The trouble with dear Margaret always was that you never *quite* knew where you were with her.

Pity Margaret wasn't a little more honest, and Hanna a little less so.

The boys were all right too. Rugby they played. They used to play hurley in the country, of course, and poor Father Eugene thought Rugby was West British, but Rugby was what the Belvedere boys played. They watched Rugby now, and played golf. Dick was going to be captain of his club. One of the best clubs they said, Hermitage. Those were the games all their friends talked about. None of them had any use for the G.A.A. and this 'ban'. Bigoted. All the same the G.A.A. was catching on in Limerick and Tipperary. People like David when he was young. If the G.A.A. had been there when David was young he would have been in it. But that was what Belvedere did for you. Good careers at the Bar. Dick clever and hard-working. Brooks scholar. Wish he would take better care of his health. Eugene nice and ordinary. Suitable marriages, a little property. Nothing to be ashamed of.

And now, Kathleen, the youngest and the gentlest. Too biddable really, you'd have thought. Never should have let her take up Irish. None of the others did. Since she came back from Aran her own mother and father aren't quite Irish, she thinks.[5] Our generation betrayed the language, she says.

[5] See James Joyce's *The Dead*. The conversation of Miss Ivors in that story is based on the conversation of Kathleen Sheehy, after a long visit to Inishmaan, in the Aran Islands.

I told her if we hadn't betrayed the language she wouldn't be able to talk like that. That Gaelic League! All either Protestants or penniless; none of our kind of people at all. So now Kathleen finds herself a young man who's both penniless and the next worst thing to a Protestant. He talks to poor David in this grand English accent (which he didn't get at Synge Street Christian Brothers School) and explains how David ought to be more Irish. He was Auditor of the Literary and Historical Society in the Royal, or I wouldn't have let him into the house. Tom and Frank both think he's clever, and he thinks so too. But we've put our foot down. I've explained to Kathleen that there's no question of her marrying Cruise O'Brien. . . .

The form in which the struggles of that time reach me, and the form in which they are interpreted here, is affected by this small, but for me decisive debate: the debate over whether I was to come into existence or not. The hitherto united Sheehy family split over this issue, with emotions no less intense than those with which the party had split twenty years before. Grandmother's bitter opposition to the marriage was dynastic, but not merely mercenary or merely ambitious: my father was small and delicate without adequate compensating advantages in her eyes: she did not think the marriage would work out. Also, once the debate was engaged, there was a question of her authority. David Sheehy would normally have agreed with his wife in such a matter, but he had a special reason for agreeing in this case. Cruise O'Brien was one of the most obnoxious of the new intellectuals in the party organization, critical of the party leadership—including David's venerated chief, John Dillon—and rich in, if little else, the power to say wounding things in a memorable manner.

Most of the younger Sheehys took the side of their parents: Dick and Mary vehemently so, Eugene and Margaret more passively. Tom sympathized with my mother but sided with Mary. Only Hanna and Frank Skeffington, took my mother's side. At the height of the long debate, an argument between my grandfather and Frank Skeffington grew so hot that Dick Sheehy threw Frank Skeffington bodily out the front door and down the steps of 2 Belvedere Place. Frank simply got up, knocked on the door, said 'Force solves nothing, Dick' and resumed his argument with grandfather.

Grandmother was afraid of Hanna: a force of will and intelligence equivalent to her own, and a moral force which she had it in her to respect. Hanna had intended to be a nun; she would have made a great reforming Mother Superior in a medieval order. When she took up a cause she did not let go. In this case her affection for her youngest sister was encased in the armour of a cause: Women's Rights included Kathleen's right to marry Francis Cruise O'Brien.

Grandmother began to back away. A simple exercise in parental authority could not stand against the spirit of the age, incarnate in the Skeffingtons. She tried delay, combined with indirect pressure. Mary put the pressure on. She was the nearest to my mother in age, beautiful, emotional, vehement, with the prize of Tom Kettle, M.P., in tow. The argument was that Mother was not forbidding the match, but that if it took place it would kill her. Tom Kettle confirmed this: I imagine with a wary eye out for any Skeffingtons who might be passing in the neighbourhood of Belvedere Place. The 'killing-mother' strategy—variants of which of course have been used through the ages in countless families—was particularly appropriate in this case because it negated the dangerous Skeffingtonian issue of *rights*. Of course Kathleen had the *right* to marry Cruise O'Brien—thereby killing her mother—if she chose to exercise this right. She did, and Grandmother survived though not indefinitely.

This family division was partly genuinely healed, partly patched over. My mother was fully reconciled to her sister, Mary, who mattered to her most, and to the others in a general sort of way. My father, on the other hand, never forgave Mary, or any of the Sheehys who had opposed the marriage. He was civil to them for my mother's sake, but it was only for the Skeffingtons that he felt real liking and respect.

The quarrel over the marriage left in this extended family, under the surface, an emotional division which tended to reflect wider divisions in the society. Those who had opposed the marriage—and *their* extended families—remained invariably practising Catholics, and in politics generally at the conservative end of the Catholic/Nationalist spectrum. No doubt in their attitude to the marriage—which took place in a Catholic Church and in relation to which religious issues played no significant overt part—there had entered 'traditional' reflexes about parental authority, and also feelings about property and prospects which, in wider arguments, pushed them to the Catholic right.

The Skeffingtons were agnostics, so was my father. My mother, in the middle as usual, ceased to practise her religion for a while, then resumed it. Politically the Skeffingtons were on the left: militant, though pacifist, socialists. My father was active in the agricultural co-operative movement: he was Sir Horace Plunkett's secretary, and wrote for AE's *Irish Statesman*. Here, and increasingly in his social life, my father came into contact with Protestants and Unionists much more than the Sheehys did, or even at this time the Skeffingtons. He worked with a Protestant, Guy Lloyd, on an edition of Lecky's *Rise of Rationalism in Europe*. He understood Protestant fears about Catholic domination in an independent Ireland, because he shared these fears. He was not reassured when Dick or Mary, or even Tom, told him that all shades of opinion would be respected.

The events of this time, and of much later—up to 1932 at least—reached me through this filter of family attitudes, alliances, antagonisms and sympathies earlier and deeper than through the process known as 'learning history'. The filter, of course, affected that later process too and affects the way in which I understand and try to analyse the events of those times and of our own. Each one of us is similarly affected in relation to the recent history of his own place: some more simply, because nearer to the centre of a tribe, others in more complex or painfully divisive ways. My own consciousness of these factors is no doubt exceptionally heightened by the fact that the dispute which distributed the older members of my family (and their children) in the patterns in which I found them, was a dispute which hinged on my own right to existence.

# 5

# The United Kingdom and Ireland Disintegrate

*'She hears the ocean protesting against separation
but she hears the sea protesting against union.
She follows therefore her physical destination
when she protests against the two situations—
both equally unnatural—separation and union.'*

HENRY GRATTAN

The year 1910 brought in the political conjuncture which Catholics in Ireland had hoped for, and Protestants had feared, since the death of Gladstone. Once again at Westminster a Liberal Government depended on the Irish Party for office. The last time this had happened—in 1892—the House of Lords had vetoed Home Rule. But by August 1911, the House of Lords no longer had a full veto power, only the power to delay, over three sessions. Home Rule seemed imminent. And Protestant Ulster prepared to resist Home Rule. In this, Protestant Ulster was encouraged by the Tory party and by the British military establishment. The ensuing struggle convulsed the political and social life not merely of Ireland but of Great Britain from 1912 to 1914. Never since the seventeenth century had the control of the British parliament over the armed forces looked so insecure as it did at this period. Indeed, had the Liberals persisted in their original policy of including all Ulster within Home Rule Ireland—and had not the outbreak of the First World War intervened—it seems likely that Britain would have undergone some form of military *coup d'état,* carried out in the name

of loyalty to the Crown and to the integrity of the Empire.[1]
How far the resistance of Protestant Ulster would have
gone, without the support of the British Tories and of many
senior army officers, we cannot know. *With* this support it
went far indeed. Virtually the entire adult Protestant population signed Ulster's Solemn League and Covenant binding
the signatories to use 'all means which may be found necessary
to defeat the present conspiracy to set up a Home Rule
parliament in Ireland' and to refuse to recognize the authority
of such a parliament should it be set up. On the basis of the
Covenant 96,000 Ulster Volunteers armed and drilled under
licences from Justices of the Peace, who were in full sympathy with this unusual movement: loyal in relation to the
Crown—so long as the Crown was loyal to Protestant
supremacy—subversive in relation to the authority of a
Parliament in which papists seemed to wield decisive influence. In March 1914 the incident known as the Curragh
Mutiny made it clear that the British Army could not be
counted on to enforce the inclusion of all Ulster in a Home
Rule Ireland. The following month a major consignment
of arms for the Ulster Volunteers was landed at Larne. The
month after that (May) the Government declared its intention of amending the Home Rule Bill. The partition of
Ireland was now inevitable, although no one yet knew where
the line would be drawn.

Catholic Ireland—and those Protestants who, like Roger
Casement, identified with its cause—witnessed this sequence
of events with astonishment and indignation. Those who
understood it best—the Irish Parliamentary Party, who were
closest in touch with what was happening in England and in
the North—were most discredited by it. This was not unjust,
for they had, over thirty years, encouraged the belief that
Home Rule—*for all Ireland* went without saying—could and
would be won by parliamentary action, and they had per-
sistently minimized the importance of Ulster Protestant
opposition (see above). By May of 1914 they knew that their
Liberal allies probably could not, and certainly would not,

---

[1] See George Dangerfield, *The strange death of Liberal England* (London 1933),
and A. T. Q. Stewart, *The Ulster Crisis* (London 1967).

deliver Home Rule for all Ireland. John Redmond, John Dillon and their followers had to explain to the Catholic people that the Home Rule they were going to get would not be for the whole island, at least not immediately.[2] To most Catholic people this meant betrayal by England. England's material might was one of the facts of life which had been impressed on them most strongly. They were also accustomed—as their ancestors had been accustomed—to think of 'England' as a monolith. The facts that Englishmen were as passionately divided on the subject as Irishmen (of different religions) were, and that an English government could not enforce Home Rule for all Ireland without bringing England, as well as Ireland, to the verge of civil war, were simply not assimilable, as far as most Irish Catholics were concerned.

It was some twenty years later, and I must have been about twelve years old, when I first heard, from my mother, the detailed story of those years. She was a fair-minded woman, a teacher by profession, and an exceptionally good teacher. Her account—more detailed than I have given here—was clear and accurate in political narrative. It was by no means an 'extreme' or chauvinistic account. Yet the impression left on my mind was one of betrayal by the English Prime Minister: betrayal of the Irish Party, and of Ireland. Underlying this were the assumptions that the Ulster Volunteer Movement and the British officers who sympathized with it, were bluffing and that Asquith, instead of calling their bluff, engaged in a form of collusion with them, e.g. asking the officers what they would do in a hypothetical situation, instead of simply assuming that they would obey orders. I can no longer share all of these assumptions but they were sincerely held, and reasonably argued, by my parents, and I believe by most intelligent and politically-minded Catholics of their generation.

(My mother's historical retrospect had also significant overtones in relation to our family's political role and fortunes, but I shall come to that aspect later in the story.)

[2] 'Temporary exclusion' of certain counties was the formula first used to break the news of partition.

Inevitably the threat of force by the Ulster Volunteers gave new impetus to the ever-present idea of using force, on behalf of the Catholics, to free Ireland. The Irish Volunteers were founded in November 1913, as in effect a counter-force to the Ulster Volunteers. Yet the leaders of the Irish Volunteers did not wish to see themselves in precisely this light. On the contrary Patrick Pearse, Eoin MacNeill and others praised the Ulster Volunteers for arming. The general idea of 'arms in the hands of Irishmen' was intoxicating and, to the most rebel-minded among the Irish Catholics, Carson's defiance of 'England' had something vaguely attractive about it, from a distance. Also these 'extreme' groups were grateful, in a sense, to Carson's movement for calling the bluff of the constitutional nationalists, rehabilitating the idea of physical force, and increasing the prestige of the organization associated with that idea.

Following the example of Larne, Erskine Childers and Conor O'Brien[3] ran guns for the Irish Volunteers to Howth and Kilcoole in July 1914. *Not* following the example of Larne, the British authorities did attempt—but unsuccessfully—to interfere with these proceedings. Three people were killed along a Liffey quay, when British troops fired on an insulting but unarmed crowd. These proceedings increased the bitterness and determination of those who were already beginning to think in terms of an armed rising against an England now engaged in war against European enemies.

'England's difficulty is Ireland's opportunity', Wolfe Tone's old slogan, was also that of the men who were to lead the Rising of Easter, 1916. But what did 'Ireland's opportunity' mean when Ireland was divided? The essential political factor behind the Rising of 1916 was the rejection of the Home-Rule-with-partition package which Redmond had accepted and for which Redmond—most unwisely—had advised Irishmen to go and fight in Flanders. But how, in the teeth of what the Ulster Volunteers meant, did the leaders of the Rising think an unpartitioned Ireland could be won? Or *did* they think it could be won? What were their thoughts about Ulster, and in particular about the Protestants of Ulster?

[3] God-father and eponym of the present writer.

I live today in a Catholic Twenty-six County State of which these men are venerated as the founders, although in fact their Rising was an attempt to avert the coming into existence of that which they are now revered as having founded. Today, many who passionately believe in the Republic they proclaimed—the Republic for the whole island—are still trying to win that objective by shooting British soldiers in Northern Ireland. These activities hardly look like unifying Ireland, but their claim to derive from the words, lives and actions of the men of 1916 cannot be so easily dismissed. And this claim necessarily has a powerful appeal to those who are brought up on the belief, inculcated in our school histories, that the men of 1916 were the men who were right.

Our school histories do not seriously discuss the ideas and policies of the men of 1916 in relation to the Protestants of Ulster. In fact I know of no previous discussion of this problem, at any level. I therefore propose to consider here the treatment of this question in the published writings of one of the principal leaders of the Rising, James Connolly (1868–1916). Of all the leaders of the Rising, Connolly was the most rational, the most internationally-minded, the least mystical, the least sectarian. As the only Marxian Socialist among the leaders he was more given to the explicit analysis of 'problems' than his fellows. He had studied, and he wrote persuasively about, Irish history. He had lived and worked among working people in Belfast, as well as in Scotland, Dublin and America. It is his thinking, about a Workers' Republic of all Ireland, that is the accepted corpus of doctrine of the revolutionary left in Ireland today. My own party, the Labour Party, was founded by Connolly and, while the Party never has been a revolutionary party, it is certainly urged in revolutionary directions, especially in relation to the North, by members who can quote Connolly effectively to that purpose.

It is therefore important to examine what Connolly's writings have to tell us about Ulster Protestants and about how unity between Catholics and Protestants in Ireland might be achieved.

Connolly wrote two historical works: *Labour in Irish History* (1910) and *The Reconquest of Ireland* (1915) The first of these works was written at a time when few Irishmen, outside Ulster, were paying much attention to the Ulster question. By the time the second work was written, the Ulster Volunteers had brought that question to the centre of the stage.

In *Labour in Irish History*, Connolly takes as his starting point the Williamite war. His thesis, generally in both these books, is that, as the Protestant rank and file were, in his belief, betrayed by their aristocratic and capitalist leaders, their real interests were the same as those of the oppressed Catholics, with whom in fact they formed one people or nation. Or did they? The fact is that Connolly sometimes writes as if they did or do and sometimes as if they did not or do not. His writing like almost all Irish nationalist writing, is touched by a curious flicker or stammer when this question comes in view. Thus he says in the second chapter of *Labour in Irish History* that 'the subject people of Ireland' had a chance to make a bid for freedom (while England was in the grip of civil war) but that instead 'the subject people took sides on behalf of the opposing factions of their enemies'. This is clear: the 'subject people' here are both Catholics and Protestants. But in the very next sentence, Connolly refers to 'the Catholic gentlemen and nobles who had the leadership of the people of Ireland at the time. . . .' Here 'the people of Ireland' can only be the Catholics: Protestants did not follow any such leaders. And when Connolly uses the term 'the Irish race'—as he does quite often—it always seems to be the Catholics he has in mind. At one point (Chapter 8) he speaks of 'two nations' (in the eighteenth century), promptly divides these again into four, and then reduces them again to two (or possibly three) along class lines: 'In fact, in Ireland at that time, there were not only two nations divided into Catholics and non-Catholics (*sic*), but each of these two nations was divided into another two, the rich and the poor. . . . The times were propitious for a union of the two democracies of Ireland. They had travelled through the valleys of disillusion and disappointment to meet at last by the unifying waters of a common suffering.'

This may do service as a way of referring to the temporary rapprochement between some Catholics and some Protestants in the movement of the United Irishmen. *But what happened after that?* Connolly does not tell us. Having discussed 'the United Irishmen' and 'The Emmet Conspiracy' in Chapters 8 and 9, he then breaks off to tell us about an early nineteenth century Cork socialist, William Thompson, and then passes on to other matters: Daniel O'Connell's attitude to trade unionism, the great famine, the Young Ireland movement, Fenianism, the Land League.

The astonishing and ominous absence in *Labour in Irish History* is nineteenth century Belfast. The story of labour in Ireland's only large industrial city during the high period of the industrial revolution is simply left out. There is no attempt to explain this omission, unless the opening words of Connolly's final chapter are to be understood as explaining it:

This book does not aspire to be a history of labour in Ireland; it is rather a record of labour in Irish History. For that reason the plan of the book has precluded any attempt to deal in detail with the growth, development, or decay of industry in Ireland, except as it affected our general argument. That argument called for an explanation of the position of labour in the great epochs of our modern history, and with the attitude of Irish leaders toward the hopes, aspirations, and necessities of those who live by labour.

It is hard to know just what to make of this. What exactly is the distinction between 'a history of labour in Ireland' and 'a record of labour in Irish History'? If 'history' includes social history—as one would think it should, for Connolly— then how can you separate 'a history of labour' from 'a record of labour in history'? I suspect that it is the words 'Ireland' and 'Irish' that transform the proposition, instead of merely localizing it. Irish History—Connolly's capitals— seems to mean for Connolly what it has meant to most Irish Catholics: the history of the Irish nationalist (alias national) movement. The 'great epochs' were the periods of revolt against England, and of serious challenge to English power. It is only if this is what is meant by Irish History that the omission of nineteenth century Belfast from a record of labour in Irish History begins to make some kind of sense. For most of the working class in Belfast do not belong in 'Irish History', thus conceived. 'The people of Belfast' belonged in Irish History, in this sense, in the eighteenth century, and Connolly dwells on them at that stage of his narrative. But in the nineteenth century 'the people of Belfast' have somehow left Irish History, and we are not told why. More than that, the Protestant workers, by leaving Irish History leave the working class itself. The last chapter of *Labour in Irish History* is entitled: 'The Working Class: the Inheritors of the Irish Ideals of the Past—The Repository of the Hopes of the Future'. In this chapter Connolly refers to the hold of the Fenian movement upon the Irish masses in the cities: But the Fenian movement had no hold at all on the largest masses in Belfast: indeed the word Fenian in the mouth of a Belfast Protestant worker even today is a deadly insult, and often a prelude to violence. The only 'masses' that Fenianism had any appeal to anywhere were Irish Catholics.

It is hard to resist the conclusion that the Protestant workers of Belfast, *as they actually were and with the feelings and loyalties they actually had*, were not consistently felt by Connolly to be part of Irish History, or of the record of labour, of the working class, or of the masses.

The Protestants stepped silently out of the narrative of *Labour in Irish History* at the end of the eighteenth century. They return to the Ireland of 1910, just in time for the peroration—as they often did and do in nationalist speeches—but they return as imaginary beings in the shadowy robes of unfulfilled prediction: 'In their movement the North and the South will again clasp hands, again will it be demonstrated, as in '98, that the pressure of a common exploitation can make enthusiastic rebels out of a Protestant working class, earnest champions of civil and religious liberty out of Catholics, and out of both a united Social democracy.'

In *The Reconquest of Ireland* (1915) Connolly is naturally more acutely conscious of the Ulster problem—'Ulster will fight' was in the air all round him as he wrote—but his analysis of it is hardly more satisfactory than in *Labour in Irish History*.

The general picture of Catholic and Protestant common people both dispossessed is basically the same as in *Labour in Irish History* but somewhat sharper:

Thus, in Ulster the Celt returned to his ancient tribelands, but to its hills and stony fastnesses, from which with tear-dimmed eyes he could look down upon the fertile plains of his fathers which he might never again hope to occupy, even on sufferance.

On the other hand, the Protestant common soldier or settler, now that the need of his sword was passed, found himself upon the lands of the Catholic, it is true, but solely as a tenant and dependant. The ownership of the province was not in his hands, but in the hands of the companies of London merchants who had supplied the sinews of war for the English armies, or, in the hands of the greedy aristocrats and legal cormorants who had schemed and intrigued while he had fought. The end of the Cromwellian settlement then found the 'commonality', to use a good old word, dispossessed and defrauded of all hold upon the soil of Ireland— the Catholic dispossessed by force, the Protestant dispossessed by fraud. Each hating and blaming the other, a situation which the dominant aristocracy knew well how, as their descendants know today, to profit by to their own advantage.

The explicit acknowledgment of the mutual hate is new: so also is the acknowledgment that this is a continuing force. Then came (Chapter II—Ulster and the Conquest) Connolly's clearest acknowledgment, or claim, that the Protestant workers and small farmers—the children of 'the rank and file of the armies of the conquerors'—are part of the Irish nation:

The children of these men of the rank and file are now an integral part of the Irish nation, and their interests and well-being are now as vital to the cause of freedom and as sacred in the eyes of the Labour Movement as are the interests of the descendants of those upon whom a cruel destiny compelled their forefathers to make war.

The rest of this chapter deals mainly with the ill-treatment of Protestant 'rank and file' and especially Presbyterians, during the eighteenth century, and praises some acts of revolt by them. The chapter ends with the words:

The thin clothing and pale faces of honest Protestant workers are still in evidence in Belfast. Let us hope that they will ere long be marching again to storm the capitalist system which has for so long imprisoned not only the bodies but the souls of their class.

Chapter II is 'Ulster and the Conquest' (mainly eighteenth and nineteenth century). Chapters III and IV, rather bewilderingly in point of sequence, deal with 'Dublin in the Twentieth Century' and 'Labour in Dublin' (same period). Chapter V brings us back to 'Belfast and its problems'.

But it is a twentieth century Belfast.

In *The Reconquest of Ireland,* just as in *Labour in Irish History,* Connolly simply skips nineteenth century Belfast, and the nineteenth century history of Ulster generally. One would think that a writer impressed by that eighteenth century meeting of Catholics and Protestants 'by the unifying waters of a common suffering', and anxious to bring about this meeting again, would be correspondingly anxious to examine the question of why that unity—such as it was—had totally disappeared. The period when it disappeared in Ulster was the nineteenth century and the nineteenth century is suppressed.

Connolly does have a kind of explanation of the division. In 'Belfast and its problems'—after acknowledging that Belfast is municipally better run than Dublin—he goes on:

The things in which Belfast is peculiar are the skilful use by the master class of religious rallying cries which, long since forgotten elsewhere, are still potent to limit and weaken Labour here, and the pharisaical spirit of self-righteousness which enables unscrupulous sweaters of the poor, with one hand in the pocket of their workers, to raise the other hand to heaven and thank God that they are not as other men.

Why should the master-class in Belfast be more 'skilful' than elsewhere, and is it only their extraordinary skill that makes 'religious rallying cries' still potent there? And why—in heaven's name, one might appropriately say—could James Connolly of all people say that pharisaical self-righteousness among employers is 'peculiar to Belfast'? No one knew better than he did how prone the employers of *Dublin* were to exploit religion for the sake of profit.

In the rest of the same chapter Connolly describes the wretched conditions of industrial workers in Belfast. Then he goes on: 'The majority of the poor slaves who work under such conditions and for such pay, as also the majority of the mill and factory workers amongst whom consumption claims its most numerous victims are, in Belfast, descendants of the men who "fought for civil and religious liberty at Derry, Aughrim and the Boyne." If these poor sweated descendants of Protestant rebels against a king had today one-hundredth part of the spirit of their ancestors in question, the reconquest of Ireland by the working class would be a much easier task than it is likely to prove.'

The rest of the short book does not discuss Ulster or the religious problem. So the explanations we are left with of the religious split are:

1. Belfast employers are exceptionally skilful in using religious catch-cries.
2. Protestant workers are exceptionally lacking in spirit.

James Connolly was a great pioneer of the Trade Union movement and—in the last phase of his life—a revolutionary leader. His historical writings are secondary to his militant activities and were designed to help these activities. It is obvious, therefore, that Connolly does not give us his full thinking on the subject of 'Ulster'; he gives what he thinks will be useful. But the things which he thought useful to say, in the conditions existing just before the First World War, have long outlasted those conditions, and have acquired a retrospective increase in importance as a result of Connolly's heroic fight and death in 1916. Even without this, *Labour in Irish History* would remain important, as a first sustained attempt to apply the methods of Marxist historiology to Irish history. Connolly's plain, powerful prose, with the force of his extraordinary character behind it, strikes home to many intelligent young Irish men and women with the effect of a revelation. Unfortunately in Ireland the idea of revelation is associated with canonization, and canonization, once attained, is not conducive to rational enquiry.

As far as Catholic-Protestant relations are concerned,

⟨Connolly's practical work as a trade unionist and politician reflects—as we should expect—a similar pattern to what we find in his historical writings. In Belfast in June 1911, he brought out his deep-sea dockers—who were Catholics—on strike in sympathy with the cross-channel seamen, who were Protestants. To draw attention to his conception of working-class solidarity cutting across religious lines he started a 'non-sectarian labour band'[4] which continued bravely to make itself heard in the troubled Belfast of the Home Rule crises.⟨

At the same time, Connolly by committing his socialists to Home Rule for Ireland—a Home Rule for all Ireland, with Protestants in a minority—brought about the result that his following among the Belfast workers was necessarily almost entirely Catholic. He had a bitter controversy with a Protestant socialist—and anti-Home Ruler—William Walker, in the course of which Connolly alluded contemptuously to the subject he generally skirts so delicately in his historical writings: the *actual* allegiance of Ulster Protestants. Walker had referred (rather irrelevantly) to Protestant nationalist and agrarian leaders in Irish history. Connolly replies: 'We do not care so much what a few men did as what the vast mass of their co-religionists do. The vast mass of the Protestants of Ulster, except during the period of 1798, were bitter enemies of the men he has named, and during the bitter struggle of the Land League, when the peasantry in the other provinces were engaged in a life and death struggle against landlordism, the sturdy Protestant Democracy of the North were electing landlords, and the nominees of landlords, to every Protestant constituency in Ulster. . . . All these men will live in history because they threw in their lot with the other provinces in a common struggle for political freedom. In the exact measure that we admire and applaud them must we condemn and deplore the sectional and parochial action of Comrade Walker.'

The 'vast mass' here treated so dismissively are of course exactly the same people as those 'children of the rank and

---

[4] I should very much like to know the composition by religious persuasion of the non-sectarian band. Also the routes it followed.

file [whose] interests and well-being [are] sacred in the eyes of the Labour movement' in *The Reconquest of Ireland,* written at about the same time.

Connolly, who in argument with Walker shows himself fully aware of the actual allegiance of Ulster Protestants, yet tried to treat this more lightly than seems to befit the allegiance of a 'vast mass'. William McMullen, who worked with him in Belfast at this time, tells a revealing anecdote:

He, no doubt, found the Northern environment trying and uncongenial and it was only with difficulty he could be patient with the odd stolid Orangeman whom he encountered in his propaganda work up to this. One such occasion was when he was speaking at Library Street on a Sunday evening and was expatiating on Irish history when one of this type interrupted him, and drawing a copy of the Solemn League and Covenant from his pocket brandished it in the air and remarked there would be no Home Rule for Ireland and that he and his thousands of cosignatories would see to it. Connolly, with a sardonic smile, advised him to take the document home and frame it, adding 'your children will laugh at it'.[5]

The children have not laughed, nor are the grand-children laughing.

As soon as partition was mooted, Connolly came out against it in passionate and seemingly prophetic words, still often quoted today. Partition, wrote Connolly in *The Irish Worker* (14th March 1914), would mean 'betrayal of the national democracy of industrial Ulster', would mean 'a carnival of reaction both North and South, would set back the wheels of progress, would destroy the oncoming unity of the Irish Labour movement and paralyse all advanced movements while it lasted.

'To it, Labour should give its bitterest opposition, against it Labour in Ulster should fight even to the death if necessary, as our fathers fought before us.'

Many Irish socialists have found this argument extremely persuasive, since indeed the results of partition seem to be what Connolly foresaw: in both parts of the divided island

[5] Introduction to *The Workers' Republic* (Dublin 1951). This introduction is a valuable source for Connolly's Belfast period.

the Labour movement is weak, and conservatives exploit sectarian prejudices. But the question should be asked—and has not been at least until recently: what kind of an Ireland would we have if it had become separated from Great Britain as an island unit, including the Catholic majority which favoured that solution *and* the Protestant minority that opposed it? How could such a result have been achieved, and what consequences would have flowed from it? I shall return to these questions.

When we compare Connolly's historical writings with the policies he pursued, and with his recorded sayings and journalism, I think that despite all the ambivalence a fairly clear and internally consistent picture of what he thought on the subject emerges. It could be summarized as follows:

Protestant workers and small farmers rightfully belonged to the Irish nation, and to the Labour movement, and when they took their place in that nation and, movement they should be warmly welcomed. (Implicitly: by the Catholics, but Connolly might have rejected this formulation.) Protestants who refused this place, however, were necessarily motivated by lack of spirit, ignorance and stupidity and were the dupes and instruments of capitalism and imperialism, and what Connolly calls 'the ruling class and nation'. Connolly explicitly admits that 'the vast mass' of Protestants not only are but have long been in this condition. So the Protestants generally are seen as having excluded themselves from the consensus of the Irish nation and the working class, which are in practice overwhelmingly composed of Catholics, who also of course make up the majority of the population of the island. The Irish nation so composed, has a right to independence, and the territory to which it has a right is the whole island. Protestants are to be incorporated in this unit, even against their will. Their resistance is not expected to be very serious or prolonged, but if necessary should be overcome by force: against partition 'Labour in Ulster should fight even to death if necessary'. After an independent, united Ireland is won, Protestants will be reassured, cherished and re-educated and will speedily forget their misguided earlier loyalties (laugh at the Covenant).

Exceptional in so much else, James Connolly was by no means exceptional in holding these views. In their national aspects (that is, leaving aside the specific emphasis on the working class) they represent the general assumptions of Irish nationalist thought on the subject, with the important exception that relatively few people at this time went as far as Connolly in seeing force as justifiable to prevent partition. They were fully the assumptions of the 1916 leaders and their followers, and as such were to enter what became the official ideology of the independent Irish State.[6] But they entered it in the form of assumptions, several of which remained unspoken. The logic of the system pointed towards Irishmen fighting Irishmen but this conclusion was so uncomfortable that vagueness covered it.

The Rising of 1916 was, of course, a blow struck against England, and struck in circumstances that precluded all hope of military victory. Thus the problem of 'what to do about Ulster' cannot have presented itself with any urgency to the men in the General Post Office in April 1916.

Yet 1916 and its aftermath affected Ulster too. It was another tightening of the siege.

Tom Kettle came back to Dublin, on leave from the Western front, in the early summer of 1916. He went to the house of his sister-in-law, Hanna Sheehy-Skeffington, where his daughter Betty was playing with her cousin Owen. When the children saw him coming they ran away. He was in uniform.

Men in that same uniform had ransacked that house in April. They had been looking—unsuccessfully—for evidence, which could be used to justify the murder by firing-squad in Portobello Barracks, Dublin, of Tom Kettle's brother-in-law, Francis Sheehy-Skeffington. Skeffington as a pacifist, and also as a socialist and nationalist, had opposed the war, and his anti-recruiting activities had naturally made him unpopular with the military authorities. He was picked up as a hostage and then shot on the orders of an officer named Bowen-Colthurst. He had earlier witnessed a murder com-

[6] See, for example, the writings of Thomas MacDonagh. MacDonagh, like Connolly, was executed after the Easter Rising.

mitted by the same officer, and had said he would denounce the murder. Bowen-Colthurst was found 'guilty but insane', and released after some months in Broadmoor. Hanna Sheehy-Skeffington went to America, to tell the story of her husband's death, and to rouse Irish-American opinion against America's entry into the war as England's ally.

The executions of the 1916 leaders, the Skeffington murder, and other murders committed during the suppression of the Rising, caused a great change in the politics of nationalist Ireland. Anti-English feeling, always present but in reduced heat during the period of nationalist alliance with the English liberals, now flared up in full intensity. The men who, like Redmond and Kettle, had favoured 'fighting for England' began to look like traitors, or at best dupes. Tom Kettle was killed at Guinchy in the autumn of 1916. If he had come back he would have been rejected, for essentially the same reason that made his daughter run away, his uniform.

In the general election of 1918, nationalist Ireland voted out the old Irish Parliamentary Party, and voted in its place for Sinn Féin, the party now committed to the Republic proclaimed by Pearse and Connolly. David Sheehy was among those who lost his seat in this election, after thirty-three years in parliament.

The Sinn Féin members, refusing to take their seats at Westminster, constituted themselves into Dáil Eireann, claiming to be the parliament of all Ireland. In their assembly the roll-call was read for all the constituencies in Ireland. The members for constituencies with Protestant majorities— that is, most constituencies in eastern Ulster—did not answer. Protestant Ulster had voted Unionist as usual.

From the point of view of Protestant Ulster, the significance of the shift in nationalist (Catholic) opinion was that the Catholic leaders who had reluctantly accepted partition, and the idea of remaining within the Empire, had fallen, and been replaced by men who totally rejected partition and the Empire, and who were committed to the use of force for securing full independence for an island unit. This was— from an Ulster Protestant point of view—the open proclamation of a siege which had long been more covertly conducted.

The Irish Republican Army, more or less under the authority of Dáil Eireann, began its guerrilla campaign against the British. Generally speaking, the writ of Dáil Eireann ran throughout Catholic Ireland, and the guerrilla was sustained by the Catholic population. In Belfast, Protestant workers conducted anti-Catholic pogroms

Failing to suppress the guerrilla, the British Government put through a measure partitioning the country—the Government of Ireland Act of 1920—and setting up two parliaments, the Parliament of Southern Ireland in Dublin and the Parliament of Northern Ireland at Stormont, Belfast. The one at Stormont was for an area of six counties: Antrim, Armagh, Down, Fermanagh, Londonderry and Tyrone. This was the area selected by the Unionist leaders when they were in a position to select the optimum: the period of the war-time coalition government.

When King George V had opened the Stormont parliament, Lloyd George opened negotiations with the leaders of Dáil Eireann. Lloyd George's objective was to get these leaders to accept the substance, if not the form, of the Government of Ireland Act: to accept, that is, limited self-government for the Catholic-majority area. In this, Lloyd George was successful. His success was based mainly on the force of things: the rather obvious fact that there was nothing better, from Dáil Eireann's point of view, to be had. But he also encouraged the hope that a Boundary Commission, set up under the Anglo-Irish Treaty of 1921, would cause the border to disappear, or at least bring about the transfer of the extensive Catholic-majority areas included in Northern Ireland. Michael Collins, on the Irish side, believed that, after this transfer, the remaining area would not be economically viable. As no transfer has yet taken place, this belief has not been put to the test.

A minority in Dáil Eireann rejected this settlement. Its rejection hinged much more on formal and symbolic matters —notably the question of an oath of allegiance to the Crown —than on partition: no doubt because the political leaders knew that partition was inevitable. To many—probably most—of their followers, however, it was partition that constituted the great betrayal.

Catholic Ireland, in the twenty-six counties—the Southern Ireland of the Government of Ireland Act, now known as the Irish Free State, moved towards internal civil war. For a time the two sides compromised their differences through a secret agreement to encourage and help guerrilla activities in the North (defence of the Catholics). This broke down and the forces of the Irish Free State—those who had accepted the Treaty—moved against, and rather speedily crushed, the irregular forces who, in the name of the Republic proclaimed in 1916, opposed the Treaty.

By 1922, the essential framework of Lloyd George's Government of Ireland Act had been accepted, at least *de facto*, in both parts of the partitioned country.

# 6

## The Catholic State

*'While leaving to Caesar the things that are
Caesar's they [Catholic Bishops] must, however,
concern themselves with the things that are God's.
From the nature of their office they have the right
and the duty to intervene when religious or moral
issues are involved.'*

ARCHBISHOP D'ALTON OF ARMAGH

It was never officially called a Catholic State, of course. Its
territory (twenty-six counties) was what Lloyd George had
defined as 'Southern Ireland'. Its first official title was the
Irish Free State. That lasted from 1922—the effective date of
self-government—to 1937, when Mr. de Valera gave the
State a new Constitution. Then the name of the State became,
in the Irish language, Eire and in the English language
Ireland—with the confusing exception that, in the English
version of the Preamble to the Constitution, the name of the
State was Eire ('We the people of Eire. . . .'). There was
another confusion. This Constitution, enacted by the people
of the twenty-six counties, claimed to be the Constitution of
the whole island (thirty-two counties). The name of the
State was the name of the island. This led to difficulties on
the rather frequent occasions when it was necessary to refer
to the actually existing State as distinct from the island, and
without the State's metaphysical penumbra of asserted
jurisdiction. The proper official way of referring to the State,
thus shorn, was: 'Ireland, exclusive of the six north-eastern
counties, pending the re-integration of the national territory'
(IEOTSNEC PTROTNT). In practice, somehow this never quite
caught on. In the twenty-six counties people called the State

'Ireland', with a sense of vague uneasiness about what exactly it was they were talking about. In Northern Ireland people —both Catholics and Protestants, oddly enough—generally continued to refer to the twenty-six counties simply as 'the Free State'. Occasionally, however, they used 'Eire' which they usually pronounced 'Eerie'. I once heard the expression 'the Eerie Free State', and thought it appropriate enough.

The matter of nomenclature was further complicated when, in 1949, the government of John A. Costello changed the designation of the State to 'Republic of Ireland'. As a matter of convenience, people now began to use 'the Republic' to mean the twenty-six county State. But legally the 1937 Constitution remained in force, the name of the State continued to be Ireland (Eire), its *de jure* claim to be the whole island remained unabated, and the new designation 'Republic' was no more than a description of the State defined in the Constitution, and thus implied the same claim.

In the North, people generally continued to call the place whatever they had called it before.

However defined, named or described, the State remained within the boundaries of Lloyd George's 'Southern Ireland' and retained the essential characteristic of that entity: that of being that part of the island which was inhabited, in overwhelming majority, by Roman Catholics—the population is 95 per cent Catholic at the time of writing.

I was less than five years old when the new State came into existence, and I grew up in a somewhat murky and suspicious relation to it.

None of my family was whole-heartedly attached to the new State; most of them disliked it, but for reasons which varied widely.

My mother's brother, Eugene Sheehy, was the nearest, in our family, to being a whole-hearted supporter of the new order of things. He seemed, in fact, a minor pillar of that order. He was Judge Advocate-General in the Free State Army in the Civil War period, and later a Circuit Court Judge. He was one of the rather numerous middle-class Catholics who, having formerly supported the Irish Parliamentary Party, rallied to the support of the pro-Treaty

Cumann na nGaedheal party, on 'law and order' grounds at the time of the Civil War. The new Government needed such allies, but its relations with them were necessarily a little constrained. Eugene, after all, had been in the British Army at John Redmond's call throughout the World War, including 1916. The new Government was made up of Sinn Feiners, all of whom had denounced the wearing of British uniform as treason to Ireland. Eugene could hardly forget this. The new Government could hardly forget it either. Allies like Eugene were needed, in the struggle against the extreme Republicans, but they were compromising allies. The Republicans claimed that those who accepted the Treaty were traitors, and this claim was made more plausible by the appearance on the Treaty side of men like Eugene, whom all Sinn Féiners, in the days when they were united, had denounced as traitors.

At the other end of our political spectrum, Hanna Sheehy-Skeffington, Eugene's elder sister, belonged to the most uncompromising faction of the Republicans. Her murdered husband had been a pacifist, and Hanna, in some sense, seems to have considered herself still a pacifist—as well as a feminist and socialist. Yet in practice, as a result of Frank's murder, she had been drawn into close association with violent revolutionaries. She had been a judge in the revolutionary Sinn Féin system (according to family tradition), and supported the Republican side in the Civil War. This cost her her job—as a teacher of German in a Technical School —in the post-Civil War period. The generally acknowledged leader of the Republican side at this time was Eamon de Valera. But when, in 1927, de Valera took—or was deemed to take—the Oath of Allegiance to the British Crown, then required for admission to Dáil Eireann, Hanna was among those who broke with him, thus putting herself in the small minority of extreme Republicans, permanently opposed to both main parties in the State, and to the State itself.

Strictly speaking, Eugene was, from Hanna's point of view, a double traitor—once for his British uniform, and once for his Free State one—while Hanna, from Eugene's point of view, was a criminally irresponsible firebrand. Actually, they never broke with one another, but maintained relations of gingerly affection, as if something might break at any moment, on an unguarded word. So when the family met at Eugene's house—as it did on rare occasions—politics was not directly discussed. The trouble was to find anything else to discuss—Hanna's interests being now almost exclusively political, while Eugene liked to talk golf, Rugby or horse-racing, topics which Hanna regarded with mild incredulity. In the event they usually played charades, to amuse the young and because it was a family tradition from the happier pre-war time. As it happened, it also provided the elders with a convention in which they could communicate with the minimum of mutual shock—rather like the 'joking relation' which certain African tribes maintain with one another.

Eugene and Hanna did not meet often. Those who did meet often were three sisters; Hanna, Mary and my mother. I remember Hanna and Mary mainly as talking politics: my mother as listening. Ideologically, the strongest bond between them all was militant feminism. They were also all against the government, but for different reasons. Hanna's I have already described. Mary's were partly feminist—she saw the Free State government as what would now be called male-chauvinist, and she saw the Catholic priesthood in the same light (although she was a practising and devout Catholic). But Mary was also human enough to reveal her resentment at the fact that our family had come down in the world. For her, all the varieties of Sinn Féin were upstarts: 'the people who think the world began in 1916'. Tom Kettle, too, had been killed in that year but Tom was without honour in the new Ireland, because he had been killed in the wrong country and in the wrong uniform. True, there was a project to put up a memorial to him—the bust that now stands in Stephen's Green—but for a long time the unveiling had to be put off for fear of incidents (which did in fact occur, even many years later). Mary was very handsome, with 'good bones': cheeks blazing, eyes flashing, she looked the part of the indignant aristocrat. I don't know how much of these feelings Hanna and my mother shared. They did not talk in this strain themselves, but they did not seem to object to Mary's doing so.

Grandfather, David Sheehy, lived with Mary. He was absent minded in his old age, and she was inclined to bully him. Was she unconsciously punishing him for having lost his parliamentary seat in 1918, and for our dynasty's decline? In any case, he went to Mass six times a day—one for each of his six children—and walked out of one such Mass, on hearing that it was for the repose of the soul of Timothy Michael Healy, the first Governor-General of the Free State. The family, including Mary, regarded this action as showing a proper spirit. Tim Healy had been a renegade from the old Irish Parliamentary Party, and honoured precisely for that by the new regime: his soul could find such repose as it was entitled to, without the specific assistance of David Sheehy.

My father was not in sympathy with many 'Sheehy family' attitudes, but he had no more liking for the new order than they had. He had been a secretary of Sir Horace Plunkett, had worked for Plunkett's co-operative movement, and his ideal of reconciling Catholic and Protestant, unionist and nationalist, through emphasis on social and economic rather than political and constitutional aims. Plunkett's co-operative creameries had been burned down by the Black-and-Tans: Plunkett's own house had been burned down by Republican irregulars in the Civil War. The *Freeman's Journal*, the old Irish Party paper, for which my father had also worked, was burned down too. After that, my father worked for the *Irish Independent*. He, like the *Independent*, had generally supported the Free State Government, as against the policies of its Republican adversaries, but he was increasingly repelled by the pervasive and ostentatious clericalism of both the paper and the government. This gave him some common ground with Hanna, whose character in any case he admired. He could talk with Republicans—one of his close friends had been Rory O'Connor the leader who triggered off the Civil War and was executed during it. But on the whole, and increasingly, his friends tended to be those with whom he foregathered at the United Arts Club in Dublin: intellectuals, liberals, nationalists, often of Protestant background—people who were increasingly out of sympathy with the new order, not because of any Republican leanings but by repulsion from what they felt to be the oppressive pieties of the Catholic State. R. M. Smyllie, the editor of *The Irish Times*, was a member of this club. So was W. B. Yeats.

My father died on Christmas Day, 1927, when I was ten. By this time I was already attending a Protestant school, Sandford Park, Dublin. My cousin, Owen Sheehy-Skeffington —nine years older than me—had also attended this school. Owen had attended it not because his mother felt any special attraction towards Protestantism, but because:

(a) The Catholic Church had excommunicated the Republicans during the Civil War
(b) At a Protestant school of liberal type—like Sandford Park—the position of a 'Catholic agnostic' could be, and was, respected.

There was a snag, however. Politically, Protestants, however liberal, were generally Unionist by tradition and symbolic habit. True, they accepted the new State (which was, of course, more than Hanna did). But the aspect of the new State which Protestants then most liked to emphasize was the fact that it remained (at least up to 1937, and perhaps up to 1949) part of the British Empire. This was, of course, precisely the aspect that Hanna rejected. So at Sandford Park, and at Trinity College—where one went from Sandford Park—they played God Save the King on Armistice Day, and wore poppies. (Aunt Mary wore a poppy too, but this was for Tom and so all right.) God Save the King, poppies —and later, at Trinity, the Loyal toast—were out for Owen and me, just as Protestant religious instruction was out. The fact that we were attending a Protestant school, and had inherited little love for the Catholic State, was not to mean any breach of loyalty to the Irish nation—in the sense in which a tradition prevalent among Catholics envisaged that nation.

In fact we had to be all the more loyal to the idea of the

nation in that we were rejecting the institutions in which for most of its members it was embodied: its Church and its State.

All this was tricky enough for both of us. In one way, however, it was trickier for me than for Owen. Hanna was an agnostic, and Frank had been an atheist. My father, too, was an agnostic but my mother was a practising Catholic (though not without some hesitations and interruptions). For a Catholic parent at this time to send a child to a Protestant school was adjudged a mortal sin. Battle for my soul (and my mother's) went on over my head. On one side were my father, Hanna and Owen: on the other Eugene, Mary and the traditional theology. My mother was in the middle. So I had gone to a Protestant preparatory school, then to the Dominican Convent at Muckross, Dublin, for First Communion. After that to Sandford Park, and more mortal sin.

After my father's death, the pressure on my mother to withdraw me from this school must have been strong. Another widow, in a similar position, had withdrawn her boy not long before from Sandford. She had been told that by keeping the boy at a Protestant school she was prolonging her late husband's sufferings in Purgatory. Whether this argument in this form was put explicitly to my mother I cannot say, but she was certainly aware of its existence. In any case I stayed on at Sandford Park. The Skeffington factor was no doubt in part responsible, but there was another reason. My father's friends had raised some money for my education, and this could be used at Sandford Park, not elsewhere. The Catholic Church in Ireland has always had a healthy respect for a good *material* reason in favour of a given course of action and I think the existence of such a reason in this case may well have eased the pressure on my mother. In any case I not merely stayed on at Sandford, but was allowed while there to be confirmed (in the Catholic Church at Haddington Road), an unusual, though not unique concession at this time. The process of obtaining this concession was, however, distasteful. I remember standing with my mother one winter evening outside the front door of

the Parish Priest of Rathmines, while that ecclesiastic—a
purple, pear-shaped person—spoke gruffly to my mother
through a chink in the door.

'. . . The oppressive pieties of the Catholic State.' It is hard
to convey to the outsider just how these worked. An anthology
of 'abuse of Catholic power' case-histories—such as one finds
in the works of Mr. Paul Blanshard—may be accurate enough
in detail, but leaves a false general impression, excessive in
darkness. On the other hand some critiques of the Blanshard
position, also literally accurate, also end by leaving a wrong
impression: too bright, too sweet, too light and airy.

It can be argued that it is misleading to use the expression
'the Catholic State'. A recent excellent and scrupulously fair
study, *Church and State in Modern Ireland*, by J. H. Whyte shows
that it is difficult to define exactly what these relations have
been, but that a simple picture of 'the State under the thumb
of the Church' will not do. Political parties—especially the
most successful of these, Mr. de Valera's Fianna Fáil—have
on occasion rejected advice from the Catholic Hierarchy,
and continued to flourish. Also the hierarchy's advice is
seldom sought by the State, and seldom spontaneously
tendered. Protestants—5 per cent of the population—enjoy
the same political rights as everyone else and flourish economically, and their leaders have repeatedly—perhaps too
repeatedly—testified to the fair, and even generous treatment
they have received from the State.

'Home Rule means Rome Rule', was the slogan of Ulster
Protestant resistance in Edward Carson's day. It still represents the substance of the reason why Ulster Protestant
workers and farmers reject, despise and fear 'the Free State'
which claims jurisdiction over them.

Has it been demonstrated by now, after fifty years of self-
government, that Home Rule does *not* mean Rome Rule?

In the literal sense, it certainly has been demonstrated.
There is no known case of the Pope's interfering in the affairs
of the Irish State, and even the Irish Church is in practice
self-governing and its hierarchy co-optive. Indeed at the
height of aggiornamento under Pope John, when one realised
the sullen distaste with which powerful Irish clerics eyed the

activities in Rome, it was possible to wish that the concept of Rome Rule had more reality, as far as the Irish Church was concerned.

But of course only the most literal-minded of Ulster Protestants (not, admittedly, an altogether negligible sub-category) ever supposed that Home Rule would mean personal rule by the Pope. What the slogan implied was the general condition of being priest-ridden, the over-riding authority of Catholic bishops and priests, the Catholic State.

In this sense, it would be much harder to claim that experience has entirely disproved the old slogan.

It is true—and interesting considering the overwhelming Catholic majority—that the Irish State has never officially proclaimed itself to be a Catholic State. Why did this not happen?

At the beginning of self-government, in the Irish Free State, the Government *could* not have proclaimed a Catholic State. The original Constitution of the Irish Free State is an impeccably liberal document, stressing freedom of conscience and religion, and recognizing no special position for the Catholic Church. In very much later times—in the 1970's—the Fine Gael party, the ideological descendants of the founders of the Free State, have been taking pride in the liberalism of the Free State Constitution, as compared with the more specifically Catholic character of its successor document, Mr. de Valera's Constitution of 1937. It is interesting, and significant, that such liberalism should now evoke retrospective pride. But what the modern Fine Gael spokesmen generally forget or leave aside, is that the liberalism of the 1922 Constitution was by no means a spontaneous product of Gaelic and Catholic minds. That Constitution was based on the Anglo-Irish Treaty of 1921, and its liberalism was of English inspiration. The English Liberals had had to face, ever since Gladstone's 'conversion' to Home Rule in 1886, the Tory argument about Rome Rule. Their answer had to be one that became familiar in later decolonizations: that of 'built in guarantees' to ensure that the emancipated colony would behave in a manner acceptable to the norms of metropolitan public opinion. Paper is a fragile safeguard,

as the Tories did not fail to point out, but it was the best
safeguard the Liberals could offer, and to drop the 'built in
guarantees' would of course supply the Tories with new
ammunition. The Lloyd George Coalition of Liberals and
Tories was under the same pressure, once it decided to treat
with the Irish rebels, since many backbenchers were deeply
suspicious of such dealings, and would become more so if
they found that guarantees which even Liberal governments
had judged indispensable had been dispensed with by the
Coalition. So the guarantees were written into the Treaty:
the new State could not establish or endow any religion, and
was bound (as Northern Ireland also was) to respect freedom
of conscience and religion.

The Irish Free State became constitutionally a secular
State, because the conditions through which it became a
State at all precluded it from having any other kind of
constitution.

The affairs of the new State were not however long administered in a purely secular spirit. The Catholic hierarchy
had supported the Treaty, and had excommunicated those
who opposed it in arms. The Government, therefore, appeared
to be 'better Catholics' than their opponents, and they
encouraged this image of themselves. They introduced and
carried a motion preventing divorce, in 1925. It is not clear
whether they were asked to do this by the hierarchy, either
officially or informally, or whether they sensed it was expected of them, or acted in accordance with their own
consciences (trained, by Catholic instructors, to abhor
divorce), or whether they judged it politically expedient, as
strengthening their *de facto* alliance with the clergy and
reinforcing the respectability of their image. Probably a
combination of several of these elements was at work.

It is interesting to consider the position of the Protestants
of the Free State, in the face of this move.

Protestant attitudes to 'the power of the priests' were
traditionally equivocal. On the one hand, Protestants felt
distaste for the existence of this power, based as they believed
on ignorance and superstition, and they tended to despise
both those who wielded this power and those who endured

it. On the other hand, power is power. In the days of their ascendancy, Protestants—and the British Government—had tried to turn priestly power to their advantage. In so far as priests exhorted their flocks against extremism, Fenianism, the Land League, then the only complaint that the organs of Protestant opinion made about 'the power of the priests' was that it was inadequate: that the Catholics did not defer to their priests on these important social matters as much as they did on things of much less moment. The ambivalence and political variability of Protestant attitudes to priestly power had emerged in a remarkable way at the time of the fall of Parnell. After the Divorce Court verdict, and *before* the Catholic hierarchy had spoken, Protestant newspapers— in Belfast and elsewhere—had attacked the hierarchy for condoning immorality by their silence. But after the hierarchy had spoken, and when its disapproval was brought to bear with cruel and crushing force, then Protestant opinion veered in favour of Parnell. To a considerable extent, these were tactical political options. Protestants, North and South, favoured the union with Britain, and the union seemed safer when the Bishops and nationalist politicians were at logger-heads. On this ground it must have seemed attractive *both* to provoke the hierarchy into action *and*, when it had acted, to encourage the resistance of the weaker party, thus pro-longing the struggle. Yet, if there were tactics in it, there were emotions too—a certain amount of old-fashioned Catholic-baiting in the first phase and, in the second phase, pity and terror for the great Protestant leader—as he seemed in his fall—hounded by the Catholic mob. Not only the young Yeats—deviant, in being a nationalist—but the far more typical Oenone Somerville and Violet Martin (Somer-ville and Ross), strong unionists, felt this way. And there was fear in it too. A Home Rule Ireland dominated by the forces that broke Parnell would seem to most Protestants—and quite a few Catholics too—an ugly place to be locked up in.

Yet, by the time self-government actually came, most Protestants felt rather well-disposed towards the power of priests. The priests after all excommunicated and otherwise discouraged the Republican forces who, in their retreat towards the South West, burned the houses of leading Protestant families. It is true that the burners—like the Wexfordmen in 1798—thought of themselves as acting, not against Protestants, but against landlords and traitors, enemies of the people, England's garrison in Ireland. But most Protestants had been Unionists and therefore, in Republican eyes, part of the said garrison, and liable to similar treatment. Most Protestants were middle class, and most middle-class people supported the Free State government against the Republicans, and were glad to have the Catholic clergy as their powerful allies. But Protestants were more vulnerable than middle-class Catholics to Republican extremism—because of their traditional allegiance— and therefore more in need of priestly aid and protection.

There were, of course, exceptions. Indeed it seems that Protestant Sinn Féiners—a tiny minority of Protestants of course—were more likely than others to take the Republican side in the post-Treaty split. I remember three good Republican ladies, friends and associates of my Aunt Hanna's: Madame MacBride (alias Maud Gonne) in her dramatic widow's weeds, tall and gaunt, towering over her tiny and pugnacious friend, Madame Despard, Lord French's sister; also Constance Markiewicz (*née* Gore-Booth) with her thin brown face and high monotonous upper-class voice:

> *That woman's days were spent*
> *In ignorant good-will,*
> *Her nights in argument*
> *Until her voice grew shrill*

I thought of them as Protestants, and so did everybody else, though I believe that two of them were converts to Catholicism. Such conversions, however, were not taken very seriously, socially speaking. Catholics, if they were Republicans, took such conversions simply as further establishing what very decent friendly Protestants these people were. Non-Republicans, especially Protestants, took the conversions as a further and superfluous proof that the people concerned were 'cracked'.

For the majority of Protestants, the divorce motion of

1925, presented a difficult and delicate challenge. On the one hand there was no doubt what it was: a specifically Catholic measure, departing from the spirit if not the letter of the 1922 Constitution and perhaps (as proved to be the case) setting a precedent for other measures in relation to which Protestants would be made to conform, at least outwardly, to the requirements of Catholic public opinion. On the other hand there were more important issues than divorce—the rights of property for example, and the still smouldering Republican threat. Also, in the Ireland of the 1920's, divorce was a very nasty issue, socially speaking, to have to take a stand on. In the Parnell divorce crisis over thirty years earlier, Catholic Parnellites had been only too apt to say that, whereas adultery and divorce were forbidden to Catholics, Protestants were 'different' (i.e. could not be expected to know, or behave, any better). Protestants naturally resented this and it became accepted doctrine among anti-Parnellites, whether Catholic or Protestant, that 'decent Protestants' were just as opposed to divorce as Catholics were. Between the 1890's and the 1920's, Protestant opinion on this question evolved somewhat, but Catholic opinion did not. Thus in 1925, a Protestant who vigorously opposed the law against divorce would be endangering his status as 'a decent Protestant' in the eyes of his neighbours. In these circumstances, it is hardly surprising that Protestant criticism of the new law was muted or that it fell short of withdrawing support from the Government that initiated the legislation. There was a distinguished exception. W. B. Yeats denounced the Bill in the Senate with majestic vehemence as inflicting a wrong on the Protestants of Ireland. The language he used implied that Protestants were an elite group, or caste, who should not have laws made for them by their inferiors. Naturally the speech annoyed Catholics, but most Protestants also thought it unwise. Yeats was speaking out of disappointment: as a Protestant nationalist he had imagined that Protestants, by reason of their abilities and education, should get, as he said, 'considerable government' into their hands. Now he was finding that the majority of his own community, the Protestant Unionists, had indeed had reason to fear Catholic power in the new Ireland. The paradox was that they, who had entertained such fears, were now rather cheered to find that things were not so bad as they had thought they might be.

In the same year, 1925, in which this divorce legislation was carried, the Government, unfortunately for its future, was obliged to recognize the partition of the island. The Boundary Commission, on which the negotiators of the Treaty had pinned such extravagant hopes, prepared a report generally confirming the existing border, but proposing some minor changes, including some that would have handed over portions of the Free State to Northern Ireland. In order to parry this, the Government rushed through a measure confirming the border as it stood. This was satisfactory to the British and Northern Ireland governments. Perhaps it was also satisfactory to the opposition in the Free State, led by Mr. de Valera, since it saddled the Government party with responsibility for something which neither the government nor the opposition had had any power to avert.

Subsequent Free State sectarian legislation—against contraception, and setting up a Censorship of Publications, to exclude 'immoral and obscene' literature—presented Protestants with the same kind of problem as the divorce legislation, resolved in essentially the same way: guarded and 'responsible' criticism, combined with continued general support for the Government.

Republicans, who had hoped that the sectarian legislation would damage the Government by losing it Protestant support—more important financially than psephologically—were now correspondingly disappointed, and rather contemptuous of Protestants. My aunt Hanna was often heard to say that she could not understand why they were called Protestants, since they never protested. On the other hand, the only daily paper that had opposed this new legislation in any degree had been 'the Protestant paper'—the *Irish Times*. Especially after the crass administration of the literary censorship began to drive many Irish intellectuals, writers and artists into a sort of interior emigration, it was to 'the Protestant paper' that these people, mainly Catholics, turned.

If they lived in the country, and were cautious, they had their *Irish Times* delivered in plain wrappers.

From 1922 to 1932 the government of the Free State was in the hands—through democratic elections—of the winners in the Civil War of 1922, supported—at least for the Civil War and its aftermath and also, though less explicitly, up to 1932—by the Catholic hierarchy.

Among those who resented the clericalism of the first Free State government, many—though not all—believed that the new Government, the Fianna Fáil party headed by Eamon de Valera which came to power in 1932, would rule in a more liberal spirit. The main reason for believing this was that these were the party of the excommunicated, during the Civil War. They had, that is to say, shown independence of judgment (even if their judgment on that specific issue had been bad) and capacity to resist even the most extreme form of clerical pressure. This combination did not necessarily add up to liberalism, but in Irish conditions it had quite a powerful appeal to such liberals as were around, and to many of the young.

For most Protestants, however, Mr. de Valera's independence of judgment seemed less relevant than the use he had made of that judgment. He was feared as an extremist, anti-English, subversive of the economic order, and hostile to Irish Unionists—that is to say to the Protestant community in its political aspect. It was also feared—by the middle classes generally—that Mr. de Valera might prove 'a Kerensky'—not a Communist himself, but opening the way to Communism.

Such fears, and corresponding hopes, lent a portentous and dramatic air to the turning-point of 1932. I was fifteen then and rejoiced in the change, but as from a distance. Most of my family had disliked or distrusted de Valera. My mother, however, voted for him. She was impressed by his grave and dignified demeanour, and by his courteous rarefied speech: he was a gentleman. He was also from our part of the country and had been a parishioner of Father Eugene Sheehy who was known to have had a strong influence on him. His devotion to the Irish language also attracted her, and prob-

ably too—though she was not explicit about this—his
position as a good Catholic whose relations with the Church
were somewhat strained.

As for me, the idea of putting out a government which
has been in as long as you can remember has natural attrac-
tions for a youth of fifteen. Also, as a healthy young animal,
I was respectfully tired of the atmosphere of honourable
defeat in which our family lived. It would be nice, for a
change, to be even remotely on the side of someone who
was winning. There was more than that to it, however. 1932
brought to most Irish people a new sense of *legitimacy* in the
institutions of the new State. Up to 1932, the State and the
pro-Treaty party had seemed one thing, and the idea of the
State, and consequently the quality of Ireland's independence,
seemed limited and tarnished thereby. When the government changed, through democratic elections, the citizens felt
better about their State and about themselves.

In my own family, for example, while criticism of Mr. de
Valera continued lively, the State itself was no longer treated
dismissively or derisively. It was now a State it would be
proper to serve, as our family had believed it would be proper
to serve a Home Rule State.

It was shortly after this that I decided that what I wanted
to do, when I graduated, was to join the Irish Foreign
Service. Most of the family smiled, approved, encouraged.
Even my Aunt Hanna, though still rejecting the regime,
thought the project not dishonourable. I think now that all
of them could no more repress such a tendency in myself,
than a particular kind of tree stump could repress the emergence of a particular kind of shoot.

Grandmother would have been pleased.

In office, Mr. de Valera consolidated his position with
such skill that his party has remained in office ever since,
with the exception of two three-year periods of coalition
government (1948–51 and 1954–57). Mr. de Valera succeeded in the difficult feat of reassuring people who had been
frightened of him, without unduly disappointing his original
followers. His Church policy was among the means whereby
this result was attained. He did not repeal the sectarian

legislation of his predecessors. On the contrary, in his Constitution of 1937 (discussed below) he made sectarianism the law of the land in a far more permanent sense than his predecessors had done. Yet, even while doing this, he managed to convey the impression that he and his followers were somehow more independent of the Church than their predecessors had been. Partly, this was a question of style: Mr. de Valera's air of aloof dignity was such that one felt whatever he did was done without exterior prompting. Partly it was a question of tradition. Mr. de Valera represented (or, as my aunt Hanna thought, misrepresented) the political tradition in Catholic Ireland thought most capable of standing up to the Church: the tradition of Irish Republicanism, the Fenian tradition. Hanna thought that he looked as if he could stand up to the Church, without actually standing up to it, just as he looked as if he were a Republican, without actually being one. This was unfair. Mr. de Valera did stand up to the Church, where he thought the Church was wrong—about the Irish Republic. But on issues like divorce, contraception, obscene literature, there was no question of standing up to the Church because Mr. de Valera —a good Catholic, in the traditional sense, from rural Ireland —agreed with the Church on such matters. It is true that he was aware of the argument that to make laws on such questions which were more restrictive than those existing in Northern Ireland, and which were believed to be demanded by the Catholic Church, had the effect of reinforcing partition. But here the concept of the decent Protestant came to the rescue. Decent Protestants did not want such things any more than we did.

But the main reason why Mr. de Valera succeeded in conveying an impression of independence is that this impression was correct. His independence was rooted in the fact that he knew he was right. When his opinion differed from that of another person, it was that other person who was wrong. His cold certitude on this point was at least the equal of that possessed by an Irish Archbishop. The Bishops knew of this characteristic and had a certain grudging respect for it. They were no more anxious than he was to provoke a

confrontation which if it ever did take place—and it did not
—would have to be of epic proportions.

The nature of Mr. de Valera's strange symbiosis with his
Church is perhaps best conveyed by Maxim Gorky's epigram
on Tolstoy: 'With God he maintains very suspicious relations.
They are like two bears in one den'.

Mr. de Valera's Constitution of 1937 was designed to show
that the State, under Fianna Fáil, had won a freedom not
achieved under the first Government of the State. By good
luck he came to power at a time when it was relatively easy
to make such a demonstration. The Irish Free State had been
a part of the British Empire. Under Mr. de Valera—until
after the Second World War—the State in question, under
a new name, remained within the British Commonwealth.
But the Commonwealth was different from the Empire in
more than name. Through the efforts of, among others,
Mr. de Valera's predecessors, the Commonwealth had
developed in such a way that a member State possessed in
fact complete freedom of action, as far as legal ties were
concerned.

Mr. de Valera later explained that he stayed within the
Commonwealth in the hope that doing so would make it
easier for the North to rejoin the rest of the country. But if
indeed he was interested in wooing 'the North'—in practice,
the Protestants of Northern Ireland—his Constitution of
1937 was an odd bouquet to choose.

Article 2 of the Constitution declared the national territory
to be 'the whole island of Ireland, its islands and the territorial
seas'.

Article 3 asserted—while leaving in suspense for the time
being 'the right of the Parliament and Government established by this Constitution to exercise jurisdiction over the
whole of that territory'.

Article 44.1.2 recognized 'the special position of the Holy
Catholic Apostolic and Roman Church as the guardian of
the Faith professed by the great majority of the citizens'.

Thus, the Protestants of Northern Ireland were declared
incorporated *de jure* into a State which recognized the special
position of the Roman Catholic Church.

It would be hard to think of a combination of propositions more likely to sustain and stiffen the siege-mentality of Protestant Ulster. Mr. de Valera reinforced the effect two years later when he stated in a broadcast to America: 'We are a Catholic nation.'

In terms of twenty-six county politics—of which Mr. de Valera was the apparently absent-minded master—the Constitution made some telling points. Mr. de Valera's predecessors had 'recognized partition'. Mr. de Valera withdrew that recognition. Mr. de Valera's predecessors had made a Constitution with no mention of Catholicism. It was Mr. de Valera who repaired their omission, although they had claimed to be better Catholics than he.

How could Eamon de Valera brought up on a muster-roll of Protestant patriots—Tone, McCracken, Emmet, Davis, Mitchel, Parnell—make the statement: 'We are a Catholic nation'? When he said that, was he throwing away, for twenty-six counties electoral advantage, the Irish Republican tradition, Tone's 'common name of Irishman'. I do not think he consciously intended anything of the kind. I think that the real answer lies in the peculiar nature of Irish nationalism, as it is actually felt, not as it is rhetorically expressed. The nation is felt to be the Gaelic nation, Catholic by religion. Protestants are welcome to join this nation. If they do, they may or may not retain their religious profession, but they become, as it were, Catholic by nationality. Recognizing, as they must, at least the overwhelming primacy and preponderance of the Gaelic and Catholic component of the nation, they are not expected to quibble or jib at such an expression as 'We are a Catholic nation'. And in fact Mr. de Valera's following included a few decent Protestants, members of the Catholic nation. But Protestants who neither sought nor acknowledged such membership might well be annoyed, as well as puzzled, at finding the territory where they were in a majority claimed as part of a State constituted by the Catholic nation. One other point could not escape their notice: the more 'the Free State' asserted its independence the more explicitly it also asserted its Catholicity.

Mr. de Valera, however, stopped short of defining the

State, in the Constitution, as a Catholic State. The 'special position', recognized in Article 44, was in fact a compromise between formal proclamation of the Catholic State and the non-denominational Constitution of 1922. Possibly Mr. de Valera felt that by refraining from formally proclaiming a Catholic State he was holding out some kind of olive branch to Ulster Protestants. The lack of response to this modest peace-offering may have affected his state of mind when he said, later, 'We are a Catholic nation.'

If the State which he governed was the State of a Catholic nation—with a deviation of only about 5 per cent—then the State itself was substantially Catholic. Its failure to proclaim itself formally as such might well strike Ulster Protestants— to whom it laid claim—as devious rather than generous.

This matter seems quite important in retrospect. It did not seem so important at the time, partly because in the middle and late thirties people had other things on their minds and partly because of the kinds of opposition Mr. de Valera was receiving. The main opposition party, Fine Gael, was not at this time complaining—as some of its spokesmen were to do many years later—about Mr. de Valera's abandonment of the relative liberalism of the first Constitution. On the contrary its members were abusing him, from a militant Catholic standpoint, for continuing to recognize Republican Spain. A few years earlier they had adopted, for a short time, some of the symbols and style of Fascism, in the Blueshirt movement. By the late thirties, the Irish Christian Front, no less Fascist in tendency but more explicitly Catholic in language, had taken the place of the Blueshirts, and its language was echoed by the main official opposition party. At the other end of the spectrum the extreme Republicans in the Irish Republican Army claimed to fight the Fascist threat, but the hollowness of this ideological position was to be demonstrated during the war when their leaders tried to bring 'help to Ireland' from Nazi Germany. Their object was to oust or coerce the neutral Government in Dublin and to end partition with the help of the Wehrmacht.

By 1937 my earlier enthusiasm for Mr. de Valera had cooled; I was already a member of the Irish Labour Party.

But Labour was a minority party. It was rather clear that the defence of Irish democracy, in the conditions of the thirties, depended most immediately on Mr. de Valera and his party —appropriately enough, as they were the most obvious beneficiaries of the system in question. It was also clear, Mr. de Valera being what he was and his people being what they were, that democracy in Ireland had to be taken with a tincture of theocracy.

The 1937 Constitution is still in force, unamended, at the time of writing. Divorce and contraception are still forbidden. The laws remain, and the social climate which produced them remains constant in a sufficient degree to ensure resistance to any change in the laws. (See below, Chapters 9 to 11.) Yet the climate has changed, since the late fifties, sufficiently at least to permit serious discussion of such changes. The Taoiseach (Prime Minister) Mr. Jack Lynch has indicated that he might initiate Constitutional amendments including the redrafting of Article 44 (the special position of the Roman Catholic Church) and also that he might consider changes in the laws affecting divorce and contraception. The Primate of All Ireland, Cardinal Conway, has said he would have no objection to the repeal of Article 44.1.2. This article remains, however, unchanged at the time of writing, nor has any concrete move been made towards its repeal. Resistance is stiff towards any serious attempt to change the laws on the specific issues of divorce and contraception. In the early part of 1971, the Labour Party at its Annual Conference in Galway passed, by a large majority, a resolution calling for the repeal of the anti-contraception laws. A Bill for the repeal of these laws has been introduced in the Senate by two young independent Senators. When it was reported that the Government might accept the substance of this Bill, the then Archbishop of Dublin, Dr. J. C. McQuaid, issued a Pastoral letter condemning any such proposal, in terms which the *Irish Times* described as 'druidical' and declared that the legalization of contraception would be 'a curse upon the country'. Cardinal Conway also opposed the change, in language of a slightly more contemporary character. The Government, which had earlier put out hints that it might be about to repeal the laws in question, promptly retreated. It denied even a first reading—i.e. permission to print the proposed Bill—to the repeal measures, in the Senate in 1971 and in the Dáil in 1972.

The hierarchy has not, however, stood entirely still. In 1970, it rescinded its long-standing ban on Trinity College, so that it is no longer a mortal sin for Catholics to attend Trinity College. It is not known how this decision will affect the eschatological status of Catholics who attended Trinity while the ban was in force.

Northern Protestants tend to think of democracy in 'the Free State' as a farce. The real rulers are the Catholic hierarchy: since they can tell the voters what to think, they can tell the government what to do. The great exhibit in support of this view has been the case of Dr. Browne, in 1951. Dr. Noel Browne was Minister for Health in a coalition government. He proposed a Mother and Child Health Scheme without a means test. The Catholic hierarchy condemned such a scheme, as contrary to the moral law. When Dr. Browne tried, none the less, to persist with his scheme, his colleagues demanded and obtained his resignation. The then Taoiseach, Mr. John A. Costello, was profuse in declarations about how unthinkable it would be for a Catholic government not to obey a ruling of the hierarchy on such a matter.

Yet the incident does not prove, so neatly as is often supposed, that the hierarchy are 'the real rulers of the country'. The Government which had shown itself exemplary in obedience to the hierarchy fell and was not re-elected. Dr. Browne's own party—which had expelled him—was shattered at this election and is no longer in existence. Dr. Browne increased his vote in his Dublin constituency, and is still a significant force in Irish politics at the time of writing, and the main beneficiary of the affair was Mr. de Valera's Fianna Fáil party which had maintained an austere silence on the Church-State issues, and which, when re-elected, carried a measure containing much of the substance of Dr. Browne's scheme.[1]

[1] For a very detailed account of this episode see J. H. Whyte, *Church and State in Modern Ireland.*

It would not be true to say that 'when the Church has spoken the case is finished'. On the contrary, no one can know what might be started if the Church should again intervene in a political issue.

(Contraception law is a border line case, since the Churchmen concerned are known to be genuinely convinced that contraception is a moral, not a political issue. At the same time, the State laws are products of a political assembly, and Church pressure on this Assembly to maintain them makes the enforcing itself political.) Both politicians and Bishops therefore like, where possible, to avoid areas of possible confrontation. Bishops do so from prudence and dislike of publicity. But the politicians have an even more urgent incentive to avoid confrontation since the politicians, unlike the Bishops, are responsible to a constituency and are removable. The influence of the Church on the State should be measured—if in fact it were measurable—not by the frequency or intensity of confrontations, but by the assiduity with which politicians avoid such confrontations. Quite recently in the Dáil, the then Minister of Justice, Mr. Micheál O'Móráin, in answering some questions about adoption law, used the cryptic phrase: 'There's a stone wall there.' He did not develop the allusion, and a foreign reader of the Dáil Debates might well be puzzled by it. No one in the Dáil was puzzled. The Minister's 'stone wall' was the veto of the Catholic Church. The Bishops do not want Protestants—or partners in 'mixed marriages'—to be allowed to adopt Catholic children, even if the alternative is for the children in question to remain in institutions. Irish adoption law reflects this Catholic position, and the Minister considered himself as having no power to change it. That was the stone wall. The Minister's reference to it was unusual, not for its cryptic nature, but for the mere fact of being a reference to a subject on which complete official silence is the norm.

It has to be, because it is the Church, not the State, that teaches where the stone wall runs. The State has never disputed Cardinal d'Alton's doctrine (see epigraph to this chapter) that the Bishops have the right and the duty to intervene when religious and moral issues are involved. But it is also the Bishops, not the State or any arbitrator, who decide whether religious or moral issues are involved or not in any given political proposal. During the 1960's there were signs that the State was anxious to exert more authority in this matter. In fact, however, Church control in this area was not seriously challenged. Indeed it looked, during 1971, as if the authority of the Catholic Church were about to be extended—under a Community Schools scheme—over the one type of post-primary instruction that it did not already control, Vocational Education.[2] These proposals encountered strong criticism, however, and were substantially modified early in 1972. But primary and secondary schools remained firmly in clerical hands.

In general the population of 'the Catholic State' has become more permeable to outside—and non-Catholic—ideas and influences than it used to be. This tendency has been favoured by the ecumenical movement, but television has probably been a much more powerful agent of change. The eastern part of Ireland—where most of the population is—is now exposed to British television, both B.B.C. and Commercial, and the nature of this competition has affected Irish television also. In these conditions—and considering the numbers who watch television, as compared with those who read books—the book censorship became obsolescent in fact, while remaining in force as law. Open discussion of formerly taboo topics—notably contraception—became the norm, not just in the *Irish Times,* but in the rest of the press, owned, written and read by Catholics.

The Catholics of the Republic are probably now somewhat more anglicized than they were when Ireland was actually ruled by England. Television is a more powerful agent of acculturation than are bayonets. Conversely, the Protestants of the Republic are being progressively absorbed in the Catholic nation. Their numbers have fallen steadily, not mainly through emigration—in fact they have a slightly lower propensity to emigrate than Catholics have—but

[2] Readers of Mr. Whyte's *Church and State in Modern Ireland* should note that that book was written before the education controversy of 1971 and the contraception controvesy of the same year. These would require some modifications in the author's estimate of church power.

through mixed marriages, the offspring of which are generally brought up as Catholics, this being a condition of the acceptance of such marriages by the Catholic Church. The expectation of the probability of such marriages has its own social momentum. A Protestant mother, in rural Ireland, knowing that her daughter's chances of being married at all will be diminished if marriages with Catholics are ruled out, may well not choose to hand down to these daughters the heritage of the reformed faith in as uncompromising a form as she herself received it from her parents. And this will make the Catholic marriage more probable. With the exception of a few unreconstructed older people, and of some Northern Protestants residing in the Republic for business reasons, the Protestants of the Republic no longer hold a political allegiance distinct from that of the Catholic majority. 'The Protestant paper' the *Irish Times* has shed the last vestige of its unionist tradition. So has 'the Protestant University' Trinity College, and some expect the character of Trinity to change further in a 'Catholic' direction, following the lifting of the hierarchy's ban.

The State of the (95 per cent) Catholic nation can fairly be criticized for a certain insensitivity in relation to the rights and claims of the 5 per cent minority. But that minority, having made its adjustment, resents this insensitivity only to a slight extent. This is appropriate enough for, as injustices in the world go, these are slight injustices.

As far as Northern Protestants are concerned, the injustices and insensitivities are not particularly important: the rulers of Northern Ireland are not themselves squeamish on such matters. Two things, however, remain important in Northern Protestant eyes, about the State with which they share an island:

The first is the tendency of Southern Protestants to be absorbed in the Catholic State and nation: a tendency expressed—in the shift in political allegiance and—even more in dwindling Protestant numbers.

The second is the claim of the Catholic State to jurisdiction also over the Six Counties of Northern Ireland, and over its predominantly Protestant population.

# 7

# The Protestant State and its Enemies

*'We know the war prepared*
*On every peaceful home*
*We know the hells declared*
*For such as serve not Rome.*
*The terror, threats and dread*
*In market, hearth and field*
*We know when all is said*
*We perish if we yield.'*

RUDYARD KIPLING, ULSTER, 1913

One does not need to write 'the Catholic State and its enemies'. The population of the Catholic State is 95 per cent Catholic, and the remaining 5 per cent have no desire to overthrow the State. But more than a third of the population of the Protestant State are Catholics, and most of these have never acknowledged the legitimacy of a State in which they were included against their will.[1] Of this alienated fraction a very small but dangerous minority—in the form of the Irish Republican Army—has always sought to bring down the State through combined political and military action. This small minority has always enjoyed widespread, if nervous, sympathy among the Catholic population of Northern Ireland. Applying Mao's famous metaphor, about one-third of the population is 'water' capable, in certain conditions, of supporting the 'fish' of the guerrilla.[2]

[1] Most—not all. A survey directed by Professor Richard Rose in the summer of 1968 shows 33% of Catholics as approving 'on balance' the Constitution of Northern Ireland. Subsequent events presumably reduced this. See Rose, *Governing without Consensus*, p. 189.

[2] Rose's survey shows only 13 per cent of Catholics as favouring 'any measures' to end partition; 83 per cent as disapproving 'any measures'. But such opinions are generally unstable under pressure.

The remaining two-thirds is land.

Northern Ireland is not, of course, a sovereign State. It is a part of the United Kingdom of Great Britain and Northern Ireland. The limited powers of its parliament have derived entirely from, and may be revoked by, the United Kingdom parliament. In addition, the legislation of the Northern Ireland parliament is subject, legally, to veto from Britain, through the power of the governor—the Crown's representative—to 'reserve' a Bill, which then lapses unless royal consent —in practice consent of the British Cabinet—is granted within one year. Also the Government of Ireland Act (1920), which remains the fundamental law of Northern Ireland, forbids the Northern Ireland parliament, among other things, to 'give a preference, privilege or advantage, or impose any disability or disadvantage, on account of religious belief, or religious or ecclesiastical status. . . .'

Thus, on paper, it seemed entirely possible to ensure that conditions in Northern Ireland should conform to those in the rest of the United Kingdom, as regards basic questions such as civil rights and equal franchise.

Yet in practice what developed in Northern Ireland, from 1921 to 1969, was an institutionalized caste system, with the superior caste—Protestants—in permanent and complete control of government, and systematically ensuring special privileges for its members in relation to local franchise, police, jobs and housing. This was most flagrant in the case of Northern Ireland's second city, Derry. The population of Derry was two-thirds Catholic, but the City Council, through gerrymandering, was two-thirds Protestant, and used its powers predictably. All this developed without significant interference from Britain, up to 1969. A convention even grew up that Northern Ireland internal affairs should not be discussed at Westminster. In general, the relation of Northern Ireland to Westminster came to resemble that of an American Southern State to Washington between the end of Reconstruction and 1957.

How could the very specific prohibition of religious discrimination, in the Government of Ireland Act, be reconciled with Northern Ireland practice?

The official answer—until the Cameron Commission *Disturbances in Northern Ireland* (Cmd 532, 1969) in 1969 officially acknowledged facts that had long been notorious —was that there was no religious discrimination.[3] This seemed like a plain lie, but it was not as simple as that. Defenders of the *status quo* would acknowledge, in private, that there *was* discrimination, but would deny sincerely enough that it was *religious* discrimination. No one, it was argued, was imposing any 'disability or disadvantage, on account of religious belief etc.' The *religious* beliefs of Catholics were their own affair. Their *political* allegiance and intentions were another matter. Politically their allegiance went to neither of the lawfully constituted parliaments, in Stormont and in Westminster, but to 'a foreign country': the Free State (Eire, the Republic). As a community, the Catholics aimed at the destruction of Northern Ireland, and the further disruption of the United Kingdom. Some of them were trying to accomplish this by force and violence, and the rest of them were either sympathetic to this endeavour, or—at best—unwilling to co-operate with the authorities in bringing it to an end. In these circumstances, the Northern Ireland government could not trust the Catholic community—as a social and political grouping, not on theological grounds— and was fully justified in taking such precautions, in relation to that community, as the security of the State might require. And the Northern Ireland government, with its intimate knowledge of the local scene, was in a better position than the British Government to say what these precautions should be.

If the Home-Rule-with-partition settlement could have been carried out in peace, this line of argument would not have been fully available, and to the extent it was available would have carried less weight with British governments. But of course the settlement had been shaped by a threat of force from the Protestant community (the Ulster Volunteers),

---

[3] This was also the opinion of 75 per cent of Protestants answering Rose's 1968 loyalty survey (*Governing without Consensus*). 75 per cent of Catholics thought there was discrimination. In general, however, Rose's survey tends to show Catholics as less dissatisfied than was assumed in the South.

and the actual use of force supported by the Catholic community. Such British sympathy as was forthcoming for any section in Ireland went to 'loyal Ulster'. British antipathy to Ireland, historically a much stronger force, concentrated on the 'Sinn Fein murderers' and their Catholic supporters. Many Englishmen felt the 1921 treaty with the said murderers to be a humiliation, and there was a compensatory reflex further favouring loyal Ulster. This was again intensified by the treaty's sequel—the Irish Civil War—which seemed to show that Ulster had been right in resisting a Home Rule which—as Ulster had foreseen—was leading to anarchy. That argument was dubious enough: the Northern Ireland of 1922 was hardly an oasis of peace in a desert of anarchy. It was torn by two conflicting fears of terrorism: that of the I.R.A., for a time encouraged by the Dublin Government, and that of the pogroms against Catholics, carried out by elements of the Orange Order, which was the main prop of the Stormont government.

Yet, whatever doubts may have been felt about the intellectual, moral and physical arguments of the rulers of Northern Ireland, it was clear that they were right about one thing: any serious attempt, either by Dublin or London, to impose Home Rule for all Ireland as a unit would precipitate a civil war far more bitter and devastating than the actual intra-Catholic civil war of 1922.

In these circumstances it is not altogether surprising that the Ulster Unionists were left a free hand in Northern Ireland. One half-hearted effort was made to restrain them. The Government of Ireland Act had laid down proportional representation as the electoral system for both Northern Ireland and Southern Ireland: Paradoxically, although the Act was accepted for Northern Ireland and rejected—formally at least—for Southern Ireland, it has been Southern Ireland (the Free State, the Republic) which has kept proportional representation, while Northern Ireland dropped it. Proportional representation was intended as a protection for the religious minority in each area. The Catholic State did not fear its 5 per cent Protestant minority: the Protestant State did fear its 33 per cent Catholic minority. So the

Catholic State felt able to keep Proportional Representation while the Protestant State dropped it as soon as it could. The law abolishing proportional representation for local elections—the Local Government Act (N.I.) 1922—passed through all its stages in the Northern Ireland parliament by 5th July 1922, but did not receive the royal assent until 11th September 1922. This hesitation of two months and six days was to remain for forty-seven years the most vigorous attempt recorded on the part of the Westminster government for the upholding of the safeguards for the minority laid down in the Government of Ireland Act. Proportional representation in parliamentary elections in Northern Ireland was abolished in 1929.

But in fact, even in the same year in which the Local Government Act was passed, the British Government itself, under pressure of the struggle with the I.R.A., had set up an institution whose composition and practice made nonsense of paper guarantees for minorities. This was the Ulster Special Constabulary, an armed force drawn, inevitably, from loyalist elements: that is to say, overwhelmingly from the Protestant population, and especially from the Orange Order and the Ulster Volunteers. The Special Constabulary, created by the British Government, were handed over to Northern Ireland control in 1921. The 'B Specials'—the part-time reserve of this constabulary—remained, until after the crisis of 1969, an important part of the structure of the Protestant State, and a standing reminder of its character. Both its friends and its enemies saw it as the Orange Order, armed and in uniform. There were few, if any, legal limits on the uses to which the Northern Ireland government might put this force. The Civil Authorities (Special Powers) Act (N.I.) 1922 empowers the Minister of Home Affairs to 'take all such steps and issue all such orders as may be necessary for maintaining order'. It also provides that 'if any person does any act of such a nature as to be calculated to be prejudicial to the preservation of the peace or maintenance of order in Northern Ireland as specifically provided for in the regulations, he shall be deemed to be guilty of an offence against the regulations'. The Special Powers Act was renewed annually up to 1933, when it was made permanent. From the point of view of the British government, it was a legitimate, though regrettable, reply to the subversion and violence of the I.R.A. From the point of view of the rulers of Northern Ireland it was that too, but also—and inseparably—an instrument of Protestant control over the disaffected community which harboured the I.R.A.: the Catholics.

The great losers by the settlement of 1921 were undoubtedly the Catholics of Northern Ireland. Of them alone could it be truly said that they were much more fairly treated under direct British rule (before 1914) than they were under the new system. The Protestants of the Free State had also been better off, in terms of acknowledged social standing, at least, under British rule—but for many years, and certainly since 1886, their situation had been obviously precarious, and their status under the new dispensation was quite tolerable, and better than they had expected. The reverse was the case with the Catholics of Northern Ireland. Their position had been improving: they had, in some cases, achieved control over local government (under the 1898 Act). They looked forward with hope—and a degree of confidence up to 1914—to the coming of Home Rule for all Ireland, and through it an end to Protestant supremacy in Ulster. But Protestant supremacy, in the latter years of British rule, had lacked an institutional framework. In certain circumstances, most conspicuously when the Liberals were in power, a British controlled constabulary (made up in large part of Irish Catholics) protected Catholics from Protestant violence (as in 1886). The Ulster Volunteers, the I.R.A., and devolution of power from Westminster to Stormont changed this situation drastically. As was to happen with many another minority as imperial power declined the Catholics of the North were in fact delivered into the hands of their enemies. In the Republican tradition of course the Ulster Protestants were not enemies but misguided brothers. But the Catholics were to find—as Ibos and Bengalis have found—that the power of a misguided brother can be more oppressive in practice than that of a remote and indifferent foreigner. And Ulster Catholics are in fact rather less partial to the 'misguided brother' theory of history than are the orators of Dublin.

The Catholics, as a body, originally boycotted the parliament of Northern Ireland (following the elections of 1918). Later, after a twenty-six county parliament had been set up in Dublin, and the Northern Catholics found themselves abandoned by their brothers in the rest of the island, their elected representatives began to take their seats, although a Republican and 'abstentionist' element continued to be critically important among them. But whether they took their seats or abstained made little difference: they were in permanent minority. They might hope that their higher birth rate[4] would eventually produce a Catholic majority, but this was largely offset by a higher migration rate, which reflected in part the policy of the Protestant State in job and housing opportunities and in part the fact that the Catholics, even before the Protestant State came into being, were generally worse off than the Protestants, having a higher proportion of poor farms and unskilled jobs. The difference is, however, less than is often claimed. Professor Rose's 1968 survey found 'a limited tendency'—13 per cent differential —'for Protestants to have a higher occupational class than Catholics; the median Protestant, like the median Catholic, is a manual worker'.[5] Rose also notes that, in Northern Ireland, *there are more poor Protestants than poor Catholics* (his italics). The basic fear of the Protestants in Northern Ireland, Captain Terence O'Neill was to say in 1969, is 'that they will be outbred by the Roman Catholics'. If so, it was foolish of the Unionist leadership to incorporate so much Catholic-majority territory into Northern Ireland. In fact of course the 'basic fear' was also the basic stock-in-trade of the Unionist Party. The relation of violence to this whole situation is worth considering. A British government might—in theory —have divided the island in accordance with the known

---

[4] For 1968, Professor Rose reports: 'The median Protestant parent interviewed had three children and the median Catholic four children'. (*Governing without Consensus.*)

[5] *Governing without Consensus.* Proportionately, however, Catholic manual workers are two-and-a-half times more likely to be unemployed than Protestant ones.

wishes of its inhabitants, as made clear in every successive general election since 1885. That is, the British could have acted on the general principle that areas in which there was a home rule majority should be part of a self-governing Irish State, while areas with a Unionist majority should remain part of the United Kingdom, under the United Kingdom parliament and government. This would not have been easy to work out fairly, in relation to marginal areas. But the result would have differed significantly from the present border which reflects the greater proportionate political influence of Protestants as against Catholics, swinging the balance in all marginal cases. But nobody in Ireland wanted a fair border, because everybody wanted everything. The Unionists wanted to keep all Ireland in the Union, the nationalists wanted to take it all out. The British government, having originally upheld the Unionist position, then came —under the Gladstone liberals—to accept the position of the nationalists. The wishes, and allegiance, of the Unionist minority were to be simply overborne, even in relation to those areas where the Unionists were in a clear majority. The Unionists broke this position, and secured partition, by the threat of force. The Nationalists, under Republican leadership, tried to undo the work of the Ulster Volunteers, and win a united self-governing Ireland through the actual use of force. They failed. Their failure left the situation no worse—though not substantially better—in relation to the twenty-six county area, than it would have been under the kind of Home Rule the liberals were envisaging in 1914. But the real victims of the armed struggle for a united self-governing Ireland were the Catholics of Northern Ireland. Their position, within an entity set up in response to a Protestant demand, would in any case have been difficult. But the attempt at force made it much more difficult, and this for three reasons. First, the Ulster Protestants, seeing the Catholics as involved in an attempt to subjugate them by force, were correspondingly alarmed and correspondingly vindictive in their triumph. Second, the British Government, in the formative period of the new province, disliked the Catholics as 'Sinn Féiners', and were correspondingly disposed to leave the treatment of Catholics to the discretion of the Loyalists who ruled in Northern Ireland. Third, the proclamation of the Republic in 1916, the blood-sacrifices which followed, and the mystique that accompanied them, led succeeding generations of Catholic young men (and a few deviant Protestants) to reject all compromise, and offer further blood-sacrifice to win back the Fourth Green Field. And their actions made the rulers of Northern Ireland feel justified in treating Catholics generally as a fifth column.

Each side with its historians and orators inevitably sees its own actions as defensive, and the other side as the aggressor. Thus Liam de Paor—whose *Divided Ulster* (London 1970) is one of the best studies of the subject from an Irish Republican point of view—refers to 'the effort on the one hand to bludgeon the people (*sic*) into submission to the new Ulster ascendancy and on the other hand to the reprisals carried out by the armed nationalists'. For the Unionist political scientist, R. J. Lawrence, on the other hand, it is the Unionists who are retaliating against Catholic provocation. Of the Catholics he writes, tersely: 'The measures provoked by their own intransigence gave them ample ground for complaint' (*The Government of Northern Ireland*: Oxford 1965). Lawrence goes on to say that the 'vituperation and violence' of the Catholics —against Special powers, internment without trial, abolition of proportional representation, gerrymandering and discrimination—'ranged the majority of the population solidly behind the Unionist Party'. Thus Catholic protest is seen as setting the seal on what Catholic intransigence originally provoked.

The significance of such formulations as those of Mr. de Paor and Mr. Lawrence lies in the fact that, far from being propagandist in intent, they are expressive of what seem to members of the two communities to be self-evident truths.

The acceptance by the Free State Government of the Boundary in 1925 (see above p. 116) might perhaps have been expected to lead—through a feeling that the siege was being relaxed or even abandoned—to some kind of loosening of politics inside Northern Ireland. But this did not happen: Protestants continued, and continue, to vote Unionist,

Catholics continued, and continue, to support varied forms and tactics of anti-Unionism. The Unionist Party and the Orange Order, the political and social products of the siege-mentality, had a vested interest in maintaining the tautness of the siege-mentality. An important characteristic of this mentality is a settled distrust of 'the others'—in their overtures no less than in their assaults. The Unionist Party and the Orange Order fanned this distrust annually in the great parades of July and August, triumphing over the Catholics of the North, and defying the Catholics of the South.

In any case the policy of official recognition by the Dublin Government of the Northern regime lasted only seven years. In 1932, the coming to power of Eamon de Valera and Fianna Fáil marked a more or less open renewal of the siege. The 1937 Constitution (Chapter 6) in effect repudiated the Boundary Agreement, and formally laid claim to Northern Ireland. This document, as seen by Northern Protestants, constituted and constitutes, a standing vindication of the Unionist Party's call for unremitting vigilance.

The Second World War, in its course and in its outcome, strengthened the Protestant State. The Catholic State (Ireland/Eire) was neutral.[6] The Protestant State, being part of the United Kingdom, was at war (although conscription was not imposed in Northern Ireland, for fear of Catholic resistance, and consequent damaging repercussions in the United States). Naturally this ensured that Northern Ireland got a very much more favourable press, in Britain and in the allied countries, than Ireland/Eire did. In particular, the landing of American troops, allies of Britain, in Northern Ireland and their use of a base there, near Derry, greatly encouraged the rulers of the Protestant State. America, after all, had been the great, though distant and usually latent, threat to their security. As American power grew, in proportion to that of Britain, internal influences on American policy became influences on British policy also. And one of these influences was the Irish Catholic ethnic vote in the

[6] On the reasons for neutrality see the present writer's essay 'Ireland in International Affairs' in *Conor Cruise O'Brien Introduces Ireland* (London & New York, 1969).

American cities. That had made itself felt in the 1880's and 1919–21. It might make itself felt again, and some future British Government might 'sacrifice Ulster' for the sake of relations with an ally which was—or seemed to be— taking on the dimensions of a protector. The fact that the ports of Northern Ireland were available to the United States in its hour of need, while the ports of Ireland/Eire were not, seemed an important insurance for the future.

Correspondingly Ireland/Eire felt the cold breath of international disapproval, in the aftermath of the war. The country was not admitted to the United Nations for many years—not until 1955–56—whereas the United Kingdom of Great Britain and Northern Ireland—under that title— was a founder member, and permanent member of the Security Council.

Wisely, Mr. de Valera, in the immediate post-war years, had little to say about partition. But when he fell from office, in 1948 he decided to tour the world, in an effort to arouse its conscience to the iniquity of partition. This put pressure on his successors, the Inter-Party Government headed by Mr. John A. Costello—with Mr. Sean MacBride, Maud Gonne's son, as Minister for External Affairs—to show at least as much sense of urgency about the problem as Mr. de Valera was doing in opposition. Thus when the Inter-Party Government decided that Ireland/Eire (twenty-six counties) should leave the Commonwealth, this step was proclaimed to be—on no very clear line of reasoning—a step towards the unity of Ireland. In Britain, Mr. Attlee's Government responded by—in effect—leaving relations with Ireland (Eire) (twenty-six counties) now a Republic, just as they were before the Republic, but at the same time reassuring the Northern Ireland Government that this implied no change as far as they were concerned either. Mr. Attlee's Ireland Act (1949) reaffirmed that no change in the constitutional position of Northern Ireland would be made without the consent of its parliament. This seems in retrospect a minimal response, but it came as a shock to people who had been speaking as if unity were already in sight. The Dublin response was the formation of an All-Party Committee,

which sponsored the publication and international distribution of a series of pamphlets on the theme of Ireland's right
to unity. The money for this effort was raised by public
collection and the collection, as is normal in the Catholic
State, was made outside the churches after Mass on a Sunday
morning. Some money was collected outside the Protestant
churches too, but a low proportion of the total. My sister-in-
law remembers a very frosty reception when she tried to
collect from the local Protestant congregation.[7] So it became
known in the North as 'the chapel-gate collection': a satisfactory symbol of the nature of the siege. It was also satisfactory when the whole episode, and the Inter-Party
Government itself, came to an inglorious end, amid the
fulminations of Catholic churchmen, after the dismissal of
Dr. Noel Browne in 1951. (See above, chapter 6.) The
Northern Ireland Unionist Party, which normally preferred
to take no official notice of happenings in the South, issued
a pamphlet about the affair, featuring the Dail debate.

From 1948 to 1955, first under the Inter-Party Government, and then under the Fianna Fáil Government which
succeeded it, I was officially concerned, in the Department
of External Affairs, with policy towards the North, and
especially with the projection of policy. I was Counsellor,
in charge of the Information Section of the Department and
also Managing Director of the Irish News Agency, founded
on the initiative of Mr. Sean MacBride, and rather grudgingly
sustained for a time by his successor, Mr. Frank Aiken. After
an interval (1955–56), during which I was Counsellor of the
Irish Embassy in Paris, I returned to headquarters as head of
a new United Nations section, and in 1960 became Assistant
Secretary, heading the Political and Information Sections,
as well as the United Nations Section, so that I was again
concerned with policy towards the North.

In accordance with the general plan of this book, this
therefore seems to be the point where I should say something
about my own associations with the North.

[7] Much later, in the harsher climate of 1972, some Protestant congregations
in the Republic were warned that the *amounts* collected from them 'for the
support of families of internees' would be publicly announced in the locality.

I had no family ties with the place, except that Frank Skeffington, who was shot before I was born, was an Ulster ex-Catholic. At school I met many Protestants, but hardly any Ulster Protestants. We had one Ulster Protestant teacher, however, Dr. J. J. Auchmuty, and I learned from him, at the age of seventeen or so, the interesting fact that Northern Ireland had a Protestant majority. Most Irish Catholics are left to find this out for themselves: some, I believe, never do find it out.

At Trinity, I got to know many Ulster Protestants, some of them well. In 1938 I became engaged to Christine Foster, daughter of the headmaster of a well-known Protestant secondary school, Belfast Royal Academy. In 1939 we were married.

Christine's family took in an even wider span of the Northern Protestant spectrum than mine did of the Southern Catholic one. Her father, Alec Foster, was a Derryman, a rather ecumenical Presbyterian at that time, a classical scholar, former Rugby international and ballad-singer, with an inexhaustible appetite for every form of Irish folk-tradition and all varieties of song. No man had less of the siege-mentality, as far as personal relations were concerned, yet the siege of Derry was always in his heart and often on his lips. When we first met, he kept enquiring whether I would eat a rat. This was a test of worth, derived from the conditions of Derry in 1689. Christine's mother's family, the Lynds, were Presbyterians of Huguenot origin. Her grandfather had been pastor of May Street Church, and Moderator of the General Assembly. It was one of the few Presbyterian families to retain significant traces of the old liberal-radical Presbyterian tradition. Christine's uncle, Robert Lynd, the essayist, had supported Home Rule, written a book called *Ireland a Nation,* and opposed the Solemn League and Covenant. Her mother and three of her aunts, Dolly, Lucie and Ina, had belonged to the Gaelic League. Not very representative Ulster Protestants, it would seem, so far. Yet another aunt, Laura, was married to a pillar of the orthodox Protestant Establishment, the extremely conventional Bob Jones, headmaster for many years of the Royal Belfast

Academical Institution. Ina—who had once belonged to the Gaelic League—married William Lowry, a genial, capable and truculent figure who later became Minister for Home Affairs, and whose son Robert is now Chief Justice of Northern Ireland. (Bill Lowry's resignation was called for by many Catholics, after he was questioned by Orangemen about allowing an Orange Hall to be used by the u.s. Army for a Catholic religious service. Bill's reply was that it could always be fumigated.)

The Lynds resembled the Sheehys in many ways—not least in being well satisfied with their genes—and, as with the Sheehys, their family affections went deeper than their political differences. Neither family had wanted Ireland to be divided, but the Sheehys had found it natural to come to terms with the Catholic State, the Lynds with the Protestant one.

The families knew and respected one another. Robert Lynd and Tom Kettle had been friends. But that was before the war. Now, not only religion, but partition cast their shadows. Sheehys knew that, in the Protestant State, where the Lynds seemed to be doing quite well, thank you, the Sheehys could only be second-rate citizens: a preposterous state of affairs. And Lynd knew, even better, that in the public sector of the Catholic State, Lynds were unlikely to be more than marginal figures, tolerated and discreet irrelevancies. Three of them were in fact living there, holders of comfortable jobs left over from the British days, working towards their pensions. They were all three unmarried. The married Lynds were all in the Protestant State, or in England.

It was not, and it was, a question of religion. Hanna Sheehy-Skeffington and Anne Lynd-Foster agreed about religion. They were both against it. They also agreed about men: they were against them. As educated emancipated women of the same generation they agreed about many things. Yet they were in a fundamental, permanent, almost existential disagreement. It came out clearly one evening in our flat in Dublin in 1941. Anne was visiting from Belfast. We had invited Hanna to meet her. Anne spoke about the

war news, and how much better it was. We should soon put
Italy out of the war, she thought. There was a sharp intake
of breath. Then Hanna said, in a low outraged voice, simply:
'WE.'

The evening was not a success.

Neither lady was quite real to the other. Since Anne was
Irish she could not, in Hanna's system, be British and therefore to identify with the British was affectation, pretence.
What really hurt about that 'we', I think, was its entire
naturalness, transparent lack of affectation, thoroughly in the
character of the lady who spoke the word. Anne did not fit
into Hanna's system. She ought either to be Irish, in the sense
in which Hanna understood the word Irish, or to be a fake.
She was quite obviously neither. Mentally, Hanna made her
disappear.

Anne, for her part, knew about Irish nationalism, had
been a nationalist herself in her Gaelic League days, and
she knew Hanna's history. So, if she thought about it, she
would have known how 'we' would affect Hanna. But she
didn't think about it. Irish nationalism had been, I think,
for her not much more than a hobby: you took it up, put it
down, meant to think about it again some day. But, with a
war on, her instinctive reactions were those of an Ulster
Protestant. The world in which she had thought of herself
as an Irish nationalist, the world in which one at least adapted
one's speech to the feelings of Irish nationalists, dropped
below the horizon of her mind. Mentally, she made Hanna
disappear.

This little exchange was representative of most of what
passed for dialogue between Catholic and Protestant in and
about Northern Ireland.

The Northern Ireland I came to know through Christine's
relatives was that of the Protestant middle classes, mainly in
Belfast. Most of them were people of liberal views; nobody
spoke unkindly of Papists; everyone was kind, or at the
worst polite, to me personally. But somehow there were no
local Catholics around. One of Alec Foster's sisters had married a Catholic named Alf, but they lived in England. Alf was
referred to once, in the presence of our son Donal, then a

toddler, by Alec's parents—Alec's father was Registrar of Births, Deaths and Marriages in Derry. Alec's mother, talking to her husband, said something about Alf's marrying a Protestant: her tone must have carried a note of disapproval. Donal, playing on the floor, asked 'What's wrong with marrying a Protestant? Conor married a Protestant'. The old pair were troubled by this intervention, and in some strange way impressed.

Later, through my official work, I came in touch with an entirely different Northern Ireland: that of politically active Catholics.

One of my functions was to provide a kind of liaison between the current Minister for External Affairs and Northern nationalist (Catholic) leaders. Another was to introduce foreign journalists, and others studying Northern Ireland, to the nationalist circles which their official Northern Ireland guides would steer them clear of. This last activity sounds redundant, but in practice at this time—when the interest of the media in all aspects of Ireland was languid—it was not unusual for a journalist to come to Belfast, to get 'Northern Ireland's side' and then come to Dublin for 'the Republic's side'. In Dublin the journalist would see me and if I found, as I usually did, that his contacts in Belfast had been exclusively Protestant and Unionist, and if it seemed sufficiently important, I would take him to meet Catholic and nationalist leaders, usually in Belfast, Derry, Armagh and Omagh—renewing my own contacts there at the same time.

I remember in particular, from one journey (in 1952 I think) various epiphanies. I was acting as guide to an English Jesuit, Father Wingfield-Digby, who was carrying out an enquiry for his Order into the condition of Catholics in Northern Ireland.

In Armagh, Senator J. G. Lennon showed us the electoral map of the city, providing the necessary key of religious denominations by area, and touring the city boundary. What he showed us was a classical gerrymander, thorough to the point of pedantry: at one point the city boundary, following the line of a certain terrace, suddenly skipped behind the back-gardens of three houses, homes of Catholics. Gerry Lennon explained these things, with controlled indignation, but at the same time a faint touch of local pride: it was not everywhere you could see the like of this abomination. But Father Wingfield-Digby was simply disgusted by such an example of rustic bigotry. 'Good Heavens!' he exclaimed. 'How perfectly stupid!' Gerry Lennon looked sourly at the Jesuit. 'In the name of God,' he asked, 'what's *stupid* about it?'

Later that day, in Derry, I brought Father Wingfield-Digby to see Mr. Eddie McAteer, M.P., and some of his friends. The Jesuit was already a bit worried at this stage about the tendency for politics and religion to run together when they should, he thought, be separate. He wanted to know, in the case of Derry, for example, how many Catholic Unionists there were, and how many Protestant Nationalists.[8]

Mr. McAteer and his friends looked at one another: the Jesuit might have been enquiring as to the prevalence of Unicorns in the vicinity. But they applied their minds to the question. There had been a Catholic Unionist—and they named him—but the Protestants snubbed him of course, and the Catholics boycotted him, and he gave up. Protestant nationalists? Well. Such indeed there might well be. Professor ——, for example, at Magee College, a thoroughly decent man: 'He must be a nationalist really, but of course he calls himself a communist. It's safer, you see.'

From Derry we drove back to Dublin. When we crossed the border, the Jesuit sighed with satisfaction. 'It feels like coming home,' he said. It was an odd remark, since he was leaving the United Kingdom, to which he belonged, and entering a foreign country. Yet he was a very English Englishman, and I had the impression from him that he didn't mean that the Republic was 'like home' because it was Catholic, and so home for Jesuits. I think he meant that the Republic was more English than Northern Ireland.

Crossing Co. Monaghan the Jesuit looked at his notes. He still seemed troubled. He said what fine people Mr.

[8] The Civil Rights movement later changed this situation a little. Mr. Ivan Cooper is a Protestant, anti-Unionist M.P. But the basic equation remains true.

Lennon, Mr. McAteer and their friends were. I agreed. 'Just one thing,' said Father Wingfield-Digby. 'Can you be quite sure they're . . . well . . . loyal?'

I could have said they were as loyal as sixteenth century English Jesuits, or twentieth century Western Communists: that is, fanatically loyal to something other than the State in which they lived. But it hardly seemed worth while.

I never learned what Father Wingfield-Digby reported. I expect it was to the effect that the disabilities of the Northern Catholics were real, but due, not to their religious faith, but to their misplaced political allegiance. No action.

Fairly early on—certainly by 1951—I had realized that propaganda about 'Ireland's right to unity' was futile. I knew, after all, something about Northern Ireland Protestants: not a lot, but much more than most Southern Catholics did. I thought, however, that concentration on a reality—the repression of the minority in Northern Ireland—might achieve better conditions for that minority. In fact, efforts in this direction achieved very little. One reason for this was the grievances in question, though oppressive in the daily life of those who experienced them, were unspectacular and even humdrum, and that far more brutal repressions were taking place elsewhere in the world in the aftermath of the Second World War. Journalists, at this period, were apt to regard Northern Ireland and its problems as quaint rather than serious and potentially tragic. Also, no Dublin government, during the fifties and sixties, wanted to concentrate on this aspect. What Dublin governments wanted to emphasize in the fifties—whenever they concerned themselves with the question at all—was 'Ireland's right to unity', the basis of which was the undoubted fact that there was a Catholic and nationalist majority in the whole island. To the fact was added a claim—or, more often, an assumption —that the only unit for self-determination had to be the island of Ireland, held to be a natural geographical and historical unity, inherently indivisible. To concentrate attention on conditions inside Northern Ireland might seem like abandoning the basic claim that partition itself was the root of all evil.

From the point of view of the Northern Ireland Government, on the other hand, the maintenance by Dublin of its claim to incorporate the North was a standing justification for the repression of the Northern minority, the Fifth Column. This justification was reinforced by a revival of the activity of the Irish Republican Army—that is, the effort to 'unite Ireland' by the gun—at the end of 1956. This resurgence was repressed, not only by the Northern Ireland and British Governments, but by the Dublin Government—under Mr. de Valera (1957–9), and then under his chosen Fianna Fáil successor, Mr. Seán Lemass (1959–66). Using power available to it under a war-time statute, the Offences against the State Act, the Government re-introduced internment without trial in the Republic, and interned I.R.A. members and sympathizers in considerable numbers. By 1962, the I.R.A. campaign had petered out.

With fateful and largely unexpected results, the Lemass Government determined on a new policy line towards the North. Mr. Lemass did not formally drop the claim to unity —he could hardly have done so and kept his party intact— but he made it a remote, platonic ideal. In the present, his emphasis was on economic co-operation and friendly relations with the Stormont Government. Reassured by Dublin's attitude during the I.R.A. campaign, Captain Terence O'Neill, who succeeded Lord Brookeborough as Prime Minister of Northern Ireland in 1963, decided to accept the outstretched hand. On 14th January 1965, he received Mr. Seán Lemass at Stormont to discuss 'possibilities of practical co-operation in economic matters of mutal interest'.

'Things,' Mr. Lemass commented afterwards, 'will never be the same again' so far as North–South relations were concerned.

In retrospect, there is a true tragic irony in those words.

If the Protestant State had been as homogeneously Protestant as the Catholic State was Catholic, then the Lemass-O'Neill *rapprochement*—followed up as it was by various 'official level' contacts—might indeed have given the results hoped for: the burying of old animosities, the adoption of a modern, pragmatic, developmental approach:

better business, more tourists, a pleasanter 'image' for all concerned.

As it was, it wasn't *just* a question of 'North-South relations'. There was the much more intractable question of the internal equilibrium between the communities inside Northern Ireland. The Lemass-O'Neill contacts began to change that, but with the reverse—as it seems at the moment of writing —of the results the protagonists hoped for.

'The present disorder of Northern Ireland', wrote Mr. Iain Hamilton in the summer of 1970, 'is basically the product of Lord O'Neill's attempt to liberalize the Unionist regime's attitude to the Catholic community. Since Lord O'Neill's first meeting with Seán Lemass in 1965, events have borne out Tocqueville's dictum that a grievance, while it may be patiently endured so long as it seems beyond redress "comes to appear intolerable once the possibility of removing it crosses men's minds".'[9]

Mr. Hamilton's 'basically' is incorrect, and so is his implied assumption that if O'Neill had only left well enough alone, members of the minority would not have discerned, by the mid-1960's, any 'possibility of removing' some of their grievances. But his comment on the price of liberalization is to the point; we do not know what the price of further 'not an inch' would have been, or when it would have had to be paid.

The feelings of the two communities towards one another were not susceptible of being turned off or turned on by politicians in Belfast or Dublin. I remember one discouraging Northern journey, on the instructions of Frank Aiken, Seán Lemass's Minister for External Affairs. The object was to convey to various nationalist/anti-Unionist/Catholic leaders and publicists the wish of Mr. Aiken and the Dublin Government that they should take a more active part in public life, cease to boycott local official ceremonies, and associate with Protestants to a greater extent. Most of them heard me with resignation, but without manifest assent. A typical comment was that, although Frank Aiken had been

[9] Article 'From Liberalism to Extremism' in *Conflict Studies* no 17, November 1971.

born in Armagh he had been away from it a long time.
There was one man, however, a local chieftain in a remote
village in a desolate hilly part of South Armagh who made
no reply at all to my message. He was sitting in front of his
little shop and looking out across the glen in the stillness of
the summer evening. Uneasily, to break the silence, I asked
him whether there were were many Protestants in the district.
Then he spoke, quietly: 'There's only one Protestant in this
townland. And with the help of God, we'll have him out of
it by Christmas.'

To many Catholics, feeling themselves prisoners in the
Protestant state, the Lemass-O'Neill fraternization seemed
like a final abandonment. The old emphasis on anti-partition
might not have done them much good—it had not, in fact,
done them *any* good—but at least it had encouraged them
to hope that, in some way, Dublin would manage to come
to their aid. Now even that small hope was dimmed.

In the pre-Lemass days, Dublin's failure to focus attention
on the plight of the Northern Catholics had been justified
in terms of the need to 'put unity first'. Now unity itself was
de-emphasized, but discussion—at least public discussion—
of the condition of the Northern Catholics became more
taboo than ever. It might endanger the possibilities of
*rapprochement* with the Stormont Government, from which it
was hoped improvement in the conditions of the Catholics
might eventually flow. This hope, however, was denied (as
far as the public was concerned) by Stormont's insistence
that all discussions with Dublin were confined to the question
of economic co-operation between the two governments.

My connection with the Dublin Government ended in
December 1961[10] so that I had no direct experience of the
heyday of the Lemass-O'Neill fraternization. But even by
1960–61 the official mood in Dublin was one not merely of
reaction against the excesses of the chapel-gate collection
period, but one of impatience with the Northern Catholics,
and a degree of aversion from them. They had brought, it
was felt, most of their troubles on themselves, and it was
now up to them to come to terms with reality.

[10] See *To Katanga and Back* (London and New York 1962–3).

In New York, in I think 1960, I drafted proposals for a possible approach to the problem at the United Nations. The idea was that the Irish Government should formally disclaim any intention of absorbing Northern Ireland, against the known wishes of the majority there, but at the same time should invite international attention to the condition of the minority, and to the contravention of the Universal Declaration of Human Rights which this condition involved. No intervention by the United Nations was to be sought or expected, but the tabling of the issue, and its continued presence on the U.N. agenda, would exercise a certain pressure on the United Kingdom and on Stormont, while reassuring the Northern Catholics that a policy of improved relations between Dublin and Belfast did not involve the abandonment of their community. At the same time Stormont would have the less reason to oppose the reforms, in that the principle of no-unity-without-consent would now be proclaimed, for the first time, by Dublin. The Irish Delegation, in the Special Political Committee of the General Assembly, had helped Austria to forward a rather similar approach, in relation to the treatment by Italy of the German-speaking minority in South Tyrol (*alias* Bolzano/Bozen). Austria was pleased with the results: a similar approach seemed worth trying on our own account.

It wasn't tried, however. It is easy to see why. The pragmatists, who were trying to shape the *rapprochement*, saw how vehement the immediate reaction of Stormont would be to anything of the kind. The traditionalists, who felt queasy enough already about the *rapprochement* idea, could not stand the explicit announcement of no-unity-without-consent. The Permanent Head of Ireland's Mission to the United Nations at this time belonged to the first school; the Minister for External Affairs to the second: the ideas died.

The *rapprochement* effort, combined with diminishing interest in the Northern minority, continued through the first half of the sixties, culminating in Mr. Lemass's call on Captain O'Neill in 1965.

The date was unfortunate, for the following year was a

great commemorative year, a year in which ghosts were bound to walk, both North and South.

In 1966, the Republic—and also many of the Northern Catholics—solemnly commemorated the Easter Rising of 1916. These celebrations had to include the reminder that the object for which the men of 1916 sacrificed their lives— a free and united Ireland—had still not been achieved. The general calls for rededication to the ideals of 1916 were bound to suggest to some young men and women not only that these ideals were in practice being abandoned—through the Lemass-O'Neill meetings and in other ways—but that the way to return to them was through the method of 1916: violence, applied by a determined minority. The Dublin Government tried to discourage these last conclusions, but there is in fact no way of discouraging them effectively within the framework of a cult of 1916. The numerous commemorations of similar type that had to follow could only reinforce this trend, favouring a revival of the Sinn Féin-I.R.A. movement, in various forms.

Ulster Protestants, in the summer of 1916, commemorated not only their usual seventeenth century topics but also the fiftieth anniversary of the Battle of the Somme, when the Ulster Division was cut to pieces at Thiepval Wood. From the perspective of those who commemorated these events, the commemorations in Dublin seemed a celebration of treachery, and at the same time a threat to 'Ulster'. Captain O'Neill in his fraternization with Mr. Lemass, had seemed to say that the Republic was no longer a threat. But the spirit and character of the Dublin celebrations showed that the leopard had not changed his spots.

Just as the 1966 commemorations in Dublin favoured a recrudescence of the I.R.A., so the Northern commemorations, clashing with those in the South, favoured the recrudescence of armed Protestant extremism. The Ulster Volunteer Force, pledged to war against the I.R.A., began in this year, and was declared illegal by Captain O'Neill, after two Catholics had been murdered.

It was also in this year that the Reverend Ian Paisley, the Free Presbyterian minister, attracted international notice.

Mr. Paisley's huge, rocky face, with small, shrewd, watchful eyes, seemed a symbol of the besieged Ulster fortress for which he stood. For him, the enemy was Rome, and matters apparently so diverse as the ecumenical movement, the I.R.A. and the Lemass-O'Neill *rapprochement* were simply different tactics for the fulfilment of Rome's strategy against Protestants, and in particular the exposed Protestant redoubt of Ulster. Mr. Paisley's concepts and language seemed so laughably archaic that they concealed from many his very real intelligence.

The Northern Catholics, abandoned as they felt by Dublin, were exposed during and after 1966 to increasing Protestant backlash. After the experience of 1959-62, and given the attitude of Dublin, there seemed little hope in immediate recourse to armed force. It was in these conditions that the Civil Rights movement began to make its appeal to the mass of the Catholic population, and its fateful impact on the equilibrium of Northern Ireland.

# 8

# Civil Rights: the crossroads

*Civil Rights Association—Crafty Romanist Agitators*
PROTESTANT SLOGAN

i

During most of the 1960's I was outside Ireland—from 1962 to 1965 in Ghana, and from 1965 to June 1969 in New York, but spending part of each summer in Ireland, mainly in Dublin and Kerry. My contacts with the Civil Rights movement in Northern Ireland—a movement which began early in 1967 and first came to public prominence in the late summer of 1968—were sparse and intermittent.

The first such contact came in late October, 1968,[1] when I addressed a large, mainly student audience at Queen's University, Belfast on 'Civil Disobedience', a subject of which I had been acquiring some small direct experience in New York, in the movement against the Vietnam war. It was already *the* topic in Belfast. The Vice-Chancellor of Queen's was urged to ban the meeting, and compromised by excluding the press from it. Earlier that month, on 5th October 1968, a Civil Rights march in Derry had been clumsily and brutally dispersed by the police, who thereby precipitated a Catholic-Protestant riot. These events had concentrated international—and British—attention on Northern Ireland to a greater extent than at any time since 1914. (In the post-1918 period, attention was concentrated on Southern Ireland; Northern Ireland being then, and for long after, thought of as 'settled'.)[2]

[1] My return to New York was delayed that year, for personal reasons.
[2] For a good report of this and other major public episodes of 1968–69 in Belfast, see Max Hastings, *Barricades in Belfast: The fight for civil rights in Northern Ireland* (New York 1970).

Queen's University was one of the focal points of the developing Civil Rights movement. The left wing of that movement, under the name of People's Democracy, was just then beginning to move; it did not become widely known until a few months later, but the names of a few student, ex-student and student-based leaders were being heard: Eamonn McCann, Michael Farrell, Cyril Toman, Bernadette Devlin.

The Vice-Chancellor's obvious anxiety about the meeting was an excellent advertisement for it in student eyes, and the student audience was large, with a high proportion of vaguely left-wing students, and of Catholics, with the two categories overlapping to a considerable extent.

The main point of my lecture was that civil disobedience, in Northern Ireland, was likely to prove an effective lever for social change. In places like South Africa—where the ruling group acknowledged no superior authority and had no inhibition about using any kind or degree of force necessary—civil disobedience had failed. But in conditions where there was, as it were, a right of appeal, civil disobedience could work. Thus, in the Southern States of America, the local whites had been able to oppress the blacks, with the tacit assent of the Government in Washington, as long as the blacks themselves passively accepted their subordination. But when the blacks, by civil disobedience, obliged their white rulers to use force against them, then they revealed, in a glaring way, the contradiction between their conditions and the values professed by the wider society. Washington had been forced to intervene, when President Eisenhower sent Federal troops to Little Rock, Arkansas eleven years before. Similarly London could be forced, by an effective application of civil disobedience, to end its long collusion with Stormont's Protestant State.

The analogy and the prediction were accurate enough, as far as they went. They left out of account, however, a set of factors which did not seem important then. *The analogy stops at the Border.* It would be perfect, either if Northern Ireland were an island to itself, off the shores of Great Britain, *or* if there were a sovereign black-majority state to the South of Dixie, which claimed to incorporate Dixie. In the first case, Northern Ireland would now be a fairly peaceful part of the United Kingdom. In the second case, Dixie, not long after Little Rock, would have become a theatre of guerrilla and race-war, with Federal troops being fired on by blacks, and whites preparing for the day of Federal evacuation and the final show-down.

Neither lecturer nor audience, in that autumn of 1968, attached any immediate importance, consciously at least, to the idea of the unity of Ireland. Unity was not 'where it was at'. The left-wing of the Civil Rights movement regarded— or thought it regarded—the government of the Republic as just as corrupt and oppressive as Stormont. They did not want help from Dublin, or greatly favour the involvement of Southerners in their struggle. Southerners, they rightly thought, should busy themselves putting their own house in order, and shut up about partition. The Lemass government had at least shut up about partition. Ireland—as the student activists saw it—was now ruled by two corrupt capitalist governments, in collusion with one another, and with London. The people of Ireland would have to deal with these governments, by militant activity culminating in revolutions.

It was assumed that the result of these revolutions would be a united Irish socialist Republic. But *unity* in itself was not consciously thought of as the object of the revolutionary effort. The object was *social* revolution: a united Ireland was simply assumed to be the only conceivable framework for this.

This was of course the Catholic assumption, natural in a movement which—despite consciously sincere protestations of non-sectarianism—was always fundamentally a movement of Catholics.

The Northern Ireland Civil Rights Association was formed early in 1967, on the initiative of the Campaign for Social Justice in Northern Ireland (Dungannon). It was 'non-sectarian' meaning, as usual in Northern Ireland, Catholic-based with a few Protestant sympathizers. Its strongest visible local bases were the Catholic Housing Action

Committees and its earliest success, in the summer of 1968, concerned a flagrant case of discrimination against Catholics in housing, at Caledon, Co. Tyrone. (See Hastings, *Barricades in Belfast*, also Martin Wallace, *Drums and guns: Revolution in Ulster* [London 1970].)

No one criticized me for omitting an aspect of reality: the existence of the hope and threat of the unity of Ireland. What I was criticized for, quite heatedly, was for *mentioning* an aspect of reality: the existence of two separate communities, Catholics and Protestants.

This was held to be 'irrelevant', a favourite all-purpose student knock-out word at the time, in Belfast as well as in New York. 'Religion', one student said, 'is a red herring'. I said if so it was a red herring about the size of a whale. 'No, no,' said another student, 'no one in Ulster is the least bit interested in religion.' 'Not even in Sandy Row?' I asked. Another student said he himself came from Sandy Row, and could report that no one there cared whether a man was Catholic or Protestant. This thumping lie was loudly applauded. Hearing the applause, the speaker seemed to have some doubts about what he had uttered. He added, hesitatingly, 'They just come out when the drums beat, you know.' We knew. But *why* did they come out when the drums beat? Someone said, rather dreamily: 'Well, *any*one would.' The more orthodox answers soon followed; people came because they had been brain-washed, duped by the bosses. But were the bosses really so clever, the workers so dumb? And why should Protestant workers be dumber than Catholic workers? Well, the Protestant workers did have some privileges, small ones, which the bosses encouraged them to over-value. In any case, it was waste of time to speculate why these things should be so. The important thing was action; solidarity of Protestant and Catholic workers, dictated by basic, common class interest, would grow out of the struggle itself, dissipating false consciousness, while destroying the structures which perpetuated it.

It was easy to know *that* would not happen. Professor Rose's loyalty survey was carried out in this year (1968) and he states:

In so far as class differences are more important than religious differences, then Ulster people of the same class should have more similar regime outlooks than people of different classes but the same religion. The data from the Loyalty survey clearly reject this hypothesis. The difference between middle-class and working-class Protestants in support for the Constitution is four per cent, and three per cent in endorsement of an ultra position. Similarly, among Catholics, there is only a two per cent difference across classes in support for the Constitution, and a five per cent difference in readiness to demonstrate against the regime. The differences between religions are much larger. Within the middle class, Protestants and Catholics differ by 36 percentage points in their readiness to support the Constitution, and manual workers differ by 30 percentage points. In refusal to comply with basic political laws, about half of each class group is ready to endorse extra-constitutional actions against others who share class but not regime outlooks. It is particularly noteworthy that there is no consistent tendency for middle-class Ulster people to be readiest to endorse the Constitution and refrain from extra-constitutional politics, notwithstanding their relative advantage in terms of status.

This being the case—and it was quite evident at the time even to non-scientific observers—it should also have been clear that minority militancy, non-violent or violent, would widen the gap, rather than close it. It was much less easy to predict what *would* come out of the civil rights struggle. One thing, however, was certain, for anyone who had an idea of the character of the besieged state, and who witnessed the courage and confidence of the young people who marched against it under their hopeful and misleading banners. What was certain, already, was that much blood would be shed. I wrote about the prospect, at this time, in terms of the Antigone of Sophocles, the girl who deliberately, without violence, broke the law—by burying her brother Polynices, against King Creon's command—knowing that death would follow:

Antigone's action was one of non-violent civil disobedience, the breaking of a law which she considered to be contrary to a higher law. The consequences of her non-violent action emerge in acts of violence: Antigone's own violent death; Haemon's turning of his sword first against his father Creon and then fatally against himself; the suicide of Eurydice, Creon's wife and Haemon's mother. A stiff price for that handful of dust on Polynices. Nor is it possible to put all the blame on Creon. Certainly his decision to forbid the burial of Polynices was rash, but it was also rash to disobey his decision. The citizens of Thebes disapproved, and the prophet Tiresias rebuked him, but no one disobeyed except Antigone. Creon's authority, after all, was legitimate, even if he had abused it, and the life of the city would become intolerable if citizens should disobey any law that irked their conscience. Ismene, who was Polynices' sister just as much as Antigone was, would not risk life for the sake of her brother's dead body. It was Antigone's free decision, and that alone, which precipitated the tragedy. Creon's responsibility was the more remote one of having placed this tragic power in the hands of a headstrong child of Oedipus.

The play is still performed. The role of Antigone attracts the young, though those capable of playing it to the end will always be few. Creon continues the interminable series of his rash engagements: suppression of communism in Asia, suppression of freedom in Czechoslovakia, white supremacy and every other form of the supremacy of the supreme. In the press and in the pulpit, Tiresias admonishes Creon, Ismene seeks to restrain Antigone. And the rest of the tragedy unfolds, since Creon and Antigone are both part of our nature, inaccessible to advice, and incapable of living at peace in the city. Civil disobedience is non-violent, but everywhere attracts violence. The two greatest modern apostles of non-violence, Gandhi and Martin Luther King, were both murdered. The independence of India, crowning the non-violence struggle, occurred amid a hideous orgy of violence. Martin Luther King's aim, the equality of blacks with whites in America, is not likely to be achieved without great violence. The American protest movements, in favour of racial equality and against imperialist war, have elicited a powerful counter-movement—for the restoration of full white supremacy and the extension of imperialist war.

Most people in Britain knew little or nothing about Derry City until the police used force to disperse a non-violent but illegal civil rights march. Non-violence, setting off the use of violence, effectively draws attention to a grievance, since the public wants to know why these people are willing to put themselves in a position where they will be clubbed by the police. The British public learned then that there was something peculiar about the situation in Derry; a Catholic-Nationalist majority was ruled over by a Protestant-Unionist minority, holding a near-monopoly of jobs and housing. Some among those who learned of this situation thought it was contrary to democratic principle and ought to be changed. So far, this was a considerable reward for a limited act of non-violent civil disobedience. For the first time the Catholic minority in Northern Ireland seemed to have some prospects of achieving normal democratic rights. Yet the reaction of the minority to this change has not been one of unqualified rejoicing: it is more a case of bracing oneself against shocks to come. For these people know that much more is involved than the correction of an electoral anomaly: it is a question of changing historic relations between conqueror and conquered—something not likely to happen without violence. The subordination of Catholic to Protestant in Derry is a result of force and the threat of force. The condition of Derry may be thought of as one of frozen violence: any attempt to thaw it out will liberate violence which is at present static.

The disabilities of Catholics in Northern Ireland are real, but not overwhelmingly oppressive: is their removal really worth attaining at the risk of precipitating riots, explosions, pogroms, murder? Thus Ismene. But Antigone will not heed such calculations: she is an ethical and religious force, an uncompromising element in our being, as dangerous in her way as Creon, whom she perpetually challenges and provokes. Peace depends on the acceptance of civil subordination, since the powerful will use force to uphold their laws: the perpetual assertion of a higher law is therefore a principle of permanent revolution. In certain circumstances this is less obvious than in others. When Creon is far gone in overt violence—as in Vietnam—then even a humane calculator could justify civil disobedience aimed at obstructing his bloody progress. But the spirit of Antigone, which animates the bravest of the war-resisters, disdains such pragmatic distinctions: these young people are against the war, as against racism and any other form of oppression, because it is wrong: since their struggle is right, they are not concerned with its consequences or its cost.

At present every Creon thinks some other Creon is behind the Antigone that is plaguing him. The communists, thinks Creon, are behind the student activists at Columbia: the CIA, thinks Creon, are behind the Czech intellectuals. We should be safer without the trouble-maker from Thebes. And that which would be lost, if she could be eliminated, is quite intangible: no more, perhaps, than a way of imagining and dramatising man's dignity. It is true that this way may express the essence of what man's dignity actually is. In losing it, man might gain peace at the price of his soul.'[3]

[3] Published in *The Listener*, London, 24th October 1968. The last five words in this piece anticipate curiously the title of Miss Bernadette Devlin's book, *The Price of my Soul* (1969).

Reading that essay now, three years afterwards, I find myself no longer in sympathy with the conclusion. Antigone is very fine on the stage, or in retrospect or a long way off, or even in real life for a single, splendid epiphany. But after four years of Antigone and her under-studies and all those funerals—more than a hundred dead at the time of writing[4] —you begin to feel that Ismene's commonsense and feeling for the living may make the more needful, if less spectacular element in 'human dignity'. In any case the play has been moving—like so much else in Northern Ireland—*backwards*, away from the ceremonial act of non-violent disobedience, and into the fratricidal war, which precedes the action of the play.

ii

At Armagh, in November 1968, and at Burntollet Bridge, near Derry, in January 1969, occurred further severe clashes between Catholic and Protestants, set off in both cases by civil rights marches, and the reaction to them. There was collusion—especially in the second case—between the police and the Protestant rioters. In both cases the violence came from the Protestant side. The contrast between the peaceful civil rights marchers—just a handful of young men and women at Burntollet—and the brutal demeanour and behaviour of their Protestant-ultra assailants created a wave of sympathy, in Britain and elsewhere, with the civil rights cause, and with the Catholics of Northern Ireland. Demand for the reform of Northern Ireland's peculiar institutions grew. So far, the comparison with Dixie held.

The significance of civil rights marches in Northern Ireland was differently assessed by different groups of people.

For the marchers themselves, the marches were *non-sectarian* acts. They would have considered themselves to be sectarian if they had confined themselves to the Catholic ghettoes where they would have been unmolested. To break down the sectarian barriers, they had to move outside the ghetto. In doing so they thought of themselves as appealing

[4] Over four hundred and sixty at the time of going to press.

to Protestant workers and small farmers to join them in tearing down a social structure which oppressed all 'the people'. 'The people', as used by People's Democracy—responsible for the Burntollet march—was meant to include Protestant workers, and exclude Catholic as well as Protestant bourgeois.

Protestants generally saw it differently. They had no desire to tear down the structures of Northern Ireland, which they saw as *their* structures. They felt no solidarity with Catholics, and did not believe that Catholics felt any solidarity with them. The revolutionary language used by People's Democracy did not reach the Protestants as an appeal for solidarity. It reached them as a threat. Since Protestants did not want a revolution, it was obvious that the revolution of which the orators spoke was to be a Catholic revolution—an attempt to impose Catholic rule on Protestants by force. And the marches were the living embodiment of that threat. To Orangemen, especially, this seemed self-evident. They knew about marches. When Orangemen marched into, or alongside, a Catholic area what they meant was that Catholics must accept the fact of *Protestant* domination. Now, if Catholics were going to march in Protestant areas, what they meant was that *Catholic* domination was coming. That was not what their slogans and their banners said, to be sure, but what they said did not matter. Catholics were tricky people, and in no position yet to show their hand. Their words did not matter. But the fact of Catholics marching in Protestant territory mattered very much indeed. It had to be stopped.

Many Catholic youths saw the matter, not in the same light, but with the same feeling for what was significant. They were not interested in the theories of the People's Democracy, or in the socialist doctrines of Eamonn McCann, Michael Farrell or Bernadette Devlin. The idea of class-solidarity with Protestant workers was so foreign to them that it did not even offend them. But the tone and the air of civil rights militants—the sheer you-be-damned style of the thing—impressed them. They had been brought up, after all, in the customs of the ghetto; most of them had been warned not to respond to provocation, to be quiet when the drums beat, and the pennies dropped from the walls. That *they* should march in or near *our* territory had been an annually renewed fact of life, to be swallowed annually. That *we* should march in *their* territory had been considered unthinkable. Yet now the unthinkable was happening. The fury and consternation of Orangemen were unmistakable. So also was the fact that the rulers of Ulster were divided about how to deal with these new techniques, and that their divisions endangered the existence of the Protestant State. So Catholic youth came into the streets against the Protestant State. And the tricolour, the flag of the Catholic State, came with them. This was a negation of what had been the essential doctrine of the civil rights movement—that it was a movement for equality in the area itself, and for the rights possessed by other citizens in the United Kingdom, and not a nationalist movement demanding constitutional or territorial change. But the people of the ghettoes were not committed to civil rights doctrine. They were interested in the relation between 'us' and 'them', and in what promised a change in that relation: new tones of voice, new movements of feet.

The tricolour was a symbol of the desired change. In theory, the tricolour of Green, White and Orange stands for peace between nationalists and Orangemen, between Catholics and Protestants. In practice its appearance, in any district of Northern Ireland where both Catholics and Protestants live, invariably produces violence between the two groups.[5] The tricolour—illegal under the Northern Ireland Flags and Emblems Act—is the Catholic flag, just as the Union Jack, which is of course legal, is the Protestant flag. And the Catholic flag is also the flag of the Catholic State to the South, whose Constitution claims to apply to the whole island. Its appearance symbolizes the assertion by the Catholics *in* Northern Ireland—not the Catholics *of* Northern Ireland—of a majority status, based on the balance of population in the island as a whole. And majority status,

[5] In Northern Ireland, the colours of the flag are more often identified as 'green, white and *yellow*' than correctly. White and yellow are the papal colours, and their association with green must seem more life-like than the aspiration which the flag actually implies.

in the conditions known to both communities in Northern Ireland, implies domination.

The appearance of the tricolour, in the wake of mass-participation by Catholics in 'civil rights' forms of activity, confirmed most Protestants in their belief that civil rights were a euphemism for Rome rule.

But British opinion neither saw the civil rights movement in this light, nor understood the force of Catholic hope or Protestant fear. The British—that is, those among them, including members of Parliament, who concerned themselves with such matters—were disposed to be impatient with both sides (for their 'obsession with the past, etc.') but especially with the Protestants. For one thing the Protestants had been in charge of affairs for nearly fifty years, and were therefore the more responsible for present conditions. They had neither managed to conciliate the Catholics nor to put the fear of God into them once and for all. They had been allowed a free hand to run their own show, and the results of their running it were now obtruding themselves in a way that was embarrassing to those who had allowed them that free hand. Their exuberant but conditional loyalty to Britain was also embarrassing, like being embraced by an argumentative drunk. The British response to the fervent declarations of 'Ulster is British' was now becoming: 'All right, since you're so British, *be* British, and run your bit of Britain like the rest of Britain.' This meant conceding the substance of the civil rights demands.

Some such reaction from the British Labour Party was not unexpected. Labour and the Liberals had long been suspect, or worse, in Northern Unionist eyes. The new and ominous development was a certain coolness on the part of the British Tories, Ulster's traditional allies, even at one time beyond the limits of the Constitution. But 1912 now seemed a far more distant date in Britain than it did in Northern Ireland. If the Britishness of British Ulster struck many in Britain itself as a repellent parody, the parody was likely to grate on Tories even more than others, because it came closer to them. Ulster Unionism was, after all, an archaic and specialized form of Toryism. Its deportment was not suited to the image that the British Tories wanted for the late twentieth century. It was also rather clear that the policy which really appealed to so many Ulster Unionists —that of crushing the Papists by force—would have strikingly little appeal to an American President concerned with the big-city ethnic vote. This was a factor that had to be taken into consideration in these days, especially by a party which had advertised Britain's 'special relation' with America.

All this meant that any Northern Ireland Prime Minister henceforward would be under heavy conflicting pressures, specifically those most ominous forms of pressure which are described by those who apply them as 'support'. The British Labour Government, with the agreement of the opposition, 'supported Captain Terence O'Neill in his determination to implement the reform programme'. The Unionist Party 'supported Captain O'Neill in upholding the Constitution of Northern Ireland'. The expectations of the British and of the Prime Minister's 'supporters' in Northern Ireland in reality diverged. Also it was in the power of militant Catholics, as well as militant Protestants, to make them diverge further. In fact the more the militant Catholics provoked the militant Protestants, the more untenable the position of a Northern Ireland Prime Minister became. If he gave any satisfaction to the Catholics he alienated his own supporters. If he gave any satisfaction to his own supporters he alienated the British Government, on which Northern Ireland was financially and otherwise dependent.

The knowledge that this was so gave an intoxicating new sense of power to Catholic leaders. The initiative was in their hands. Their enemies were divided among themselves. The friends their enemies once possessed were no longer to be relied on. In these conditions almost anything the militant Catholics decided to do seemed likely to divide their enemies even more, and leave them even more friendless. Some Catholic leaders thought of exploiting this situation to win full equality inside Northern Ireland. Others thought of exploiting it to break up Northern Ireland, preparing the way for the unity of Ireland. For many militants the nature of the ultimate goal was less interesting than the sense of power actually wielded in the present, as contrasted with the long powerless past.

On the Protestant side the division was now between those who thought that Northern Ireland must remain part of Britain—at whatever price in terms of internal concessions to Catholics—and those who thought that Protestant supremacy had to be preserved, even at the price, in the last resort, of breaking the link with Britain. For the moment, the first school of thought prevailed. On 11th December 1968, the Prime Minister, Captain Terence O'Neill, dismissed his Minister for Home Affairs, William Craig. 'I have known for some time,' O'Neill wrote, 'you were attracted by ideas of a U.D.I. nature . . . Northern Ireland's Constitution is not in danger, for both parties at Westminster are committed to the guarantees we have been given. But what is at risk is the enormous subventions which make it possible for us to enjoy a British, rather than an Irish standard of living.' Craig wrote: 'If Mr. Wilson or anyone else should threaten to interfere in the exercise of our proper jurisdiction, it is your duty and that of every Unionist to resist.'

Much later,[6] William Craig, in opposition was to spell out his 'ideas of a U.D.I. nature', which were to become increasingly attractive to a growing section of Ulster Unionists. Northern Ireland would become a separate 'British community', possibly in close association with Britain, but with the reserved powers now held by Westminster transferred to Stormont. The essential point was that control over police and security would be entirely in the hands of Stormont: that is to say, entirely in Protestant hands. Under any form of U.D.I., of course, Northern Ireland would lose the benefits of Britain's welfare state—part of O'Neill's argument. But from the point of view of some Protestant extremists this would by no means be an unmixed loss since, in their eyes, the main beneficiaries of the welfare state are unemployed Catholics with very large families.

The O'Neill side of the O'Neill-Craig argument—which still continues—was presented in economic terms. But it is not just an economic case. O'Neill and his friends would

[6] *Belfast Telegraph,* 1st October 1971.

have liked to see Northern Ireland increasingly assimilate to the *contemporary* British—and European—way of life. Craig and his friends adhere to an older version of the British way of life, in which suspicion of Catholics and resistance to the claims of conquered peoples were important parts. Subsequent developments showed that the Craig concept of Britishness still has good hold on life in Ulster.

The manners of the two men correspond to their positions. O'Neill has an English accent, and smiles a good deal. Craig has an Ulster accent and hardly smiles at all in public. O'Neill was at one time very popular in the South—he was Man of the Year in a poll run by one of the Dublin mass-circulation papers at the end of 1968, and was pleased by this. Craig is unlikely ever to be Dublin's Man of the Year, and would suspect a trap if he were. Craig is still a force in Ulster politics. O'Neill is no longer one.

Burntollet (January 1969) came in the wake of the dismissal of Craig (December 1968) and O'Neill felt his position weakened as a result of it. He seems also to have felt that the Catholic militants had shown personal ingratitude to him, who had shown himself the friend of the Catholics. He gives the impression of being a generous, decent, impulsive man, and also sentimental and touchy; things that often go together. In any case he made an unwise speech after Burntollet on 5th January 1969. He seemed to put the blame for Burntollet and its aftermath mainly on the Catholics, and he promised, or threatened, greater use of the Special Constabulary for 'normal police duties'. It does not seem that he won back friends among the Protestants. But he certainly lost some friends he had among the Catholics and made some active enemies. This was soon to cost him dear.

On 24th January—after further disturbances following a civil rights march through Newry—Mr. Brian Faulkner, Minister for Commerce, resigned, making an ambiguous resignation statement, which seemed to place him as being 'stronger' than O'Neill, more 'liberal' than Craig. Politically, it was to prove a sound position for a come-back. Shortly afterwards, on 30th January, thirteen Unionist backbenchers called for a party meeting to discuss a change of leader. O'Neill then dissolved parliament, and put up O'Neillite candidates against the rebel Unionist members. This was a delicate manœuvre. It depended for success on attracting enough Catholic moderates to compensate for the defection of Protestant extremists. But the very fact that the support of Catholics was seen to be sought would in itself increase the number of Protestant defections. The number of 'Catholic moderate' votes required had therefore to be enough not only to compensate for the loss of existing Protestant extremists, but also for the loss of 'new Protestant extremists' who had just been able to put up with O'Neill's policies so far, but could not stomach the idea of an Ulster Premier looking for Catholic votes to defeat loyalists.

In the event, the number of Catholic votes secured proved inadequate, so that O'Neill's attempt to base stable power on a cross-denominational coalition of the centre failed, though by no great margin. Most of the O'Neill Unionists—nine of them—were re-elected. One of the most serious students of the Northern Ireland scene, Mr. John Cole, in his introduction to a selection of O'Neill's speeches,[7] puts the blame both on 'the uncompromising and bigoted Protestantism' represented by Ian Paisley, and also on Catholic conservatism. 'Catholic conservatism', writes Mr. Cole, 'was equally in evidence at the polls. All the pious talk about the need to end sectarianism did not persuade many Catholics to vote for a Protestant—however tolerant his attitudes might be—if there was a Catholic's name on the ballot. It was an odd form of conservatism, this, very much with a small "c", for it must have caused many an elderly Catholic farmer to vote for young candidates whose affection for Trotsky was stronger than their loyalty to Pope Paul. But in an election where colour—orange and green—still counted most, it was enough for a candidate to be a cradle Catholic to get the Catholic vote.'

In this analysis, it is clear that Mr. Cole had very much in mind the results in Terence O'Neill's own constituency of Bannside in these elections:

[7] *Ulster at the Crossroads* (London, Faber and Faber, 1969).

O'Neill, Terence (Unionist)            7,745
Paisley, Ian (Protestant Unionist)     6,331
Farrell, Michael (People's Democracy)  2,310

Mr. Farrell—who might loosely be described as a Trotskyite cradle-Catholic—certainly took Catholic votes which (if cast at all) would have had to go to O'Neill in a straight fight with Mr. Paisley. Mr. Farrell's candidature came near to electing Mr. Paisley and did serious, perhaps fatal damage to the sitting Prime Minister in this vital election, by leaving his margin of victory humiliatingly low. But Mr. Cole's conclusion that it was 'enough for a candidate to be a cradle Catholic to get the Catholic vote', is demonstrably wrong. In these very elections of February, 1969, a Protestant civil rights militant, Ivan Cooper, headed the poll in Co. Derry by taking the Catholic vote away from a 'cradle Catholic' nationalist. With that result in mind, Owen Dudley Edwards' interpretation of the Bannside result seems closer to the mark than Mr. Cole's: 'Had it not been for Farrell's intervention, the Captain's majority over Dr. Paisley would have been considerably greater, for the Catholics preferred to vote for a real, and not a token, advocate of civil rights once Farrell was in the field.'[8]

'Cradle Catholic' is wrong; 'advocate of civil rights' is a euphemism. What Catholics wanted, in 1969, were militant champions of the Catholic community. Since Parnell's day —and before, in different conditions—they had known that such champions might be all the more effective for being Protestant in religion, provided they were 'Catholic in politics'. There is no Protestant equivalent to this. There were no Catholic Unionist parliamentary candidates. Not even the pro-O'Neill Unionist constituency organizations dared to run such candidates in 1969, though one or two potential Catholic candidates were available.[9] This was one of the reasons why Catholics were sceptical about the liberating possibilities of O'Neillism.

[8] Owen Dudley Edwards, *The Sins of our Fathers: Roots of Conflict in Northern Ireland*, Dublin, Gill and MacMillan, 1970.
[9] Much later, Mr. Brian Faulkner put a 'token' Catholic, Dr. G. B. Newe, into his Cabinet. At the time of writing Dr. Newe is not a member of parliament.

That Catholics were prepared to vote for a politically suitable Protestant, while Protestants were *not* prepared to vote for a politically suitable Catholic was a significant but ambiguous fact. Catholics were inclined to interpret it complacently, as meaning that Catholics are less bigoted than Protestants. There is a sense in which this is true, if we take bigotry to be equalled to fear. Ulster Protestants *do* fear Catholicism. Ulster Catholics do not fear Protestantism.

The reasons for Protestant fear of Catholicism are adequate to explain the strength of the fear. The old fears of besieged Reformed communities have been kept continuously alive in Ulster—by the reality of the siege—and made even more lively by certain modern developments, such as democracy and birth control. Protestantism in Ireland has been on the defensive for more than a hundred years. In the South, Protestantism has about gone under, conquered more effectively by Catholic marriage regulations than by any material force. In these conditions, while the Catholic community can be despised for its material weakness, the strong element of fear in the relationship is projected on the Catholic *Church*. To admit an adherent of that mysterious and resourceful enemy into any inner council of Unionism would be letting a spy into the citadel. If O'Neill had tried it he would have lost his seat at Bannside.[10]

A Catholic, on the other hand, may fear the material power of Protestants, but he has no fear whatever of Protestantism. He knows little and thinks little about it; there is simply no equivalent on his side to the Protestant brooding on the Pope of Rome. His attitude *to Protestantism*—as distinct from contemporary Protestants—is condescending. His youthful impression of Protestantism was that it was founded by Henry VIII in order to have eight wives. The impression may be somewhat refined in later years—in respect of Tudor marital statistics at least—but the idea that Protestantism is not to be taken seriously remains. This is, of course, a kind of bigotry, but different to the Protestant kind. Contempt and fear enter into both forms but, from the

[10] Faulkner's decision on Dr. Newe was never submitted to an electoral test.

Catholic side, the contempt is directed at the religion and the fear at its followers. On the Protestant side it is the other way round. What Catholics take seriously about Protestants are their material prosperity and power, their hostility towards Catholics, and the politics which are the instrument of preserving their prosperity and power, and expressing their hostility towards Catholics. That politics is Unionism. A Protestant who changes his politics, without changing his religion, is welcome because he has shed the important distinguishing characteristic of Protestants, which is not their religion. And his conversion to the politics of the Catholic community is not suspect—or suspect only in a faint degree —because he is turning his back on the politics of the dominant community, and adopting the politics of the ghetto, and because the ranks of those who have done this in the past, include the great heroes and martyrs of the political tradition of the Irish Catholic community. Nowhere in Ireland, after all, is the Rosary recited with more conviction than over the grave at Bodenstown of the Protestant free-thinker Wolfe Tone, more honoured in Catholic Ireland today than any Irish Catholic patriot who died before 1916.

Similarly a Catholic who is virulently anti-Unionist— setting him, in practice, against *almost* all Protestants—is sincerely indignant when he is accused of sectarianism. He genuinely feels he does not give a curse about the religion of 'the other side'. What he hates is their politics.

The way in which so intelligent and moderate a Protestant observer as John Cole gets the Catholic viewpoint wrong tells us, I think, a part of the reason for the most crucial event of 1969: the failure of O'Neillism. The O'Neillites needed Catholic support to offset Protestant defections. But they never even started to learn the language that could win them such support. They never even learned to avoid unnecessary use of language that was all the more offensive to Catholics because the offence was unintentional. O'Neill's own speeches are rich in such material. This, for example, from a speech in the House of Commons, on 13th December 1966:

From one side came the extreme Republicans, who sought to flaunt before our people the emblems of a cause which a majority of us abhor, and who once again refused to renounce violence as a political weapon.

Even a Catholic who had little sympathy with the extreme Republicans might wonder who 'our people' were in this passage, and might reflect that Catholics also suffered, and on a considerably greater scale, from the flaunting of emblems which a majority of them abhorred. If the Prime Minister had been really conscious of the feelings of these Catholics he needed to win, the passage would have read simply:

From one side came the extreme Republicans, who once again refused to renounce violence as a political weapon.

Fortunately for his hopes of attracting Catholic support O'Neill did not become explicit about his 'Catholic policy' until after his resignation. In an interview published by the *Belfast Telegraph* on 10th May 1969 he said:

It is frightfully hard to explain to Protestants that if you give Roman Catholics a good job and a good house, they will live like Protestants, because they will see neighbours with cars and television sets.
They will refuse to have 18 children, but if a Roman Catholic is jobless, and lives in the most ghastly hovel, he will rear 18 children on National Assistance.
If you treat Roman Catholics with due consideration and kindness, they will live like Protestants in spite of the authoritative nature of their Church.

It would have been even more 'frightfully hard' to explain all this to Catholics. Although these words were not spoken while O'Neill was still Premier, the Olympian attitude which they express was perceptible, and unhelpful to his cause.
At the same time O'Neill engaged in gestures which, while highly alarming to extreme Protestants, garnered no adequate compensation in Catholic support. Being photographed with

nuns was such a gesture, eliciting much more Protestant anger than Catholic gratitude. It may even have been counter-productive among *both* Catholics and Protestants. There is a strand in the history of Irish nationalism—a strand of which Captain O'Neill may not have been aware—which means that suspicion, rather than gratitude, is the appropriate reaction to the spectacle of Unionist politicians fraternizing with the Catholic clergy.

O'Neill's error in this was, however, pardonable. Anyone who looked at the press and television screens of the Republic during this period might well have supposed that to be photographed with the clergy was a necessary requirement for getting Catholic votes.

Yet in spite of all these errors and insensitivities, Terence O'Neill, by the end of 1968, had come across to many Catholics as a decent man, who was working in the right direction. This is proved—as far as the Republic is concerned —by the Sunday paper poll which I mentioned earlier. As far as Northern Catholics are concerned, we have the testimony of one of their number who did not admire O'Neill. Miss Bernadette Devlin writes with disgust of the impact of O'Neill's television broadcast of 9th December 1968, just before the dismissal of Craig. This was the famous 'Ulster stands at the crossroads' speech in which O'Neill said: 'What in any case are these changes[11] which we have decided must come? They all amount to this: that in every aspect of our life, justice must not only be done but be *seen* to be done to all sections of the community. . . . What kind of Ulster do you want? A happy and respected Province, in good standing with the rest of the United Kingdom? Or a place continually torn apart by riots and demonstrations, and regarded by the rest of Britain as a political outcast? As always in a democracy the choice is yours.'

This speech struck Miss Devlin and her student activist friends as 'hilarious'. 'Captain O'Neill asked how could Ulster be separate without an army and navy of its own.

---

[11] He had mentioned the appointment of a Londonderry Commission— replacing the gerrymandered Corporation—reform of housing allocations, appointment of an Ombudsman.

The way it came across was "For Christ's sake, somebody tell me where the army is and I'll declare u.d.i. too", and this complete misinterpretation of what the poor man was trying to say left the students with no respect for Captain O'Neill.'[12]

But Miss Devlin admits that others were of a different opinion: '. . . all over Northern Ireland, people were clustered round their television screens, dabbing their eyes as you do at an over-sentimental film . . . The next day the country went mad supporting O'Neill. . . . In reaction to the television speech, the various civil rights bodies agreed to call a (four-weeks) truce over Christmas. . . . The students called no truce. We did cancel a march which was to have been held in Belfast on December 14th, because we hadn't time to persuade people of the hollowness of Captain Neill's appeal, and in the pro-Captain O'Neill frenzy of the moment, a march would have seemed a useless provocation.' The students put off their planned People's Democracy march from Belfast to Derry, to 1st January 1969.[13]

The 'people' Miss Devlin refers to here included (as is seldom the case in the writings about this subject) both many Catholics and many Protestants. The cancellation of the civil rights marches, and the postponement of the People's Democracy one, are evidence of the strength of the pro-O'Neill feeling at the time among Catholics. (The fact that some action seemed 'a useless provocation', if it seemed so *to Protestants alone,* would never have led to such a cancellation or postponement at this time.) For a short time after his televised speech—and after his dismissal of Craig two days later—O'Neill's support spanned the two communities in a way previously unparalleled in Northern Ireland.

This support, in both communities, was irrevocably damaged after the People's Democracy broke the civil rights truce. But it was among the Catholics that the most serious damage was done. The savage Protestant attack on the marchers at Burntollet Bridge and subsequent brutalities of the police on Bogside seemed already to most Catholics to

---

[12] Bernadette Devlin, *The Price of my Soul* (London 1969).
[13] The march that led to Burntollet.

mean, that, whatever O'Neill might say, they were still living in the bad old days. And O'Neill's speech of 5th January must have finished him as far as a great many of his Catholic admirers were concerned. Max Hastings writes: 'In the near-hysterical atmosphere following the events in Derry, it was an ill-considered speech; whatever truth there might be in what he said, it served only to infuriate further Catholics, without appeasing the Protestants. O'Neill seemed to be brushing them all aside like so many buzzing flies, to be talking to them like an irritated schoolmaster with some trying pupils. The Catholic community wanted regret and real sympathy for what had happened—also some very solid promises that nothing like it could ever occur again. This they were denied.'[14] Eamonn McCann (quoted by Mr. Hastings) said: 'At least it meant an end to the fiction that O'Neill was a fair-minded liberal, dedicated to solving social problems. No one in Derry could place any further trust in promises and assurances made by him and people like him.'

There can be little doubt that two decisions of the student militants in People's Democracy combined to break O'Neill. These were the decision to break the civil rights truce, and the decision to run Michael Farrell as a candidate in Bannside. With O'Neill perished—for a considerable time at least—the hopes of those who wanted a coalition of the centre spanning the communities. The politics of polarization had prevailed.

O'Neill lingered on for a little over two months after the February elections, but the state of Catholic-Protestant relations, steadily worsening, undermined his already weakened position. In March the jailing of Ian Paisley and his eccentric coadjutor Major Bunting for their share in the Armagh disturbances angered the Protestant right. At the end of March there was an explosion at an Electricity Board property in Castlereagh. Members of each community accused members of the other of responsibility for this, but as far as O'Neill was concerned it scarcely mattered who had done it —by further straining the relations of the two communities it

[14] *Barricades in Belfast.*

automatically weakened him. On 19th and 20th April, Civil Rights demonstrations in Derry led to Catholic-Protestant rioting, and the police, pursuing the Catholics into the Bogside, behaved brutally, some of them killing an old man, Samuel Devenney. Catholic fear and anger, especially in Derry, after this episode prepared the mood for the explosion of the following August. Shortly afterwards (23rd April) Miss Bernadette Devlin, then aged 22, and just elected for mid-Ulster, brought the mood of the Catholic people of Northern Ireland to Westminster, in a biting and extremely effective speech, with which the House of Commons was, for the moment, delighted. It is true Miss Devlin tried to convey that it was not just the *Catholic* people whose mood she was reflecting:

'It has been,' she said, 'the deliberate and unashamed policy of the Unionist government to force the image on the Civil Rights movement that it is nothing more than a Catholic uprising. The people of the Civil Rights movement have struggled desperately to overcome this image, but it is impossible when the ruling minority is the Government. . . .'

(It is not quite clear what she meant by calling a government chosen by a Parliament elected by a *majority* of the people in Northern Ireland a *ruling minority*. This may reflect the Marxist view that governments in bourgeois democracies are invariably class tyrannies, or the Irish Republican view that Northern Ireland is illegitimately ruled by representatives of *a minority in the whole of Ireland*. Or these views may run together. In any case most of her constituents would have understood her to mean that Protestants were a minority in all Ireland.)

Miss Devlin's vibrant, vivid impact increased the conviction of Protestants that the Civil Rights movement was indeed 'a Catholic uprising'. Protestant alarm and anger—directed against O'Neill—increased still further after explosions at Clady, Co. Antrim damaged the water supply to Belfast. Again these explosions were diversely attributed—to the I.R.A., or the U.V.F., according to the theology prevailing in your home. Miss Devlin, more originally, was inclined to attribute the explosions to the O'Neill government itself, 'trying to make a link between the civil rights movement and the Irish Republican Army'.[15] How the presumption of such a link would have benefited Captain O'Neill is not clear, since it was the contention of his Protestant extremist enemies that such a link existed and that, far from doing anything about it, he was trying to appease the people concerned by supposed 'reforms' designed to weaken the fabric of Protestant Ulster.

It was precisely on this issue that he fell. On 23rd April Major James Chichester-Clark had resigned from the O'Neill Government, after the Parliamentary Party had endorsed an item in the O'Neill reform package—the introduction of universal adult franchise in local government. On 28th April O'Neill resigned. 'I have no regrets,' he said in his farewell broadcast, 'for six years in which I have tried to break the chains of ancient ignorance.'

Major James Chichester-Clark, who defeated Mr. Brian Faulkner by one vote for the premiership, belonged to the same class and clan as O'Neill but lacked his sense of political purpose. He was soon to be depicted on (Catholic) posters as 'the mad Major' tossing hand grenades around. But he was not, in fact, even a hard-liner. He had been elected because he was neither pro-O'Neill nor anti-O'Neill and because he was not Brian Faulkner. The new Government in fact lacked any clear direction, and this in itself provided an extra incentive for any group to give it a good shove in the desired direction. The idea that it was shovable was encouraged by its first act, a general political amnesty under which Ian Paisley was released—on 6th May—and pending charges were dropped against Bernadette Devlin and others. To outsiders—who quite possibly in a sense included the amiable Prime Minister himself—it all sounded a rather decent, let-bygones-be-bygones sort of thing. But in Northern Ireland, where the idea of letting bygones-be-bygones is an alien and suspect concept, it just sounded like weakness: the Government was afraid *both* of militant Protestants *and* of militant Catholics. Now it was just a question of which would prove the stronger.

[15] *The Price of my Soul* (paperback edition, Pan Books, p. 176).

The time to put this to the test was coming: the summer
season of traditional Protestant triumphal rites, of which the
principal ceremonies, among a great number of lesser ones,
are the 12th July Orange parade in Belfast, and the parade
of the Apprentice Boys in Derry on 12th August. This year
the unfolding of these ceremonies would show to what extent
the Protestant-Catholic relation had been changed since
October of the previous year.

On 12th July, in Belfast, with its strong Protestant majority,
the great Orange parade went off as usual—as it was also
to do even in the general turmoil of the next two years. But
in Derry—where 'the Boyne' is a secondary but important
Protestant feast—there was trouble: stones, petrol bombs,
water-cannon to disperse the rioting Catholics. What this
meant was that the real test was about to come in the same
place exactly one month later. The calendar of the decisive
events of two hundred and eighty years earlier pre-set the
timing of the decisive events of the summer of 1969, and
succeeding summers.

Derry City[16] is a Protestant Holy City, whose citizens are
mostly Catholics. Geographically it forms part of the Inishowen peninsula, the rest of which—that is except for the
little enclave round Derry—is part of the Republic. On
demographic and geographical considerations it should have
been awarded to the Catholic State. But Derry is more than
a city, it is a symbol of the spirit of Protestant Ulster. The long
siege of Derry by King James's Catholic Army, and its relief
by King William's Protestant Fleet in 1689, belong with the
Battle of the Boyne at the centre of Ulster Protestant icono-
graphy religion and patriotism. The Boyne is a distant image
like Jerusalem, a holy place *in partibus infidelium*, a proud
memory in a lost land, down there in irredeemably Papist
Co. Meath. But Derry City is part of Ulster, and County
Derry—the rest of which is separated from the Derry city
enclave in Inishowen by the broad expanse of the River

[16] Officially Londonderry. But whether you say Derry or Londonderry is not,
as you might imagine, a Protestant/Catholic distinguishing shibboleth. True,
Catholics *always* say Derry. But Derry Protestants also say Derry, except on
particularly 'official' or Anglophil occasions.

Foyle—has a Protestant majority. So Derry could be held. Just. And because it could be held—and especially because it could only *just* be held—the force it symbolized absolutely required that it be held at all costs. Northern Ireland itself lives a siege: the image of besieged Derry, with the promise of its deliverance, is a far more poignant symbol for it than the wilted glory of the Boyne.

Derry's seventeenth century walls are still intact, and the symbolism of siege is part of the contemporary life of the city. The small area within the walls is jealously kept Protestant. The majority of the citizens—the Catholics—are outside the walls, most of them in what is called the Bogside, straggling round the walled city as King James's motley forces straggled round it long ago. And every year on 12th August, the Protestants triumph on top of the walls, looking down on the descendants of the unsuccessful besiegers, inheritors of a siege that has never been altogether abandoned.

The cost of pretence is high, and the pretence that contemporary Derry is a Protestant City has cost the Protestant State dearly. Economically, Derry has been chronically depressed with an inordinately high rate of male unemployment—the main local industry, shirt-making, employs women. The depression is ascribed in part to Derry's being cut off from its natural trading hinterland in Donegal; in part to the fact that, in the whole of Ireland, the West has not shared in the relative prosperity of the East; in part to the fact that Unionist Governments, however much they may value symbolic Derry, distrust and dislike actual Derry City, with its disloyal majority, and put what money is available into safe Protestant centres, like Coleraine. In the minds of the local Catholic majority it is the first and third factors that are significant. They feel their economic condition to be a punishment for being Catholics. The fact that under the British Welfare State, unemployment benefit and children's allowances—the same for all religions—are much higher than in Donegal twelve miles away has not altered this feeling, although many families must have put to themselves the question of how they would manage if transferred to the Republic and its present social standards.

Politically, there is no doubt that the Catholics of Derry were systematically cheated. The gerrymandered Derry Corporation had a Protestant majority of 8–4, reversing the proportions in the city itself, and the Corporation saw to it that houses and jobs went to Protestants in a similar disproportion.

The frustration and anger of Derry Catholics had been building up ever since the creation of Northern Ireland. In 1969, hope and fear were added to frustration and anger. The hope was the general, vague exhilarating hope of the Civil Rights movement: the walls were cracking, nothing would be the same again, though no one could see what the new reality would be. The fear was more concrete, born of the experiences of January and April—the fear of a still more savage 'lesson' at the hands of the R.U.C. and Specials. All this was an explosive mixture. It was touched off by the Apprentice Boys' Parade on 12th August 1969.

Max Hastings has a vivid and lifelike description of the mood of that momentous morning:

The solemn procession of the Derry Apprentice Boys began in perfect tranquillity on the morning of 12th August. There were thousands of them, in their sober suits and bowler hats with their pipe bands and flute bands and drum bands, their wives watching from the city walls all dressed up in Sunday best. The Catholics, in the Bogside below the city, complained that they felt like animals in a zoo as spectators and Apprentice Boys gazed down over the parapets to peer into the Catholic cauldren below. In the Bogside, they could hear the sound of the bands, and the Protestant tunes—the endless renderings of 'The Wearing of the Sash' and 'Derry Walls'. By general consent and after much hard work by the moderate Catholic leaders, most Catholics stayed at home during the march, sick of Protestants and police cordons and riot tenders and drumbeating. But they were irritated, ill-humoured and not a little apprehensive.

By the Foyle River, just below the Walls, the stone-throwing started. The police chased the stone-throwers off towards the Bogside. But when the police tried to enter the Bogside they met with mass resistance. Some preparations had been made for this. A Derry Citizens' Defence Committee had prepared barricades in a number of streets. Petrol bombs were ready in some places. As the police came in in pursuit of the stone-throwers the people of the Bogside rose against them. To them, the police were simply their Protestant persecutors, armed and in uniform, coming in again to intimidate and humiliate them, as they had done in January and April. The fighting went on through Tuesday night and all Wednesday. The Bogsiders, with their paving stones and petrol bombs, held off six hundred police who were supported by Protestant Volunteers.[17] The police drenched the Bogsiders in c.s. gas.

The area had one high-rise building, on Rossville Street, which was the key to its defence. The tricolour now flew on top of this building.

On Wednesday evening the Taoiseach, Mr. Jack Lynch, spoke on television. 'The Irish Government,' he said, 'can no longer stand by[18] and see innocent people injured and perhaps worse. It is obvious that the R.U.C. is no longer accepted as an impartial police force. Neither would the employment of British troops be acceptable nor would they be likely to restore peaceful conditions—certainly not in the long term.' He announced that the Irish Government had asked the United Nations for 'the urgent dispatch of a peace-keeping force to the Six Counties of Northern Ireland'. He also announced that he had 'directed the Irish Army authorities to have field hospitals established in County Donegal adjacent to Derry and at other points along the border where they may be necessary.' And the Taoiseach reiterated his Government's irredentist claim:

'Recognizing, however, that the re-unification of the national territory can provide the only permanent solution of the problem, it is our intention to request the British Government to enter into early negotiations with the Irish Government to review the present constitutional position of the Six Counties of Northern Ireland.'

The meaning of Mr. Lynch's speech in terms of the area

---

[17] For detailed accounts of the mid-August fighting, see M. Hastings, *Barricades in Belfast*, M. Wallace, *Drums and Guns: Revolution in Ulster*.

[18] The wording as given in the officially published collection of Mr. Lynch's *Speeches and Statements* (1972). Video-tape records his words as 'stand *idly* by'.

and people whom he actually governed is discussed in the
next chapter. As far as the peoples of Northern Ireland were
concerned it came as a blast of hope and fear: Catholic
hope and Protestant fear.

Catholics interpreted it as meaning that the hour of their
liberation was at hand. Irish troops or U.N. troops, or both
together, were coming in, the walls of Jericho as well as of
Derry were coming down. When I met the Citizens' Defence
Committee in Derry on the following Saturday—that is,
*after* the British troops had been deployed in Derry—I found
its members convinced, not merely that the intervention of
Irish troops *had been* imminent, but that it was still imminent.
When I told them that, in my opinion, the Irish Government
had never had any intention of intervening, they were
shocked and disappointed.

To Protestants, the speech meant that the Dublin Government was stirring up a Catholic insurrection in order to
overthrow Northern Ireland. The reference in the speech to
'the re-unification of the national territory' meant that the
mask of 'civil rights' was being finally thrown aside and the
true purpose of the agitation at last avowed. Thus, the Bogsiders were not defending themselves—as they seemed to be
doing, in the eyes of everyone except Ulster Protestants—but
were the spearhead of an aggressive assault against Protestant
Ulster.

That night, the fighting spread across Northern Ireland:
Belfast, Armagh, Dungiven, Dungannon, Enniskillen, Coalisland. In several places Catholic crowds attacked police
stations, the object being to prevent the sending of reinforce-
ments to Derry. Catholics also attacked the Shankill Road.

At 5 p.m. on Thursday afternoon (14th August), British
troops were deployed in Derry. The police withdrew.
Rejoicing the Bogsiders fraternized with the troops.

In Derry, the fighting was over. But the effects of Derry,
and of Mr. Lynch's speech, were still being felt in the rest of
Northern Ireland. In Armagh, a Catholic was shot dead by
B. Specials—the first death in these troubles. Others followed.
In Belfast, after Catholics had attacked a police station, the
police—and B. Specials—started shooting, even using

machine guns. Protestants moved in, with and behind the
police, burning Catholic houses. Thursday night in the Falls
and Ardoyne—Catholic districts of Belfast—was worse than
Derry had ever been. Catholics are outnumbered three to
one in Belfast and, with the police on the side of their
enemies, and prepared to shoot, they could not have successfully carried out the kind of resistance that had succeeded in
Bogside. Six people—including a child—were killed and
more than a hundred injured in Belfast that night; more
than a hundred houses were destroyed and over three
hundred damaged by petrol bombs. Only one of the dead
was a Protestant, and almost all the houses burned or
damaged were Catholic houses.

On the Friday afternoon, British troops were deployed on
the Falls Road. They were welcomed, as on Bogside, but
with less exultation: whatever happened, the Catholics of
Belfast were still heavily outnumbered, and the troops were
thin on the ground. That night, Protestants burned Catholic
houses in Ardoyne. Army patrols moved in slowly, Max
Hastings records—it seems ironic in retrospect—Catholic
rage at 'the army's refusal to fire on petrol bombers'.
Gradually, the fighting and burning subsided as the Army
moved in. As in Derry, the police retired from the Catholic
areas.

Although actual casualties were fairly small—there were
eight deaths as a result of the week's violence—there is no
doubt that, had the British Government not intervened with
its own forces, the Catholics of Belfast were in danger of
decimation—'After Thursday night,' writes Max Hastings,
'there was no shadow of doubt that without the army, the
Protestants would have totally overwhelmed the Catholic
area given a few more hours, and the police would have
done little to stop them.' This is an understatement, in so far
as the role of the police is concerned, and it would even be
an understatement to say that the police were *helping* the
Protestants. The fact is that the police were *part* of the
Protestant forces trying—as they saw it—to crush a Catholic
insurrection that had begun in Derry and was backed by
Dublin.

Relations between Catholic and Protestant in Northern Ireland were never the same again after the events of August 1969.

The Protestants had lost the most essential of all their powers: control of law-enforcement, control—to put the same thing in another way—of the state's apparatus of coercion. Their police, at Derry, had failed to impose their will. At Belfast, they had been imposing it, but by means which no modern British Government could tolerate. The British Army had been deployed 'in support of the civil power' but the civil power supported had not been that of Stormont. The Government in London had been forced to involve itself in the internal affairs of Northern Ireland, breaking a well-established convention that for decades had protected the Protestant State even from criticism at Westminster. Now Stormont's most vital powers were simply taken off it. The police were put under the control of the British Commander—that is, placed at the mercy of the Wilson Government in London. The Downing Street Declaration, issued after a meeting between Harold Wilson and Chichester-Clark, on 19th August, made it clear that the epoch of Westminster's benevolent non-intervention had ended. 'The United Kingdom Government have ultimate responsibility for the protection of those who live in Northern Ireland when, as in the past week, a breakdown in law and order has occurred. . . . In the context of the commitment of these troops, the Northern Ireland Government have re-affirmed their intention to take into the fullest account at all times the views of Her Majesty's Government in the United Kingdom, especially in relation to matters affecting the status of that part of the United Kingdom and their equal rights and protection under the law.'

As if to show what this polite euphemism would mean in practice, General Sir Ian Freeland, the officer commanding the British troops in Northern Ireland, ordered, on 22nd August, the handing in of all B. Specials' weapons to central armouries. It was, as Ian Paisley immediately proclaimed, the first step towards the disbanding of the Specials.

On 12th September the Cameron Report was published,

constituting a moderately worded but damning indictment of the peculiar institutions of the Province since its foundation and constituting also the justification of the Civil Rights Movement (but not the People's Democracy).

On 10th October, the Hunt report on the police was published and accepted by the Northern Ireland Government. This ended the carrying of firearms by the police, and placed the reserve police under the control of the British Army Commander. Hunt also found that a policeman's membership in the Orange Order was incompatible with 'the task of demonstrating impartiality at all times'.

In the wake of Hunt, on 11th October, the Army intervened to crush fierce Protestant riots in the Shankill. Protestants and their houses were searched for arms. They were in fact forced to undergo some experience of the condition which Catholics had known for so long: that of being governed against their will.

The humiliation of the Protestants, and their anger, were deep and bitter. The Catholics, for their part, knew that they had won a victory, but did not know how to exploit it, and also dreaded a counter-attack. The Civil Rights battle was won in principle. It was possible to complain that the promised reforms were too slow in coming. It was quite clear, after the Downing Street Declaration and Cameron, that the reforms must come. The most important of all reforms from the point of view of the Catholics—the destruction of the anti-Catholic security force—was already an accomplished fact. But after the heady experiences of August, the militants among the Catholics, and a great many of the young, were little disposed to settle for a hum-drum package of reforms, the objectives of 1968. They wanted more, much more. But more of what, exactly?

The more articulate of the Catholic militants, as we have seen, had thought, or said they thought, in terms of class-struggle, social revolution, the fight against imperialism. But what had happened was a fight between Catholics and Protestants, at the end of which the British Army—imperialists—had stepped in, to the great relief and warm welcome of the Catholics. . . .

The more emotional and romantic of the militants could satisfy themselves with the revolutionary *style* of August, 1969 in Derry: all those barricades. The most conspicuous figure on the barricades, Bernadette Devlin, saw Derry as an international revolutionary model: 'Derry suddenly found itself the centre of revolutionary Europe, setting a pattern that revolutionaries all the world over will never forget. It was very interesting to note that in Czechoslavakia in August, 1969 they followed our pattern perhaps unconsciously. As soon as the troops came in, the people raced down the side streets and put up barricades.'[19]

'The people', as used by Miss Devlin, generally means 'the Catholics', and means that here. But if Catholics are the people, what are the Protestants, and how should the people deal with these non-people? Miss Devlin treats these matters in the peroration of her book: 'The Unionists can struggle as much as they like to get back the support of the Protestant working class, but we shall get through to the Protestants in the end. Some of them have burned down Catholic houses, but we will not allow our forces to terrorize the ordinary Protestant population. One day they will realize that we have no more quarrel with people who happen to be Protestant than with people who happen to be Catholic. They will see that our only qaurrel is with the Unionist Party Government.

'For half a century, it has misgoverned us. Now we are witnessing its dying convulsions: and with traditional Irish mercy, when we've got it down, we will kick it into the ground.'

It is a chilling passage, as much in the vagueness of its assumed benevolence towards the 'ordinary Protestant population', as in the brutality of its concluding image. Apart from that image, the whole thing is hollow. If the official Unionist Party had been losing 'the support of the Protestant working class'—as it had—this was not because of growing class-consciousness, but because the Unionist Party had not been as tough with Miss Devlin and her friends, and the Catholic 'people' generally, as the Protestant working class

[19] *The Price of my Soul.*

demanded. Nor were the Catholic militants making any serious attempt, now or later, to 'get through' to the Protestant working class, nor would they even have physically survived if they had gone into the Protestant working-class areas, after August 1969, to make such an effort. Protestants can have derived little reassurance from the promise, 'we will not allow our forces to terrorize the ordinary Protestant population'. Miss Devlin controlled no forces, and when forces emerged they showed no such restraint. And how were Protestants to be reassured by being told that they were not the enemy—not they, only the party and the government that represented them and whose only fault, in their eyes, was weakness in the face of those whom Miss Devlin represented?

Mr. Eamonn McCann, another prominent figure in the Bogside that August, later wrote about the period 1968–69 generally, in a mood of candid disillusionment. 'We had been working', he wrote,[20] 'on a conscious, if unspoken, strategy to provoke the authorities into over-reacting and thus provoke a mass response. We certainly succeeded. But when the mass response came we were not capable of holding it.' 'Taking the leadership from the Left', he wrote elsewhere in the article, 'had proved as easy as taking candy from a baby.'

The fact was that, all along, there had been a fundamental falsity in the position of this group. Their activities were highly significant, but did not have the significance they themselves ascribed to them. Formally, they had been not only non-sectarian, but even anti-sectarian, their objectives class objectives. But in practice the more violent their language and gestures—nominally in the service of a revolution of all the workers—the more they were polarizing Catholic against Protestant, and whipping up sectarian/nationalist feeling in both communities. Their most decisive exploit— the destruction of O'Neill—set the two communities on a collision course. They did not just 'spark off' *one* 'mass response'. They sparked off *two*: a Catholic mass response, and a Protestant mass response. The whole population of Northern Ireland now suffered between these two great fires.

[20] Article, 'October 5th and After', in *The Irish Times*, 6th October 1971.

After August 1969, the radical orators had in fact nothing further to offer to the Catholic population; they never had had anything to offer to the Protestants. The Catholic mass response had won its remarkable gains, and also elicited a great over-shadowing danger, in the shape of the Protestant mass response. The fear of the Catholic community, under that shadow, did not call for more oratory or marches, or appeals to a non-existent class solidarity, or a revolution of the hopelessly divided working class. It called for guns to defend Catholic homes. The men who brought the guns and were able to use them would have the key to the situation in the Catholic ghettoes, and the initiative elsewhere. The stage was set for the return of the Irish Republican Army: the Catholic guerrilla.

# 9

# The Republic and the Republicans

*'For Republicans there can be no two opinions on that question. We may have to bow our heads for a time to the enforced partition of our country by a foreign Power, but the sanction of our consent that partition can never have.*
*We deny that any part of our people can give away the sovereignty or alienate any part of this nation or territory. If this generation should be base enough to consent to give them away, the right to win them back remains unimpaired for those to whom the future will bring the opportunity.'*

EAMON DE VALERA in opposition,
10th December 1925

*'The only policy for abolishing partition that I can see is for us, in this part of Ireland to use such freedom as we can secure to get for the people in this part of Ireland such conditions as will make the people in the other part of Ireland wish to belong to this part.'*

EAMON DE VALERA in power, 1st March 1933

i

I resigned from New York University at the end of May 1969, and came back to Ireland to stand as a Labour Party candidate in the general election campaign of June-July 1969.

The Nineteenth Dáil, issuing from these elections, was to be dominated by the Northern problem, from the second month of its existence on. The Government formed immediately after the elections was to be disrupted by the North within ten months of its formation. But in the elections themselves the North was not an issue at all. 'Support for the objectives of the Civil Rights movement' was common ground among all parties. This did not involve much practical activity, since it was a principle of the Civil Rights movement to depend mainly on its own efforts. The governing party— Fianna Fáil—was known to prefer the older type of straight nationalists in the North to the new civil rights militants, and especially to their left fringe, but it did not obtrude these preferences. The Irish Labour Party had contacts with the middle of the Civil Rights movement—John Hume and Ivan Cooper in Derry, Austin Currie in Dungannon, Gerry Fitt in Belfast—and some of the younger members of our party wanted close co-operation with the People's Democracy and with Eamonn McCann's Derry Labour Party, and wanted also to bring the tone and tactics of these groups into the Republic. Or thought they did. But none of these varieties of emphasis played any significant part in these elections, nor would it have been possible to interest the twenty-six county electorate in them at that time. In that electorate, sympathy with 'civil rights' was general but tepid. Nor were P.D. type tactics capable of setting off any such mass responses in the Republic as they had set off in the North. They should have been able to do so indeed if, as the radical militants held, the origins of such mass-responses were essentially economic, for the unemployed, and lower-paid workers, were *worse* off in the Republic than in Northern Ireland. But in fact the positive mass response the student left had obtained in the North had been the response of the alienated Catholic minority in the Protestant State. There was simply no equivalent to this in the Catholic State.

So the twenty-six county elections were fought on twenty-six county issues, or at least not on Northern ones. In Dublin North-East, the main Government contender was Mr. Charles J. Haughey, the Minister for Finance. Mr Haughey, before a year had elapsed, was to become associated in the public mind with the North, arms plots, Republicanism and patriotic adventure. But at this time no one identified Mr. Haughey with the Republican current in Irish politics (see pp. 202–8). Rather the contrary indeed. As a son-in-law of

Seán Lemass—co-architect of the Lemass-O'Neill fraternization policy—Mr. Haughey was necessarily suspect to
those who regarded that *rapprochement* as a betrayal of the
'indivisible Republic'. And Mr. Haughey's general style of
living was remote from the traditional Republican and de
Valera austerities. He had made a great deal of money, and
he obviously enjoyed spending it, in a dashing eighteenth
century style, of which horses were conspicuous symbols. He
was a small man and, when dismounted, he strutted rather.
His admirers thought he resembled the Emperor Napoleon,
some of whose better-known mannerisms he cultivated. He
patronized, and it is the right word, the arts. He was an
aristocrat in the proper sense of the word: not a nobleman or
even a gentleman, but one who believed in the right of the
best people to rule, and that he himself was the best of the
best people. He was at any rate better, or at least more
intelligent and interesting, than most of his colleagues. He
was considered a competent Minister, and spoke in parliament with bored but conclusive authority. There were
enough rumours about him to form a legend of sorts.
People liked him, I think, not for possession of any of
the more obviously likeable qualities, but for lending
some colour to life in a particularly drab period, and at that
time for something else too: for seeming to be 'his own man',
not perhaps in the sense of owning any deep well of inner
integrity, but in the sense at least of appearing what he himself wanted to appear, and not what others expected of him.

I thought that, if conditions ever became ripe for a charac-
teristically Irish Catholic form of dictatorship, Charles J.
Haughey would make a plausible enough Taoiseach/Duce. It
did not occur to me, though it should have, that conditions
in the North might provoke reactions in the South apparently
favourable to the ambitions of such men. I knew that the
Civil Rights movement was likely to provoke considerable
violence in the North. I ought to have been asking myself
questions about the probable effects in the Republic of
major violence in the North, but I did not ask myself these
questions at this time. Few men, as Nietzsche said, have the
courage to think even that which they know.

I attacked Mr. Haughey over certain dealings in development land, and over conflicts of interest, trying to use these
to expose the workings of the Fianna Fáil speculator-oriented
oligarchy. Fianna Fáil attacked the Labour Party as infil-
trated by Communist intellectuals, of whom I was the reddest
and most exotic specimen. Evidence connecting me with
Communism was not to be had—Fianna Fáil had to do what
it could with the fact that I had been heard to advocate
diplomatic relations with Cuba. But in fact 'Communism' is
a technical term, in the political vocabulary of the Catholic
State. Formally, in the late twentieth century, you can't be
seen to go round demanding to know when your opponent
was last at Mass, Confession or Holy Communion. This
would be sectarian behaviour, unmodern, uncivilized,
resembling the goings-on in the North of Ireland. But if
there is reason to believe your opponent may be vulnerable
in this area, you can hit him just as accurately by calling
him a Communist. This is a *political* charge, impeccably
twentieth century in character. (The fact that Senator Joe
McCarthy was eventually discredited never made much
impact on public opinion in Ireland.) But as well as being a
political term, 'Communist' carries a 'religious' message:
Communists are known to be atheists also. So the question of
the opponent's religious faith, or lack of it, comes automatically into the zone of legitimate *political* discussion. A
good Catholic, by definition, cannot be a Communist. But
a bad Catholic may well be one since he, also by definition,
being bad, is capable of anything, so may very well be a
Communist. So, if you call someone a Communist, and have
no proof of this, you may discreetly adduce indications
establishing a presumption of Communism: educated at a
Protestant school and University, first marriage ended in
divorce. These proofs are not coercive in respect of Communism, but Communism is really beside the point. The point is
to show that your opponent is a bad Catholic, so as to enlist
help of the church in eliminating him and his associates
from public life, to the benefit of yourself and your associates.
    I was vulnerable in this area, especially because my first
marriage had ended in divorce—in Mexico, by consent—in

1961 and I had married again in 1962. My second wife, Máire MacEntee, was a Catholic, and our marriage was in a Catholic Church in New York. My wife's father was a former Minister for Finance and Deputy Premier in Fianna Fáil governments and my wife's mother was a sister of the eminent Irish Dominican, Michael Cardinal Browne. It was therefore difficult for Fianna Fáil publicly to give me the full treatment, 1891 style, but they did their best, by word of mouth on the door-to-door canvass, to exploit 'the moral issue'.

The Labour Party itself was vulnerable, not only to such tactics directed against certain of its candidates, but because it had, fairly recently, taken to itself the designation of *Socialist*, and because the distinction between Socialist and Communist is not clear to all Irish minds, and especially not to all Irish clerical minds, especially when they don't want it to be clear. My wife, shortly after this time, heard a priest in Dingle, Co. Kerry, deliver a sermon on 'Communism and Socialism'. The priest gave Communism the expected treatment. Then he went on to Socialism. 'Socialism,' he said, 'is worse than Communism. Socialism is a heresy of Communism. Socialists are a Protestant variety of Communists.' Not merely Communists, but *Protestant* Communists! Not many votes for Labour in Dingle.

So the key to Mr. Jack Lynch's campaign, in that June of 1969, was a tour of the convent parlours. Like Captain O'Neill he was photographed with nuns, but unlike Captain O'Neill he knew how to talk to nuns.[1] The press and media were not present for that series of convent chats, but the word came through all the same. A Labour colleague from Munster told me ruefully of a mothers' meeting convened in his constituency by a Reverend Mother on the day before polling day. It was not, said the Reverend Mother to the other mothers, for her to advise them on a political matter. Certainly not! She only wished to remind them of their duty, as Catholic mothers, both to vote and to be very prudent about how to vote. She would give them no advice about

[1] 'Must be very tiring for you', one imagines the Captain saying, 'with all those rosary-beads to tell and so on'.

which party to vote for. That was not her province. Whatever party they voted for, however, they should be sure that it was a party which could provide stable government and which was free from any tendency to Communism. If there was doubt as to whether there might be Communists in a certain party, it would be wiser not to vote for that party. That was all!

That was one Reverend Mother to whom Mr. Lynch's message had not been addressed in vain.

Dublin, which returned Parnellite candidates after the divorce crisis of 1891, and which re-elected Dr. Noel Browne after the Mother-and Child clash, was not greatly impressed by the convent-parlour whistle-stop. Although I was the prime target of the offensive against 'Communism', I was elected easily for Dublin North-East, running second —in a four-seat constituency—to the Minister for Finance, Mr. Charles J. Haughey. But the campaign told to some extent—together with other factors—in the rural areas. Labour, which had had reasonable expectations of gaining some seats, actually lost some. Mr. Lynch had a clear majority not in total votes cast, but in terms of seats in the new Parliament.

Afterwards, when I reproached Mr. Lynch, in parliament, with making use of Catholicism, for party political purposes, similar to the use made by the Northern Unionist Party of Protestantism, Mr. Lynch refused to acknowledge any such parallel. Up to a point, Mr. Lynch was right. The use of Catholicism in the politics of the Republic is in many ways *dis*similar, especially on the surface, to the use of Protestantism in the politics of the North. The *tone* is different, for one thing. Political Protestantism in the North is ostentatious, challenging, blatant. Political Catholicism in the South has had its blatant phases—for example at the time of the Spanish War—but generally it is discreet, pervasive, sly. There are, I think, three main reasons for this difference. One is rooted in the different historical status of the two communities. The Protestants had felt no need to dissemble in a United Kingdom whose population was overwhelmingly Protestant. The Catholics, having to struggle long and hard against anti-Catholic prejudice in the United Kingdom, had been required to disclaim any persecuting or triumphalist intent, and to appeal, in tone and form, to liberal opinion in order to win concessions for Catholics. The obligation to 'learn the liberal language' stood the Catholics in good stead, as Protestantism declined in England as a political force, and as the tone and slogans of Ulster Protestantism began to sound repulsively archaic.

The second reason for the difference lies in the structure of ecclesiastical organization of the two denominational groups. There is an Erastian element in Ulster Presbyterianism and nonconformism, which also affects the tone and character of the Church of Ireland in Ulster (if only from fear of losing membership to the nonconformists). Among the Presbyterians and nonconformists, certain divines vied with one another for popular support, and the winners, from the early nineteenth century on, were those who, like Henry Cooke (see Chapter 2), were prepared to sound most militantly anti-Catholic and loyalist. In the hierarchical organization of the Catholic Church, however, the pressures were more complex. As in the world of *Le Rouge et le Noir*, so in Catholic Ireland also, ascent to ecclesiastical power was achieved not by 'roaring'—as in the celebrated case of Belfast's Reverend Hugh Hanna—but by discretion, obedience and a due appearance of humility. Even among those who have already achieved power, the life-long habit of discretion remains. High ecclesiastical pronouncements, bordering on the political area, are sparse and usually cryptic. Where a note of menace is indicated it is likely to be oblique and muffled. There is, generally, no need to raise one's voice: the knowledge of the power inherent in the source of the statement supplies its own amplification: the medium is the message. Nor are *lay* Catholic demagogues generally much in demand, except very occasionally for shouting down those who will not hear the whisper from on high. In general the Catholic statesmen most appreciated are those who emulate the reticent manner of the ecclesiastics: as Mr. de Valera did, as Mr. Lynch does.

Also, the political contexts into which religious power is

injected are radically different, South and North. In the North, there is the straightforward siege situation, Protestant versus Catholic. In the much more nearly homogeneous Republic, all the political parties are overwhelmingly Catholic in membership, support and representation. The Church has good reason to be satisfied with this situation, no desire to see Catholicism used obtrusively as a political weapon. Many of the voters also dislike any visible attempt to exploit their religion in this way. When Fine Gael used noisy appeals to Catholicity as a weapon against Fianna Fáil in the 1930's it failed hopelessly. Fianna Fáil itself, in the 1969 elections, showed a far finer flair for the real possibilities. It knew, in fact, that this was a weapon that had to be fitted with a silencer. Not loud accusation, but a quiet, just perceptible nagging doubt, whose expression Charity would fain have altogether suppressed, had not Prudence discreetly sounded her note of warning: this was the style in which Mr. Jack Lynch smothered the Labour challenge in June 1969.[2]

Sometimes travelling from Northern Ireland back to the South, I have the impression of leaving a turbulent republic of barking, snarling, yelping dogs and entering a kingdom of cats, moving on padded feet, about occasions for which undue publicity is not required. Personally I like the atmosphere of 'the South' rather better—I was born a cat after all —but I can understand that a born dog might have nightmares about being silently asphyxiated under all that fur.

## ii

The Northern question hit the politics of the Republic seriously, for the first time since 1925, on 12th August 1969, when the spectacle of the Bogside resistance filled the television screens.

For most viewers in the Republic a feeling of identification with the Bogsiders was immediate, as if instinctive, and yet

[2] It is true that in the wilder and more barren parts of the country, where a whisper would not have carried, a ruder tone prevailed among Mr. Lynch's henchmen. But Mr. Lynch managed to be adequately uninformed about this.

somehow unreal, like sympathy with a family ghost; or, more precisely, with a member of the family writing from emigration, with alarming news imperfectly understood. That they—the defenders—were our people, blood of our blood, went without saying. According to the dominant political theory in the Republic—which is Republicanism —the Ulster Protestants, in and out of uniform, were 'our people' too. The idea that they were not part of our people, were a separate people or nation, would have been totally rejected at this time by all citizens of the Republic who had received adequate instruction in the dominant ideology. Yet neither watching Bogside on the box, nor in other contexts, did actual Irish Catholics *feel* that actual Ulster Protestants were really part of 'our people'. Again and again, in the course of the controversies that began after Bogside and continue fiercely at the time of writing, politicians of the Irish Catholic people, speaking of the situation in Northern Ireland, have used the phrases 'our people', 'the people' and even 'the population' in contexts where these terms were applicable to the Catholics, and to them alone. Those who have used these words in this way cover the entire spectrum of the politics of the Irish Catholic people. Dr. Paddy Hillery, Foreign Minister of the Republic, has used this language: so have Miss Bernadette Devlin, and Miss Máirin de Búrca, the General Secretary of the official (left-lining) Sinn Féin, and many, many others. All those named, and many of the others, profess impeccably anti-sectarian sentiments, and claim Protestants as part of the nation (Dr. Hillery). Protestant workers as part of the working class (Miss Devlin, Miss de Búrca). But the way they use 'our people', etc., in their unguarded moments, reveals the reality. As one would expect, Protestant converts to the political culture of the Catholic people,[3] tend to use language in the same way. Thus, the only Protestant member of Mr. Lynch's Cabinet, Mr. Erskine Childers, recently (29th October 1971) in a televised discussion which included the present writer, claimed that Mr. de Valera's 1937 Constitution was now accepted by 'all our people'. This statement

[3] See above, pp. 48–51.

is demonstrably untrue, if 'all our people' means all the people inhabiting the territory claimed by the Constitution in question. When I put this point to Mr. Childers, he seemed unable to understand it, although he is an intelligent and highly educated man. But the gap between traditional Irish Republican doctrine, formed in the eighteenth century, and the realities of late twentieth century Ireland would confuse anyone obliged to think about the realities in terms of the doctrine—especially the doctrine as refracted through Mr. de Valera's Constitution.

It was in these terms that Mr. Jack Lynch was obliged, if not to think, at least to express himself, on that day of crisis in 1969. He had to take account of many factors, of which the potential effect of his words on the actual situation in Northern Ireland was probably the least important. The most important factor was that his response had to seem appropriate and adequate to a public in the Twenty-six Counties, the most significant components of which, as far as he was concerned, were the members of his own government and party. He had a government and party to hold together, under heavy stress. At the time of writing this— more than two years after Bogside—the stress is at least as great as it was then.

Fianna Fáil was a party which exploited a Republican-revolutionary mystique, while practising very ordinary pragmatic middle-class politics. The effect of Bogside was to bring the mystique exploited into sharp collision with the pragmatism practised.

In the cabinet, in the party and in the country, there were men and women to whose emotional lives, and to whose conception of the meaning of life and of its glory, the mystique of 1916 was central. For most of these, Bogside meant the re-lighting of the fire. They did not see the Bogsiders as demanding equality of rights in Northern Ireland, or warding off another police riot. They saw them as starting the last phase of the age-long struggle against English power in Ireland. They saw the police as England's hirelings, the Protestants who supported the police as England's dupes. Theirs was a blazingly simplified conception of history and of reality. This, and the sincerity of their conviction, made them formidable. They were made still more formidable by the fact that the doctrine they actually believed in was the doctrine which everyone else in the Republic was officially deemed to profess: Republicanism. To argue with a Republican about Irish politics is like arguing with a Catholic Bishop about religion. It is not only unrewarding in itself: it may well be socially damaging in its results. In Ireland there is one condition that is decidedly more frowned upon than being a bad Catholic, and that is the condition of being *anti-national*. Anyone who argues with a Republican, without accepting the fundamentals of the Republican position, will be called anti-national. The implications of this are serious. Sensible people—like pragmatists—therefore, avoid controversy with Republicans.

The trouble for the pragmatists, in and after August 1969, was that they could not altogether avoid such controversy. The Republicans were demanding action, preferably immediate military intervention in Derry, but failing this at least the supply of weapons and training for the resistance in the North. Real full-blooded Republicans were, it is true, exceedingly scarce in the Cabinet: scarce in the party and in the country. But people influenced, half-convinced, over-awed or downright intimidated by real Republicans were far from scarce. There were also one or two people to be reckoned with, who had not hitherto been suspected of more than conventional Republicanism but who now saw, in the resurgence of Republican passion, a new political force, capable—like other forces—of being harnessed in the service of personal ambition. With all this, the pressure in favour of the Republican demand for intervention was considerable inside Fianna Fáil.[4] At the same time the reasons for resisting this pressure were also weighty, from a pragmatic point of

[4] Not in terms of mass sentiment. A survey by a Dublin magazine, *This Week*, in May 1970 found only 17 per cent in favour of sending the Irish Army into the North in the event of a repetition of August 1969. Only 14 per cent favoured the use of force to end partition. This proportion seems remarkably stable. A *Sunday Telegraph* survey published on 12th March 1972 found 15 per cent supporting 'the present I.R.A. campaign in Northern Ireland as the best means of achieving Irish unity'. 85 per cent said 'no' to this.

view. The Irish Army, if it attempted open intervention in Northern Ireland, would most certainly be defeated, with unpredictable but alarming consequences for the Republic (Twenty-six Counties). Other armies, in similar circumstances, had ousted the Governments responsible, in the army's opinion, for neglecting the national defences. The implications of other more covert forms of military, or semimilitary, intervention were also alarming in a more shadowy way. Generally, this path, if followed resolutely, led to, at the least, such a worsening of relations with Britain as might seriously damage the economy of a Republic which lived mainly by trading with Britain.

Mr. Lynch's solution of this tricky problem was predictable. He decided to behave as much as possible like a pragmatist—which is what, essentially, he is—while sounding as much as possible like a Republican. His speech of 12th August was therefore Republican in tone and manner, while avoiding any precise commitment. Most of the points in that speech are mentioned in the preceding chapter. But there was one sentence which, as it most clearly reflects Republican pressures in the Republic, I have thought relevent to the present chapter:

'Recognising, however that the re-unification of the national territory can provide the only permanent solution for the problem, it is our intention to request the British Government to enter into early negotiations with the Irish Government to review the present constitutional position of the Six Counties of Northern Ireland.'

A few months before, on St. Patrick's Day, 1969, Mr. Lynch had said that it was 'the aim of the Government to promote the reunification of Ireland by fostering a spirit of brotherhood among all sections of the Irish people', and promised to 'continue along this course'. In August, there was no question of uniting *people*, through a spirit of brotherhood: the question was one of uniting *territory*, by appealing to the British Government over the heads of that section of the Irish people which had refused to manifest the proper spirit of brotherhood.

The renewed emphasis on the territorial claim—which had been carefully 'played down' over the past twelve years of Fianna Fáil rule—was fully understandable under the impact of Bogside. But the claim, renewed in this way, was to take on a different, more urgent significance in the aftermath of Bogside, and especially after the British troops had been deployed. Mr. Lynch said that 'the use of British troops in the Six Counties was not acceptable, nor would they be likely to restore peaceful conditions in the long term. . . .'

The re-assertion of the territorial claim was later to combine with the deployment of the British troops into an acceptable Republican tableau: Ireland's claim to justice, denied by British armed might. But that was not how it seemed, in Bogside or the Falls, that August. In Belfast the Catholics were looking for *more* British troops to protect them from the Protestants. Their leaders asked us, in the Labour Party delegation,[5] to convey this to the British Labour Party and we did, together with the demand that the B. Specials be abolished, and that Westminster take over from Stormont, which had failed. We did not support Mr. Lynch's claim to territorial unification, which we thought inflammatory in the conditions then prevailing in Northern Ireland. At the same time we did not disavow Mr. Lynch. On British radio and television at that time, questioned by an interviewer who accused Mr. Lynch of inflaming the situation, I said that the British public and parliament would do better to examine their own responsibilities, through their collusion with an oppressive sectarian system, over nearly fifty years. True enough, as we say, meaning: true, but something less than the whole truth.

The truth, at that time, even as much of it as one could grasp, was a highly confusing affair. The Catholics were asking London for more British troops. But they were also asking Dublin for guns. This was not perfidy, but a form of re-insurance. The British troops had sometimes been slow to move in Belfast, and were still thin on the ground. And could the British always be relied on, for this rather unnatural work of protecting Catholics against Protestants? Better to

[5] See Chapter 8.

be sure than sorry. Better have a gun in your house, or at any rate a few guns in your street, to be ready the next time the Prods come. A friend of mine, a Catholic M.P., an affable, blasphemous man, told me he was looking for guns and warned me not to over-do the peace bit. 'What would *you* do,' he asked, 'if your *own* — house was attacked?' A good question.

Two years later, some influential commentators in Dublin and London were dismissing talk of 'Protestant backlash', in any circumstances, as bluff. But the Catholics of Belfast in August 1969 had only too good reason to know that there was no bluff about it.

In these circumstances the Dublin government, under-standably, was under pressure to help the Catholics get guns for self-defence, and some of its members saw that they did get guns. Samuel Dowling, Chairman of the Newry Civil Rights Association, was later (January 1970) charged in the Republic with illegal possession of arms and explosives. He was acquitted, after declaring: 'Those weapons were in our possession . . . through the work of offices and agents of the Irish Government. . . . It was made clear between us that such arms would be used only for defence of those minority communities in the North when under attack.'

In practice, there was no way of ensuring that the 'defence only' condition would be kept. Not only is 'defence' a Protean concept (see pp. 229, 245) but there were people, in Dublin and elsewhere, who were interested in the provision of guns, not just for 'the defence of our people', but for the re-unification of the national territory. For them, 'the defence of our people' was a promising way of *starting* the last campaign—the opportunity foreseen by de Valera in 1925 (see epigraph to this Chapter). And for them also the real enemy was not the forces which had actually *attacked* the Catholics in August 1969: the real enemy was the force which had *protected* the Catholics at that time: the unacceptable British Army.

These views were represented in Mr. Lynch's Cabinet, with other views. Mr. Lynch himself, as soon as things were superficially fairly quiet in the North again, tried to return to the substance of the Lemass line, in a conciliatory speech at

Tralee, on 23rd September: 'The unity we seek is not something forced but a free and genuine union of those living in Ireland based on mutual respect and tolerance. . . . We are not seeking to overthrow by violence the Stormont Parliament or Government but rather to win the agreement of a sufficient number of people in the North to an acceptable form of re-unification.'

Not all of Mr. Lynch's colleagues agreed with this approach. The divergence became public on 8th December when the Minister for Agriculture, Mr. Neil Blaney, spoke at Letterkenny, Co. Donegal. 'The ideal way of ending partition,' Mr. Blaney said, 'is by peaceful means.' But: 'no one has the right to assert that force is ruled out.'

I was in Belfast when I read the report of the Blaney speech. I had realized, since August, that peace was at the mercy of even a few snipers, firing at British troops out of the Catholic ghettoes, and precipitating confrontation and conflict between the Catholics and the British Army: a situation which, to many people in the Republic, would look like a resumption of 1921. This still seemed fairly remote—it had been with *Protestants* that the Army had been clashing in the autumn of 1969, and that conflict aroused no emotions in the South—'our people' were not involved, except theoretically.[6] But any condonation, from inside the Dublin Government, of the use of force to end partition, could legitimize Catholic attacks on the British Army, and build up towards various forms of war in Ireland. From Belfast, I publicly called on Mr. Lynch to dismiss Mr. Blaney. Mr. Lynch did indeed dismiss him, but five months later, and for reasons more cogent than my appeal.

Something else happened in December, besides Mr. Blaney's speech, and possibly unconnected with it. The I.R.A. split. That is to say, the split in the I.R.A., which had begun in the aftermath of August, became definitive with the emergence of a Provisional Army Council, in addition

---

[6] The Army house-to-house search for arms in the Shankill Road on 12th October 1969 seems to have been conducted in much the same manner as the Falls Road search in June 1970—see p. 231—which aroused indignation in the Republic. The Shankill Road search did not register at all.

to the Official one. There were now two I.R.A.'s.[7] This was the last momentous event of 1969, and the most ominous one.

### iii

It is necessary here to give a very brief account of as much of the background to the modern I.R.A. as is relevant to the theme of this book.

After the general elections of 1918, the majority of M.P.s elected for Irish seats—a majority based on Catholic Ireland—refused to sit at Westminster and constituted themselves as the Parliament of Ireland, Dáil Éireann. They asserted their control over all organs of a normal state, including an army. The army was the Irish Republican Army, based on the old Irish volunteers, and in particular the survivors of 1916. In fact, the authority of the Dáil over the I.R.A. was never more than nominal. Members of the I.R.A. gave their loyalty to the Republic proclaimed in 1916, at a time when the majority of the elected representatives had been opposed to any such policy. If the elected representatives had been wrong then, and had been rightly ignored, elected representatives could be wrong again, and rightly ignored once more by soldiers loyal to the Republic. So reasoned the many members of the I.R.A. who rejected the treaty of 1921, even when it was approved by the Dáil, and when those who approved it were given a majority by the people in the elections that followed. It was the anti-treaty forces in the Civil War of 1922 who retained the honoured title: Irish Republican Army. For a time, after this defeat in the Civil War this Army, now an underground force, gave its support to Eamon de Valera, as President of the inviolable Republic. But when de Valera entered the parliament of the State set up by the Treaty, the I.R.A. officially broke with him, though many of its former members followed him. The I.R.A. continued in existence as an intermittently active

---

[7] The open political movement—Sinn Féin—which was the legal front for the I.R.A. split consequently in January 1969. We now have two Sinn Féins, known by the addresses of their Dublin headquarters. Sinn Féin (Gardner Place) representing the Official I.R.A., and Sinn Féin (Kevin Street) representing the Provisionals.

underground army. With the government in Dublin it had a curious relationship. When its activities were too obstreperous or otherwise inconvenient it was severely dealt with: many of its members suffered terms of imprisonment, or periods of internment, twelve died in prison. These repressive actions were approved, or at least accepted by the public. Yet the public, and even some members of the government which imposed the penalties, continued to hold the I.R.A. in an uneasy but high regard. Their ideals, their intransigence and their bravery did clearly put them in line with the patriot dead, even if it might sometimes be inopportune to allow the heirs of the patriot dead actually to remain at large.

The Government in Belfast, of course, suffered from no inhibitions in this respect. It agreed that the old I.R.A. and the modern I.R.A. were one and the same: the armed forces of the enemy. The existence of the I.R.A. was held to justify prudential and exclusive measures directed against the population which harboured it: the Catholic population.

In the Republic, even many of those who disapproved the continuance of I.R.A. activities directed against the Dublin Government, could see nothing wrong with such activities in 'occupied Ireland'. Men from the South, who were killed as a result of participation in the I.R.A.'s Northern campaign of 1956–62, became the heroes of ballads, which continued to be sung with deep emotion in the Republic, even through the years of the Lemass-O'Neill *rapprochement*.

In these years, after the collapse of the military campaign of 1956–62, the I.R.A.-Sinn Féin movement adopted new tactics, a new style, and to some extent new ideas. It fell under the influence of certain left-wing intellectuals, and adopted the language of social revolution. Without ruling out violence, at an appropriate time, it emphasized techniques of non-violent civil disobedience—sit-ins, squatting, fish-ins, etc.—applicable in the Republic as well as in the North. It saw its enemies as capitalism and imperialism, and most specifically British imperialism, which held in its grip, in different ways, both the Dublin and Belfast governments. Accordingly, it was not a question of revolution in the North to bring a unity with the South: it was a question of fomenting revolution in *both* parts of the country, and out of these merging social revolutions a united socialist Ireland would come.

The Sinn Féin-I.R.A. intellectuals rightly saw revolutionary possibilities in the Civil Rights movement. Stewards supplied by the I.R.A. were responsible for the orderly conduct of the major civil rights marches and rallies. At the same time Sinn Féin-I.R.A. encouraged the emergence to prominence of the orators of the left wing of the Civil Rights movement. Miss Bernadette Devlin, in one of the most interesting passages of her book *The Price of my Soul,* shows how what she calls 'the Republican Party'—i.e. Sinn Féin-I.R.A.—determined her selection as 'unity candidate' in the mid-Ulster by-election of April 1969.

The Sinn Féin-I.R.A. movement at this time was sincerely committed to an anti-sectarian policy. Its ideas on this point derived from Tone. It saw the Protestant working-class as misled. It thought that, if class issues were emphasized, and a revolutionary situation created, the 'false consciousness' of the Protestant proletariat would be eliminated, and all the workers would join together in the attack on the political and industrial establishment and on British imperialism. The fact that at no point did such a development actually begin to happen, among the Protestants, in no way deterred Sinn Féin-I.R.A. and its left sympathizers. On the contrary it incited them to speed up the tempo of agitation, and emphasize its revolutionary character. In fact the linking of Civil Rights with the I.R.A. and revolution increased Protestant resistance to Civil Rights, and deepened Protestant antipathy to the Catholic population in which—and in which alone—all this ferment was going on. As far as Protestants were concerned, this was a Catholic insurrection, and the language of class solidarity was humbug.

It *was*, in substance, a Catholic insurrection, yet the Sinn Féin-I.R.A. leaders who wanted it to be, or become, something else were in earnest. They devoted much energy to preventing sectarian confrontations, and especially to stopping Catholics from retaliating against Protestant provocation, during the ritual provocation—months of June to August.

Whether because of doctrinaire incapacity to accept the reality of growing Catholic-Protestant polarization, or because of an honourable unwillingness to exploit this trend, the I.R.A. leadership was utterly unprepared for the crisis of mid-August 1969 in Derry and Belfast. The I.R.A. had very few weapons and very few people trained and ready to use them. Their prestige in the ghettoes went sharply down. People wrote on walls:

## I.R.A. I Ran Away.

It was out of this débâcle and the consequent discredit of the Sinn Féin-I.R.A. leadership that the Provisional I.R.A. grew. To what exact extent its growth was watered by members of the Dublin Government remains in some doubt (see pp. 208–16). But the I.R.A. had always been subject to splits—especially splits between right and left—and the situation after August 1969 was obviously of the kind that gives rise to splits. The people in the ghettoes, after all, were asking for more guns and less Marxist gobbledygook. These people, under the pressure of an immediate fear and need, did not consider whether the men who came with the guns might come with other ideas than mere defence, or whether these other ideas might prove more dangerous and destructive to the people 'defended', than ever the Marxist gobbledygook could possibly have been, or the Protestant backlash was, in the presence of the British troops.

The formidable thing about the new I.R.A.—the Provisionals—was its simple relevance to the situation. Any ordinary, patriotic Catholic, clinging to the dual pieties of his community, could identify with the Provisionals. There was no 'taint of Communism' about them, nothing puzzling or foreign at all. And there was no nonsense about them either. They were not forever telling people that the Protestant workers were really on the same side as ourselves, when anyone could see—especially in and after August 1969— that these same Protestant workers were out to kill us. The Provisionals weren't telling people to turn the other cheek if a misguided Protestant brother had a bash at them. There had been enough of that. If the Protestants wanted trouble now, they could have it. These Provisionals weren't like the old crowd—they were getting the guns and they were ready to use them.

They were indeed. But not just for the defence of the ghettoes, which of course is what they emphasized in the beginning. Their real objective was the reconquest of Ireland. Here again their strength was in the simplicity of their idea. This was no complicated, fantastic scenario like the old Official one: socialist revolutions, North and South, uniting Protestant and Catholic workers and all that nonsense. No: this was a straightforward thing—the idea was to complete the work of 1916–21, by driving the British out of the last corner of Ireland which they held. What about the Protestants? Well, what about them? Some Protestants were on our side, good Irishmen. Very, very few of them. Right. What about the rest? Well, if the rest of them felt they were British, let them. As long as they stuck to that, they could get what was coming to the rest of the British in Ireland. 1798 was over, and it was no use going on about it all the time.[8]

We had nothing against Protestants *as* Protestants.

As the people they actually were, we had quite a lot against them.

Here again the Provisional conception was clear and laudable, in terms of certain traditions and ideals of the Catholic community. However, the idea of the reconquest—as distinct from that of briskly conducted defence—was not only clear and 'laudable': it was also terrifying to anyone, especially any Catholic in Belfast, who thought clearly about the idea's implications. What kind of war would it be, in character and duration, which could compel, not merely the British, but the majority in the area directly concerned, to capitulate? And what would be the condition of the Catholic ghettoes, the pivots of the guerrilla war, by the time that war was won?

The Provisionals had no interest in raising such questions.[9] And as Provisional strength in various ghettoes increased—

[8] See the following chapter.
[9] Or answering them. Visiting reporters often find Provisional objectives more mysterious than most Irish people do.

mainly through the appeal of their defensive capability—it became apparent that questions which the Provisionals had no interest in raising would not be likely to be raised in areas where the Provisionals were strong. To ask defeatist questions was 'anti-national'. And it was unhealthy to be anti-national in Ardoyne or Ballymurphy, and to a lesser extent in wider areas.

It was not through intimidation that the Provisionals established themselves in the ghettoes, or rather it was through a reaction against *Protestant* (including police) intimidation that this happened. But once Provisionals had established themselves, intimidation or—in Provisional terms—a kind of underground martial law—became a fact. The partial breakdown, after August, of the old kind of policing—essentially the policing of Catholics by Protestants—meant that what 'law and order' was available inside the ghettoes was to a considerable extent dispensed by the I.R.A. In these circumstances, very few people, in the areas so controlled, could be expected to speak out against those who controlled them. (A few people did, none the less.) No opinion poll is possible in such circumstances. My own guess is that a majority of Catholics welcomed the I.R.A., *as defenders,* in the aftermath of August, and that a majority of Catholics came to dislike the I.R.A.'s offensive campaign and dread its consequences.

The 'Officials', in the areas where they maintained themselves—for example, the Lower Falls Road—did so through the prestige of individual officers, and through showing themselves as tough as the Provisionals, even if (for a time) somewhat more selective in their targets. The Provisionals now set the tone, among the Catholics of the North, and to an increasing but still limited extent among a number of Catholics in the South as well.

The Officials in their pre-August and pre-Provisional days had backed activities which—through an effect not consciously intended—had aroused Protestant anger, but they then restrained Catholics from replying forcibly to manifestations of the anger thus aroused. With the coming of the Provisionals, that restraint was removed.

What this implied for the two communities—-and notably for the Catholics of Belfast—remained to be seen. But even if the attempt at reconquest meant the total destruction of the Catholics of Belfast, and indeed of all the Irish, it had still to be pursued. 'The nation's honour', Liam Mellowes had declared during the Treaty Debates on 17th May 1921, 'comes before the nation's life.'[10]

iv

The emergence of the Provisional i.r.a. in the North had important implications also for the Republic (Twenty-six Counties). Here again, it meant that a new pattern of i.r.a. activity fitted better, had better chances of winning both influential and popular support, than the old pattern had. The old i.r.a. had favoured revolutions, North *and* South, and the Official i.r.a. continued along this line. As very few people in the South had any desire for a revolution, this cut these movements off from popular support. This policy —and the Marxist rhetoric associated with it—especially alienated rich patriots both in the South and in the United States. By this combination therefore the i.r.a., both in its old and Official forms, was insulated, and kept relatively ineffective, or harmless.

The Provisional line, on the other hand, made sense, in terms of the dominant ideology in the Republic. They were not, they claimed, out to make trouble in the Twenty-six Counties. They rejected Marxist language (though not 'socialism') and any political alliance with Communists. They were out, they said, to liberate the six north-eastern counties of Ireland, occupied by British forces against the will of the great majority of the Irish people. Most citizens of the Republic were conditioned to think of such a policy as well-founded and laudable. They were not conditioned to think of the Ulster Protestants as an important factor in the question, or to see that the Provisionals' policy pointed ultimately to civil war in Ireland between Catholic and

[10] Mellowes may in theory be more an Official than a Provisional hero. But of this particular saying it is the Provisionals who are the true heirs.

Protestant. People might feel vaguely uneasy about the fanaticism of the Provisionals, but found it hard to answer them. It was, in fact, impossible to answer them in terms of the dominant ideology, because they were the most effective and consistent champions of that ideology. Rich and influential patriots, repelled by the Marxism of the old and Official I.R.A., had a special welcome for the Provisionals: good Catholics, good Irishmen, no threat to anyone but the British and the . . . Unionists.

It seems that some of the rich and of the influential not only welcomed the Provisionals, but helped them to come into being. After the split, the Official Sinn Féin-I.R.A. charged that certain people in Mr. Lynch's cabinet, notably Mr. Neil Blaney, Minister for Agriculture, and Mr. Charles J. Haughey, Minister for Finance, had actually caused the split. They first tried, it was alleged—it seems as early as February 1969—to get the I.R.A. as a whole to drop its political activities in the South, and concentrate on military activities in the North. When they failed with the I.R.A. leadership, they then worked at other levels in the movement, and succeeded in detaching important elements, especially in the North, promising—and to some extent delivering— money, guns and other forms of help.[11]

The exact extent and character of the involvement of members of Mr. Lynch's 1969–70 government with the I.R.A. and especially the Provisional I.R.A. in the North is still a matter of speculation. The Arms Trials of the autumn of 1970, in which Mr. Charles J. Haughey was the most eminent of the accused, shed some light, but much still remains murky.

This much is reasonably clear:

Messrs. Blaney and Haughey were the most powerful members of the Cabinet who favoured, in mid-August 1969, some form of intervention, or at least some form of undercover activity, in the North.

---

[11] This interpretation is accepted by the *Sunday Times* 'Insight' group, in *Ulster* (Penguin Special, 1972). The details of their account may be open to question—as the team put a good deal of trust in 'official I.R.A.' handouts— but, in substance, the account would now be generally accepted.

Messrs. Blaney and Haughey were also the most powerful figures—by far—in a four-man committee set up by the Lynch government to co-ordinate activities in relation to the North. These activities were nominally concerned with relief for the Catholics. But the main form of relief which pre-occupied Northern Catholics at this time was guns for defence.

Certain Irish Army regular officers sent into Northern Ireland on intelligence work at this time became active sympathizers and helpers of what became the Provisional I.R.A. At least one of these officers was in touch with, and reported to, the committee headed by Messrs. Blaney and Haughey. The Minister for Defence, on at least one occasion, carried out an instruction (for movement of guns to Dundalk, near the border) given to him by the Minister for Agriculture, Mr. Blaney. A paper, called *The Voice of the North*, was set up, inside Northern Ireland, representing the views of Mr. Blaney, which were similar, in their fervent and uncomplicated nationalism, to the views of the Provisionals, as these later became known.

Messrs. Blaney and Haughey were later acquitted by courts in Dublin, on specific charges of bringing arms illegally *into the Republic*. Their trials revealed only as much of their activities in and around Northern Ireland as was known to the prosecution and held to be pertinent to the case. It remains uncertain exactly to what extent members of Mr. Lynch's government promoted the revival of I.R.A. activity in the North, and specifically the emergence of the Provisional I.R.A. It seems certain, however, that activities set in motion by members of the Dublin Government did help, in some degree, to bring about these developments. Captain James Kelly, one of the intelligence officers in the North (tried and acquitted with Mr. Haughey and others), has made no secret of the fact that he saw it as his duty to aid the I.R.A. (Provisionals) and that he believed the Government, and specifically the Minister for Defence, Mr. Gibbons, knew and approved of what he was going. Not only Captain Kelly but also his superior to whom he reported, the Director of Military Intelligence, Colonel Michael Hefferon, later (on

retirement) joined a political organization—Mr. Kevin
Boland's AONTACHT ÉIREANN ('Unity of Ireland')—which
openly supports the Provisional I.R.A. campaign in the
North. And Mr. Blaney himself has said in November 1971:

'. . . Give them aid and money and anything else that might be
useful to them. Let the people who are carrying on the struggle
in Northern Ireland know that you are with them.'

It may be safely assumed that Mr. Blaney, while in office,
acted on these principles. It would appear that Mr. Haughey,
a patriot of more guarded character and language, gave
some help to Mr. Blaney.

How much did Mr. Jack Lynch, the Taoiseach, know
about all this? Nothing, according to himself, until April
1970—when these activities had been going on for about
eight months—and when he did find out something he
dismissed the two Ministers concerned, and brought about
the resignation of two others who sympathized with them.
Possibly Mr. Lynch did know nothing about what was happening during this period, but if so his ignorance was
deliberate. He had after all set up a committee for the North,
had refrained from serving on it himself, and had appointed
Mr. Blaney (and Mr. Haughey) to it. He knew what that
meant: none better. Not only did he know Mr. Blaney's
views: he knew his determination and his authority. Mr.
Blaney is a very forceful man indeed, with pale, piercing
eyes, a blue spade-shaped chin and a deliberate, faintly
menacing manner. He was a 'big man' inside Fianna Fáil
and it was clear that, with the support of the other 'big man',
Mr. Haughey, he would dominate the Northern Committee,
and also other Ministers—like the Minister for Defence, a
small man in the Fianna Fail hierarchy. Mr. Lynch let this
go. By doing so he reassured those who favoured a war of
liberation while at the same time, by his speeches at Tralee
and elsewhere, he was reassuring those who feared and
rejected the idea of such a war.

Mr. Lynch's greatest gift as a politician is a capacity to
reassure simultaneously two sets of people who could not

possibly both be reassured if they were both in possession of the same sets of facts.

The period from August 1969 to April 1970 saw, in a sense, the end of the border. That is, it marked the end of the border *in so far as it was a border separating Catholic from Catholic.* The government of the Catholic State had now involved itself actively with the Catholic minority in the Protestant State, in a way that had no precedent since 1922. In its military aspects this involvement was thought of primarily as providing means of defence for 'the people', but with the ultimate and more important consideration that the arming of the people would be the beginning of the liberation of the territory. Money voted by the Dáil for relief in the North was diverted in part to the purchase of arms for 'the defence of our people'.

The logic of the policy pursued in this August-May period pointed towards the resumption of Catholic Ireland's war against Britain and Britain's Protestant settlers in Ireland.

The progress of this logic was interrupted when, on 6th May 1970, Mr. Jack Lynch announced the dismissal of Messrs. Haughey and Blaney because they were reported to be involved in 'an alleged attempt to import arms from the continent'. Mr. Lynch's action came only after the leader of the Opposition, Mr. Liam Cosgrave, had revealed that he was informed of 'the alleged attempt'. Mr. Cosgrave spoke of 'a situation of such gravity for the nation that it is without parallel in this country since the foundation of the state'. The debate which followed Mr. Lynch's announcement was also without parallel: it lasted for thirty-seven and a half hours continuously on Friday and Saturday, the eighth and ninth of May, and ended in a vote of confidence in Mr. Lynch's government. It was a peculiar vote of confidence, because several of those who gave it—and without whom it would not have passed—were people who made no secret of their lack of confidence in Mr. Lynch. They included Messrs. Blaney and Haughey, and two other Ministers, Mícheál O Móráin (Justice) and Kevin Boland (Local Government), who resigned at the same time. Those who fully sympathized with 'the Blaney line'—there were at least a dozen of them in the Fianna Fáil parliamentary party, as well as many more in partial sympathy—considered it expedient to keep the Lynch government in office until such time as Mr. Lynch could be replaced by 'a good Republican' who would, in theory, resume the line in question.

A Prime Minister who rejected the idea of a war of liberation now held office by the votes of men who favoured the idea of such a war. The policy of renewing the struggle was most clearly expressed in the debate by one of the resigned ministers, Mr. Kevin Boland (who later resigned from the Fianna Fáil party, and from his seat in parliament, to found the new party, Aontacht Éireann, referred to above). Mr. Boland said the situation in Northern Ireland today was the same as in the whole of Ireland before 1916. There were two rather clear inferences from this: that it would be right for members of the minority in the North to attempt a new 1916, and that if they did it would be the duty of those who (according to the received doctrine) owed their own freedom to the old 1916 to come to the aid of the Northern lineal successors of the men of 1916.

Mr. Boland's speech, and a more passionate but less explicit one by Mr. Blaney, were applauded by Fianna Fáil Deputies. In my own speech I commented on the implications of these speeches and the applause for them.

DR. CRUISE O'BRIEN: We have just heard Deputy Blaney. He gave a remarkable performance. I am interested in the theatre, and I can find only praise for his performance as a performance. He touched the chords of passion skilfully: he wound up on a skilful and successful appeal to unity and by doing these two things he earned the applause of the majority of the Fianna Fáil Party. It was only the Ministers who sat without clapping their hands as that performance went on. . . .

Deputy Blaney touched the chords of the emotions of an old civil war, the emotions of nearly 50 years ago. . . .

It is rather hard in the circumstances of May, 1970, as we move into one of the most tense and dangerous summers in this island, to forgive someone who rakes up the emotions of an old civil war, in language, in accents which evoke old passions. Deputy Blaney says he knows the north, both Catholics and Protestants. No doubt in a sense he does as far as those can be perceived through his mythology, through his fixations and through the experiences of his youth. If he knows the north all the more shame on him for striking that note now.

Deputy Blaney said: 'I have never advocated the use of force as a means of bringing about the unity of Ireland but I cannot stand idly by while the nationalist people are subjected to murderous assaults.' We can all understand his feelings. We can all share such feelings which are only too easy to realize. What does he mean when he says 'I cannot stand idly by'? He was up there but what was he doing? He was doing something and he is still committed to the further doing of that something. What was it? He was asked from these benches what this was but he did not say. There was a hint that he was doing dangerous and patriotic things but what they might be we do not know. He specified a number of things he said he was not doing.

Deputy Blaney said that Fianna Fáil were not split. He may well be right on that. Nothing was more significant, nothing more ominous, nothing more sinister in this debate than the applause which those dismissed Ministers drew from those benches over there from people who are saying they are loyal to the Taoiseach but who applauded the men he dismissed from his Cabinet. Fianna Fáil may not be split. They may unite around those people. He said also that Fianna Fáil were leading the country in some kind of new advance. I would say this. If Fianna Fáil indeed follow the pattern which Deputy Boland and Deputy Blaney are hinting at, and which their applause proves, it will be an advance of Gadarene swine towards the gulf of civil war they are heading for. I do not believe they are committed to that path. I think they are not quite sure what they are doing themselves and for a long time they have been confused on this issue. Deputy Blaney was not very explicit about what he was doing or what he believed should be done.

Deputy Boland who is a straighter man said what he thought and I believe him. He indicated that he also ruled out the use of force as a means of reunifying the country. That has become something of a formula and something of a code language which covers something else. It is only from Deputy Boland's speech here this morning that we find out a little of what that something else is.

What is the policy which has been hinted at and which I fear has been practised? He indicated that he was opposed to illegal organizations of a military character in the 26 Counties—I suppose at this stage we should be grateful to have that assurance at least from an ex-Minister of State. I understood the Deputy to say that as regards such organizations in Northern Ireland he was not specifically approving them nor would he condemn them. They would have to make up their own minds about what they would do. He seemed to indicate a preference for their using weapons defensively only, but he would not condemn them if they took other decisions.

Deputy Blaney implied the same thing. Deputy Boland put them in exactly the same position as the rest of the country prior to 1916. That has certain implications. It has the implication that a rising, even if unsuccessful, would be justified. That is only a part of his thoughts because he also said that arms importation into the north should not be illegal; in other words, if guns were to be run across the Border from here over that famous land frontier the Government here, the police and military should look the other way even if they did not actually lend a helping hand. That is what I understood the Deputy to say in the speech that was applauded by so many gentlemen over there.

These speeches are made not in a vacuum; they have already been heard in Northern Ireland. There they fall on attentive and fanatical ears and they will raise tension which is already extremely dangerous. They may even be responsible for actual loss of life—that is not impossible. I was in Belfast last weekend. Already then the tension in that city and in other centres which I visited—and I go there openly—was very marked. When I went again last night to speak on Ulster television the atmosphere which previously had been tense and ominous, had become electric. I have never seen so many frightened people in so short a time. Deputy Garret Fitzgerald who was with me will bear that out. In the television studio we saw the tension and alarm of the producers and the controllers; we heard hostile telephone calls; we saw a little, rather pathetic, Paisleyite mob in the street, including small children whose faces were contorted with hatred and fear. The hatred and fear are being carried along by people like Mr. Paisley in the North and Deputy Boland and Deputy Blaney here—the Deputies who still sit on the benches in this House as honoured members of the Fianna Fáil Party.

The terrible thing is that a vicious circle is involved. Those who rouse up passion, the Paisleys or the Blaneys, play into each other's hands and they confirm one another's prophecies of woe. Deputy Blaney tells us that violence is not far away in the Six Counties. His speech brings it nearer and he must know that since he knows the north. . . . It is terrible also that people whose political future now depends on an upsurge of emotion to which they have appealed here, have the power of provoking such an upsurge by their words in the north and by the further impact of events in the north on the 26 counties . . .

I appeal to the Taoiseach in this crisis to think in those terms, to think of this island in danger of drifting towards the verge of civil war through the words and actions of members of his party. I appeal to him to act firmly and to repudiate these men, to withdraw from them the Fianna Fáil Whip, to turn them from his party as he has turned them from his Government. Only then will his frequently wise and prudent language on this subject ever again carry any crediblity. After what we have seen and heard I doubt if the Taoiseach will do this—I doubt whether he is any longer able to do it. I fear he may have become the prisoner of these men. Fianna Fáil are a sick party—

MR. J. LENEHAN: We will get in again.

DR. CRUISE O'BRIEN: The party is sick with a dangerous and infectious sickness. It is incubating the germs of a possible future civil war.

# 10

# A Summer Diary

*'If the Mallam[1] falls in the water, do not ask him whether his clothes got wet.'*

GHANAIAN PROVERB

During the months of June, July and August 1970 I kept a political diary, much of it concerned with the interaction between the Northern crisis and the political situation in the Republic. During the early part of that summer, political people in the Republic were concerned less with the developing situation in the North—which was vaguely felt to be perhaps settling down—than with the repercussions of the crisis of the previous year:

*3 June, Dublin:* Radio news from North: Troops gas rioting Prots. in Palmer St., Catholics chased out of Fleet St., 11 arrests, soldier and policeman injured. All arising from transfer of an Orange banner. Prelude to July. Meetings at Leinster House, Fianna Fáil meet on the leadership crisis.

Rumours of dissolution, in parliamentary sense. Other senses too possibly present. A very beautiful day the first of summer. Sport of spotting which F.F. deputies are speaking to which. My friend Eugene[2] at the rebels' table by the hat-rack (in the Dáil restaurant).[3] An unlikely rebel. In the chamber the debate is about horses, Deputies worrying about constituency organizations, possible rivals. The split, or crack, in Fianna Fáil is the

[1] Moslem holy man.
[2] Eugene Timmons, T.D., Charles Haughey's running mate and elected to the fourth and last seat in Dublin North-East.
[3] The 'rebels' here are those Fianna Fáil T.D.s who sympathized with the Provisional I.R.A. Some of these—first Kevin Boland and later Paudge Brennan and Seán Sherwin—left the party or were pushed. Others, including Mr. Haughey and Mr. Timmons, remain in the party at the time of writing. Neil Blaney remained for a time a member of the party, but was later expelled from it. Unlike Mr. Boland he retained his seat in parliament.

topic of serious men, not the Northern situation which caused the split or crack. The North was last year.

*4 June, Dublin*
Radio news: Tear-gas in the Crumlin Rd. One man wounded. Curfew.

Brendan Halligan[4] rings to say meeting I was to address at Kilkeel, Co. Down tonight has been cancelled, as an Orange parade has been announced for the same night. (Kilkeel is a Protestant island surrounded by a Catholic rural area. Kilkeel Protestants are something special. One Catholic informant, at Warrenpoint, described them to me as 'iron men'. The idea of holding the 'Unity' (anti-Unionist) meeting at Kilkeel was to make the point that the Unity candidature was non-sectarian. In the event the iron men prevailed.)

Meeting of Labour Party. Coalition question. Operation Houdini.[5]

Fianna Fáil meeting ends by withdrawing whip from Kevin Boland—60 to 11 with one abstention. The vote means that, in any crisis in the North, the Government either has to satisfy the militant wing, or rely on the Opposition for temporary survival, or fall. In such conditions what it would be likely to do is:

1. Make 'cannot stand idly by' speeches and gestures
2. Stand idly by
3. Fall

Followed by a General Election in the worst possible circumstances. And the militants have the power to precipitate the situation from which they would benefit.

Topic of conversation among Deputies. What constituency is Seán Horan[6] going to run in? Much laughter, some of it nervous. Nervousness inspired by condition of local constituency organizations, Seán Horanism etc. North seems far away, and tends to shrink to the dimensions of a factor in calculations about how long Jack Lynch will last, which in turn is a factor in calculations about whether 'X' will be a parliamentary Secretary. Deputies divisible into two classes:

1. Those who believe that anyone who is interested in the North ought to have his head examined.
2. Those who ought to have their heads examined.

---

[4] Secretary of the Labour Party.
[5] The party was at this time engaged in trying to extricate itself—as it later succeeded in doing—from an earlier commitment never to form a coalition government with the other opposition party, Fine Gael. This commitment had meant that the country had no alternative to Fianna Fáil government.
[6] Substituted name for a trade Union leader, believed to have wide popular appeal. Potentially dangerous to any Dublin Deputy.

Eugene came out of the F.F. meeting looking slightly more non-existent than before. He has been in the habit of being elected on Charlie Haughey's surplus transferable vote under P.R. But will Charlie have a surplus next time? Will Charlie be running? Will Charlie even be at large? And what is a man to do—a small, quiet man, a little on the mean side—when his local boss is defying his national boss, when the local party organization backs the local boss, and the country backs the national boss?

When the Bogside barricades went up last August, no one imagined Eugene would be among the victims. Yet he is. Not a martyr in the North, or for the North, but a martyr *to* the North.

O. Wilde put Eugene's predicament in a nutshell:
*These Christs that die upon the barricades*
*God knows that I am with them in some things.*

*6th June:*
To Armagh and Newry with Fedelma and Nicholas.[7] Armagh, the Palace, vast Palladian, servantless, black and grey in the sun. Wide lawns and rhododendrons in bloom. Canon Elliott. On Paisley: 'When he went around on his two feet and could pop up anywhere he was a great force. But now he has a seat in parliament, and he has that big, new Church in the Ravenhill Road[8] with a mortgage on it. He has become institutionalized, like ourselves.'

Later that day, I attended the inaugural meeting of the Movement for Peace, at Newry:

Father Patrick Murphy: 'Round where I live, news that people were meeting Southerners to talk about peace could be the signal for more fighting.' Brian Garrett: 'better not have one Assembly. Better have a Northern Committee and a Southern Committee.' Tom Conaty objects to the phrase 'sectarian hate' in a draft: 'It's fear and suspicion, and then suddenly violence. Hate doesn't come into it.' Perhaps. I remember the faces of those small boys outside our car, after Paisley walked out on the T.V. panel. If that

[7] My daughter Fedelma and her husband Nicholas Simms. Nicholas' father, Dr. George Simms, is Church of Ireland Archbishop of Armagh. The object of our journey, in which we were successful, was to obtain Church of Ireland support for an association called the Movement for Peace in Ireland, bringing together Catholics and Protestants concerned with checking the drift towards sectarian civil war. Canon Eric Elliott, quoted here, became an active member of this movement.
[8] The Martyrs' Memorial Church. I attended a service in this in the summer of 1969, and was impressed by Mr. Paisley's pastoral efficiency, and by the docility and respectability of his flock.

expression wasn't hate, what was it? Rage? More settled. I think it was hate, and the pleasure of legitimate hate, the presence of an identifiable enemy.[9]

That night, an election meeting:

To Downpatrick, with Michael O'Leary (Labour Party colleague and friend) speaking for a 'unity' candidate [in the U.K. general election]. Unity = Catholic *alias* anti-Unionist. Athée à Dublin, à Downpatrick Catholique. Atmosphere of polite, 'get it over with' tension. Speaking from a lorry: small knot of 'unity' faithful beside lorry. General audience strung out thinly in front of the shops other side of very wide street. I speak on anti-Unionist lines. Two young men in hippy clothes walk slowly, diagonally across the street in front of the lorry. Smiles, fading. Protestants passing a Catholic meeting. M. speaks on need for Catholics and Protestants to come together. Think he may have misunderstood the technical term 'unity'. All remarks greeted with the same thin rattle of applause from the sparse, stolid people. The meeting will have no effect on the way they will vote, which was determined before their birth. But they obviously approve of there being a meeting. The way it 'spozed to be. Home via M. Hayes's,[10] house at Strangford. Mrs. Hayes's manner reminds me of someone, somewhere. I cannot at first place it. Then I remember: Mrs. Kenneth Dike, in the Vice-Chancellor's Lodge at Ibadan, (Nigeria) in 1965.[11] Tension under hospitality. Relief at talking to the stranger, the man from outside the tribal situation. Also bafflement at the impossibility of conveying the realities of the situation to the outsider. But here there are the British troops. Without them, civil war, including sectarian mass murder, would be certain. And *with* them, what? The homeward drive, gossip, an argument about the Mayor of Limerick. Whiskey at dawn, to bed at 5 a.m.

*7th June:*
'Clinic' in Howth. Election prospects. Seán Horan, etc.
  Coming home, Máire tells me of Owen's death.

[9] Father Murphy and Mr. Conaty were representing the Belfast Central Citizens Defence Committee (Catholic). Brian Garrett represented the Northern Ireland Labour Party. The incident involving Paisley had occurred the previous month. Paisley objected to the presence of four Catholics on the panel. His parting cry 'four to one' caused a small, hostile crowd to gather outside the studio.
[10] Mr. Maurice Hayes, a Catholic moderate. The Director of the N.I. Community Relations Board. Resigned February 1972.
[11] An Ibo household, in non-Ibo territory, on the eve of the Nigerian civil war, of which Ibos were the principal victims.

Owen Sheehy-Skeffington, my first cousin by blood, had·
been in practice an older brother to me. As Senator for
Trinity College he had long been the most consistent and
outspoken stripper-down of the many hypocrisies of the
Catholic State. Also, despite his mother's Republican associations, he had been an open enemy to what he called the
'crazy militarism' of the I.R.A. Owen's influence on my own
thinking had always been strong: it seems if anything to have
increased after his death.

*13 June:*
Lunch with Dermot Ryan, a 'peace-minded' member of the
Fianna Fáil national executive. Dermot has had kerosene bombs
(!) used against his house. He says that the Blaneyites who proposed his removal from the F.F. national executive said it would
be better for his health for him to go—the attacks on his house
must be bad for him . . .

*14th June:*
Peace meeting in Belfast.
    Brendan Harkin (Trade Union leader, Catholic, well-informed)
optimistic. Not even Provisionals, he says, want a clash with
British troops. A dusty Belfast summer Sunday. 'Kunmasi omin-
ously quiet'—*Daily Telegraph.*

*15th June:*
While our 'peace' group of six met in Belfast, over twenty bus-
loads of people from Belfast met at Bodenstown.[12] Contingent led
by John Kelly, Belfast Citizens Defence Committee, now facing
trial. Provisionals addressed by Daithi O'Conaill (six bullet
wounds in Tyrone, November 1959). Recalls August when 'the
British (*sic*) forces were driven from Bogside'. Rebuilding the I.R.A.
Some of this 'will not be displayed at Bodenstown, but will find
expression in the only way that matters from now on'. To Britain
this man said: 'You set your troops to keep what you call the
peace. You forgot that peace must be based on justice: it cannot
be imposed on (*sic*) by British bayonets. The more your troops
impose their will, the nearer you bring the day of open and direct
confrontation.'
    How near? And where is the truth, between this and Brendan
Harkin's reassuring version?
    Also invited 'the Protestants of the North' to come into the
politics of the twentieth century. The appeal being launched

[12] The grave of the founder of Republicanism, Theobald Wolfe Tone.

from Wolfe Tone's grave. The cultists of 1798 appealing to the cultists of 1690 to forget the past.

To us he says—touching on the Congo in passing:—'You can no longer contain the spirit which arose from the ashes of Bombay St.' Contain it from doing exactly what?

*16th June:*
Special meeting (of local Labour Party branch) on the North. Ten-point outline. Speakers mainly interested in coalition—against same. Point of Principle. Utterances on North divided into:

    (a) Indifferent or 'sick and tired' of the subject.
    (b) Willing to use force, either for 'defence' (i.e. of Catholics) or 'in the last resort' for 'unifying the country'.
    (c) Both more or less indifferent and more or less willing to use force. Very abstract kind of force.

How much a matter of self respect, Republican sentiment, etc.? Simple posturing in some cases? Educational conditioning? Tradition. 'Connolly was right, therefore 1916 was right, therefore force is right.' No sense of crisis, North or South. Absolute assumption in all speeches that the democratic process will continue, and that (e.g.) the Labour Party can force the other parties to coalesce and then, in opposition, convert the country to socialism.

Perhaps they are right, at least about democracy being in no danger, perhaps I am alarmist, in thinking I see signs that our hum-drum, stable little democracy may be tilting towards a collapse.

Threats to my father-in-law's person (the gun) and house (fire) for having proposed Kevin Boland's removal from the Joint Secretaryship of F.F.

*18th–19th June:*
British General Election results. Take part in television marathon. Two I.R.A.'s represented on panel—Tom Mitchell (official) and Ruairí O Brádeigh (provisional) appeared on good terms: no sparring. First contact with a 'provisional', rather disconcerting. A very gentle, quiet, good-humoured man, who seemed more interested in preventing violence than on starting it. Paisley on television, singing a hymn, untunefully, after winning N. Antrim. The official Unionist John Taylor referred to Paisley as 'Paisley' until the returns came in and then started calling him Dr. Paisley.

*20th June:*
Peace Assembly meeting at Newry. Discussion of draft. The word 'moderate' is out, reminding people of O'Neill and of defeat. A

Methodist tries to get in the word 'justice'. A Catholic objects. N. comments that those who are closest to the poorest people are the most interested just in peace(rather than in a just peace) not the other way round as you might expect. Contrast between a Quaker at one of these meetings and my friend the provisional. The Quaker who devoted his life to peace had thought himself, through the concept of a 'true peace', into something like a 'peace means war' position. The provisional, presumably dedicated to the organization of eventual violence, put so much stress on the *eventual*, that he seemed like a 'war means peace' man.

*21st June:*
Bodenstown again. This time the Fianna Fáil people and—separately—the official I.R.A. Women call Jack Lynch 'Judas',etc. Cheers for Kevin Boland. The F.F. speaker alleged that: 'We are applicants with Britain for membership of the E.E.C. and alongside which (*sic*) the moving story of Tone's search for help from France to attempt to break off the connection with England may yet turn out to be an extraordinary parallel.'

Wolfe Tone would certainly have found it extraordinary.

The I.R.A. speaker said: 'We welcome arms in the hands of Irishmen, not for use against the Protestant workers in the North but for use against the British army of occupation'.

If this is really the difference between the 'officials' and the 'provisionals' then the officials are the more dangerous of the two (dangerous to 'their own side' that is).

*26th June:*
Talk with Jack Dowling (communicator, philosopher, ex-Army officer, close student of North). News of Bernadette's arrest in evening paper. J.D. doesn't believe this will trigger off major crisis.

*27th June:*
Forenoon: telephone call from Father Murphy. Can't come for peace meeting. 'Worst night since August.' Orange procession followed 'traditional' (i.e. provocative) route. Security committee had re-routed earlier procession: refused to re-route this one. British election?[13] Father Murphy thought maybe yes. Morning papers have headlines 'North erupts'. Premature. Stone-throwing in Derry against riot-shielded troops. Shooting in Belfast. Three dead. Peace meeting at Gresham (minus Father Murphy and

[13] The suggestion here is that the new Tory Government was initially less sensitive to Catholic susceptibilities, and more amenable to Unionist pressure, than the Labour Government had been. I believe this has has been a factor in the serious deterioration which set in at the end of June. But the Haughey-Blaney revelations in Dublin were also a factor.

Tom Conaty). Agreement on text. Evening of phone-calls towards a statement by Corish. Appeals to Labour Party and to Maudling. Group of T.D.'s to go North. Statement denounces provocative circumstances and timing of (Bernadette Devlin's) arrest. But warns against dangers of any word or deed leading to further escalation. Got statement on 10 o'clock news.

But if the escalation gets going, don't our own words and deeds become part of it? Or are they already part of it? Are we not participants in the reflex activity of our tribe?

*28th June:*
To Belfast, Enterprise, with Jack Dowling and John O'Connell (Labour colleague). Check on identities of *younger* men on train. Met at station by J.D.'s brother[14] and a friend of his from Newry. Both panting with excitement. Men of about thirty. 'We don't know where we're going or what we're doing.' 'We must have revolution—it can't go on like this.' They describe how frightened the *Newry* people are. Newry: If Catholics in a majority of 80 per cent are frightened.... Driving along Royal Avenue by the burnt big shops, one praises the official I.R.A. policy of burning out British-owned businesses. The other prefers the idea of burning out little shops owned by Orangemen. J.O'C. opens his eyes and his mouth.

Gerry Fitt's[15] house. The curtains of the living room partly drawn. A big, iron grid on the basement window—new since I was here last August. Coils of barbed wire in the back garden and along the garden wall—also new. Two British armoured cars across the road—not for G.F. but because Antrim Road is potential trouble spot. British regimental headquarters. British colonel comes in briefly and talks to G.F. Asks J.D. to act as intermediary in 'cooling' situation, becoming tense in Ballymurphy. J.D. leaves on this mission, driven by his brother, and accompanied by the other revolutionary.

At this particular period, both wings of the I.R.A. wished to avoid immediate outbreaks of major violence. Dowling wanted to avoid *all* violence, wherever possible. His contacts, as a journalist and ex-officer, with the British Army and with some of the I.R.A., made him available as an intermediary.

G.F., cheerful enough, talks a blue streak. Mainly a Fittocentric history[17] of the past few years. Breaks off frequently to listen to R.E. on which a speech from G.F. is due. Says Bernadette's arrest made

---

[14] Samuel Dowling.
[15] Now the leader of the Social Democratic and Labour Party. One of the most astute, courageous and unbloodyminded personalities in Northern politics.
[16] The period for which this was true was just then coming to an end.
[17] In the same way as this 'history' is Cruisocentric; no reproach is intended.

no impact on situation in Belfast, trouble entirely due to re-routing of parades, passing buildings burnt out last summer by Protestants. Suspect this reaction due to B.D.'s status as *primissima donna*: later, however, find this suspicion unjustified. Catholic Belfast not particularly interested in B.D. A wee girl from west of the Bann. Her arrest had more impact in Dublin and London than in Belfast, which is entirely taken up with its own troubles. (Derry quite different, of course.)

*Mrs.* G.F. complains about the soldiers. There was a woman who had to have a caesarean and the soldiers wouldn't let her through the lines, or almost wouldn't let her through, or anyway she had to ask permission and it was a disgrace. Gerry says nonsense. Agrees there is something wrong though. When there is trouble between Catholics and Protestants the police face the Protestants, the Army the Catholics.

(But this a natural arrangement, since the Protestants trust the police and the Catholics don't. The trouble is the Catholics don't like the Army either. Just prefer them to the police.)

To St. Peter's Church. Father Murphy, another priest, Tom Conaty. They are getting out a press release on behalf of the C.C.D.C. I incorrectly identify this as *Catholic* Citizens Defence Committee (which of course is what it really is). Father M. corrects me: *Central* Citizens etc.: 'We don't use the word Catholic.' The press release stresses the Government's responsibility for the troubles. Discussed some account of what happened at St. Matthew's Church in the Newtownards Road—a Catholic enclave in Protestant E. Belfast. The Protestants had tried to burn the Church. The British Army had been asked to guard it but couldn't or wouldn't get round to it in time. So the I.R.A. decided to defend it. In the process two of the attackers had been shot dead. Father M.'s assistant had seen the bodies. There was no doubt they were dead. One had the back of his head blown off. The priest reporting shows no signs of emotion. Perhaps he is an unemotional man. Perhaps it is just that priests are used to death. And perhaps.

Father M. looks rueful, and also sad. It is terrible, he says. Do I imagine it or is there an inflexion in his voice that means: 'even if they are Protestants'?[18]

Is it possible, in Belfast, for even the best men to avoid that inflexion in speaking of 'them' and 'us'?

No one seems to question the assumption that it is better to shoot men dead than allow a Church to be burned.[19] In fact so firm and general was the assumption that I didn't see it until afterwards.

[18] In retrospect I think this reflection unjust. His tone meant 'even if they were violent fanatics out to lynch Papists'—a different thing.
[19] But see below, p. 231.

Paddy Devlin[20] is there, warns me against being 'too moderate'. Our people need the guns. Our people.

Father M.'s office at St. Peter's is a sort of command post. He had been up all night in constant touch by telephone with the British command. Keeping the peace yes. Also defending St. Matthew's. *Did he ask the 'provisionals' to guard it?*

The 'score' is hard to estimate. Generally agreed that it is more than the official estimate. 'They' conceal their casualties if they can. So do 'we' I imagine. So did both sides in Elisabethville. It seems probable (to those present) that six Protestants were killed, and only one Catholic. What form will the reprisals take? And is there sober satisfaction in the air? A feeling that 'we' are coming up off our knees.

To Father Des Wilson's J.D. Two other priests there with Father W. I know the father of one of them—the editor of the *Irish News*. He teaches in the new University at Coleraine and the Bishop is trying to force him to resign. These are the left wing of the clergy, Civil Rights minded, disliking the Wars of Religion. They didn't know about the defence of St. Matthew's

Check in at the *Elsinore*, opposite G.F.'s. Owned and staffed by 'our own' of course. Beer and sandwiches with J.D. 'It is the Catholics who have the initiative now,' he says. 'It is the Protestants who are afraid.'

At G.F.'s again. He has a radio turned to the police communications. Reported trouble nearby on the Antrim Road. J.D. and I go to the point indicated: if there was ever trouble there, it is over. A knot of people on the corner. An army jeep. Everybody apparently bored. A shower of rain. Back to G.F.'s. Trouble in the Newtownards Road. St Matthew's again. Back to the Hotel. They get us a taxi. The hotel being what it is, the taximan's theology is predictable. He takes us across the river to E. Belfast. Army lines. 'Press' says J.D. and they let us both through.

St. Matthew's—brown Belfast Gothic, big tower and steeple. A pillar gone from the gate—knocked down by an armoured car, reversing after a petrol bomb had been thrown at it. A woman had been pinned under it, and had to stay there while Catholics and Protestants shot it out She is now in hospital, critical.

Now there is an armoured car in the grounds. Three more armoured cars in line across the road, block it, protecting the Church. A small party of soldiers, several journalists, some of whom recognize me.

Beyond the armoured cars the Newtownards Road stretches up the hill. The crown of the hill is perhaps three-quarters of a mile away. On the part of the road that is nearest us the street lights

---

[20] S.D.L.P., M.P. for Falls Road: a brave, generous, resourceful and plain-spoken man. He put the pertinent question quoted on p. 200.

are out. Visibility is reasonably good; it is about 10.30 p.m. on a midsummer night. A bit beyond the middle distance there is a crowd blocking the road from one side to the other. The crowd stands out darkly because there is a big blaze beyond it. One of the buildings on the left-hand side of the street is burning fiercely, the flames shooting well out into the street. Beyond the fire, up to the top of the hill, the arc lights are on as usual over this arterial road.

J.D. and I start walking up the hill towards the crowd and the fire. The road is littered with rocks, big chunks of paving, fragments of metal and sections of iron grating. The material of a Belfast argument. The first side-streets are silent and empty, with no outward signs. Catholic streets near the frontier. Then a side-street full of Union Jacks with red-white-and-blue bunting strung across. We have entered Protestant territory. Groups of men and women walking along the footpaths in the same direction as ourselves. Little talk.

As we got near the crowd we see they are mostly very young. Some are carrying sticks or clubs: a few have helmets, a few have gas masks. One man has an enormous sledge hammer, as used for breaking up footpaths and thus producing material for argument.

I hope people will not remember my face from T.V. and especially from the time Paisley walked off our panel on U.T.V. A couple of middle-aged working men engage us in friendly conversation: they take us for journalists, and probably English ones. This is the first time, since our arrival in Belfast on this visit, that we have talked with a Protestant.

They love Ulster, they tell us. If people don't love Ulster they ought to get out of it, oughtn't they? We shouldn't mind about the crowd. They were only boys. The big men would come later and we would see something. That morning snipers, firing from the tower of the Chapel, had killed Protestants. Wasn't it a terrible thing that the priests would let the chapel be used for that?

J.D. said that after all, if the U.V.F. had taken over the Protestant church visible further off the hill—what could the Minister do about it? Nothing said one of these men cheerfully. The Unionist Party, said the other, had betrayed the Protestant people. They had disarmed the R.U.C. They had disbanded the Specials. They had done everything they could to leave the people defenceless.

Always the people, threatened by the non-people.

But the Unionist Party was going to be swept out of existence. At the next Stormont elections there would be a Paisley man returned in every constituency. Then the police would be re-armed, and the Specials would be back.

The 'boys' are beginning to push a big delivery van along. It is to be used as a ram, one of our friends explains.

The building that is on fire is Liptons—a British-owned chain-store. Therefore presumed to be an official I.R.A. job. No one is doing anything about the fire. The fire brigade, having been pelted with rocks, and occasionally shot at, in the early hours of the morning, are not coming out at all tonight. Between them the two (or three) I.R.A.s and the U.V.F. could burn down the whole city.

The crowd shows symptoms of wanting to move off, to storm the barricades. We move off ahead of them at a brisk walk. Not many people in the 'in between' area now. We reach the British lines, pass through them and stand behind the armoured cars. Pleasant sense of security. Reasonably clear that that crowd will not get past this block. St. Matthew's will not burn tonight.

The crowd begins to advance down the street, pushing its ram. Someone in it lights a green flare: someone else a firework. A few people start a song but it doesn't catch on. The crowd are fairly close now, but the light is bad (midnight) and we can't distinguish individuals. The soldiers begin to fire tear-gas canisters. The smoke covers the crowd almost completely. They break and struggle back up the hill. Their 'ram' runs on, though, reaches the line of armoured cars, then runs up the foot-path, and sticks beside the left armoured car. The lieutenant ('you know what the Irish are like') tells us to take cover in a side street. 'This bit may be dangerous.' When we re-emerge the ram has been extricated and is behind the British line. The crowd are re-forming near the top of the hill. They may try again, but their enterprise is hopeless tonight. St. Matthew's is safe. Our taxi takes us back to the *Elsinore*.

*30th June:* Reading my father-in-law's letter.[21] I am a little ashamed. He is of the tribe, a Belfast Catholic born, but his reaction was more generous, less tribal, than mine.

*1st July:* In the Dáil the Taoiseach refuses a debate on the issue. Could 'exacerbate' the situation. What it might exacerbate would be another crack in his own party.

*2nd July:* Morning. Harassing the T. on the debate. If the Government are not fit to face a debate on the North, they are not fit to govern the country.

Haughey, etc., returned for trial: information refused in the case of Blaney. Blow to the Lynch camp.

Lunch in National Gallery with Ruairí O'Brádaigh. An affable Irregular, strongly rather than heavily built. Refuses wine.

[21] Letter from Seán MacEntee, condemning the use of lethal force in the defence of St. Matthew's.

Pleasant open face. Smiles a lot. Too much? Believed to be the leader of the provisionals.[22] Angry at assertions his organization promotes sectarian violence. They are concerned with *defence*. Their split with the I.R.A. was not the result of Blaney intrigue, but of rank and file exasperation with I.R.A. executives for unpreparedness last summer and for unrealistic policies such as alliance with Communist Party. Has no use for Blaney, or for men like Seamus Brady.[23] Opposes sectarianism, and specifically deplored Blaneyite efforts to end Orange processions in Donegal. Admits his rank-and-file are not so ecumenical; there is 'a fever' among the people. But his organization is not trying to ferment violence; they are trying to control it, so that when it occurs it will not be wholly useless. Himself volunteers the thought that the distinction between 'controlling' and 'fomenting' is a difficult one. If you don't do some fomenting you soon won't be in a position to control. In the St. Matthew's fighting the defence was improvised by some of the Defence Committee, and by 'some of our people'. On both sides, deaths of fighters will be presented as civilian casualties; a question of compensation. I ask him about the burning of the big stores. Is that an official I.R.A. line? He smiles. 'I think that is something that would be more associated with our people.' No real *rapprochement* between 'officials' and provisionals, he says. Some co-operation in local emergencies. I ask him about contacts in Belfast and Derry. He readily gives me names for Derry: Keenan, O'Conaill: Doherty's telephone number. For Belfast he gives me no names; his face clouds over. Earlier he had agreed in deploring John Kelly's[24] sectarian press release (per the odious Brady). It looks as if the Belfast provisionals are less under his control than the Derry ones. He asks me some questions about the Congo, parallels, etc. Also: a discussion of rumours (enemy lorries approaching from Ballymena or Angola or whatever) R.Ó.B. says he thinks these issue instinctively as a means of maximum rallying of the defending group. We part outside the Merrion Square entrance of Leinster House. 'Take care' I tell him. 'Oh I will,' says he.

*3rd July:* Maudling blames trouble on organized groups aiming at anarchy and the destruction of the State. *Irish Press* editorial compares people of N.I. to a huge animal teetering about. Assumes the trouble will lead—though painfully—to unification of country and urges all hands to be decent to acquired Orangemen. Also speaks of 'antics of parliamentarians'. Someone blew up an Army

[22] In fact the leader of the Provisional Sinn Féin (Kevin Street)—the more-or-less open political aspect of the Provisional movement.
[23] Editor of *The Voice of the North*.
[24] Prominent Belfast provisional, co-defendant in the Haughey arms trial.

recruiting centre in Belfast: someone else planted a bomb at Unionist headquarters in Glengall Street (removed): someone else bombed a Catholic school.

Correspondence columns taking on increasingly open sectarian tone. Terms Catholic and Protestant being used more often, and less apologetically. John Kelly implies that if the Protestants had not been shot at St. Matthew's, some nearby nuns might have met a fate worse than death, or anyway heard some bad language.

Catholic fear, pride, hope. Protestant fear, humiliation, resentment. The decisive shift in the new relations of the two groups. The incidents—all of which could have happened before—take on a new resonance and significance from the changed relation of the groups: a change very propitious to I.R.A. 'provos'.

*5th July:* To Belfast for peace meeting with Michael O'Leary: two American students—Boston Catholics—along for the ride. Just before Newry we stop. Long queue of cars. Road-block search. New experience on this road. Last August and since (in my experience) road traffic outside the cities unaffected by crisis. Michael remembers he has copies of *An Phloblacht*[25] in the car. Search for these while car-queue inches on. Finally some copies are found in and under the fantastic litter of papers behind the rear seat. What to do with them? M. opens the door and drops them out on the road. We hope driver of car behind not busy-body, or at any rate not Protestant busy-body. Search of car moderately thorough, not interested in papers. Sergeant says trouble not serious, all instigated from outside.

Or above. Or below. . .

A drive round Belfast in the summer evening. Several searches, more thorough than on the road. Soldiers mostly polite but tense: some just tense. Three youths, face to the wall hands up against the wall, legs apart being searched by soldiers. Cyprus. Aden. Elisabethville. Curfew in the Lower Falls. No one in or out, except on special military permission.

To G.F.'s house. A visitor, a big, elderly man, calm, shrewd, bitter, talks about the shipyards. Would like to see them go altogether. A Protestant preserve, heavily subsidized: craft unions, all Protestant preserves. Boilermakers. Sneers at praise for shop-stewards' efforts for peace last summer. Just did it for their own jobs and their own people, for fear of losing orders. The struggle is not a religious one. The terms used should not be Catholics and Protestants but settlers and natives. 'The people who are oppressing us are the settlers with the British behind them.' Sneers at Southern sentimentality about Northern Protestants. 'They see the name McCracken over a shop and they think

---

[25] The Provisional paper.

of Henry Joy and 1798. Has nobody told them that's all over?'

*6th July:* To Falls Road: 'curfew' lifted.[26] People going to Mass. Shock and hysteria. Women report, incoherently, atrocious behaviour of troops. We are shown a house where an old woman lived alone, which was searched in her absence by troops. Very small, very dirty room, with things flung around on the floor: nothing broken. Portrait of Joe Devlin on the wall, and a picture of an elderly couple with the lettered words: 'Till death did us part'.

We are brought to another house. There are soldiers near the door. The woman will not let us in. The soldiers move away. A neighbour tells the woman it is her duty to show us the damage. She shows us the damage done to her front door, a broken lock. We have a glimpse of her parlour, crowded with fragile knick-knacks and holy statues: did the soldiers knock nothing down or did the woman set them all up again? She does not like us looking, shoves us out the door again. Patriotic protests from the neighbour.

12 o'clock Mass at St. Peter's, Falls Road. Father P.M. preaches. Natural right to self-defence. Troops proved incapable of defending our people. Example: heroic defenders of St. Matthew's. Concluding appeal for calm and restraint. No hint that right of self-defence might be abused. No word at which any provisional might jib.[27]

Coffee with Father M. in his office after Mass. Says he was edified to see me in his congregation. I tell him I have sat in Paisley's congregation too. Sharp look. I ask him: 'do you think it right to shoot to kill in order to stop people from burning down a Church?' He answers calmly: 'No, I don't. That would not be right. But this was an attack against a community, their homes and their lives. The Church grounds were used in the defence of the people. If the defenders had been more experienced they might have been able to beat off the attackers without loss of life. But they were justified in what they did, as you would be justified in killing a robber, if you believed that only in that way could you ensure the safety of yourself and your family against this attack.'

Afterwards out in the Falls Road itself a small crowd gathers round us. One or two men are angry, almost hysterical, as well as the women. 'What is the Dublin Government doing?' 'What are

[26] This was the morning after the first big arms-search in the Falls Road.
[27] This is an accurate account of this particular sermon. But Father Murphy has been courageously outspoken and unequivocal in his condemnation of the aggressive I.R.A. violence which set in afterwards. He is probably a better judge than I might be of the right moment to start condemning.

*you* doing? Isn't this our country? Aren't you our government?'
A youngish man, tall, unshaven gets out of a car and asks whether
it's true we are against Haughey and Blaney. I tell him yes, and
try to say why. He starts shouting 'You stabbed them in the back'.
Crowd beginning to gather. Uncertain as to where all this is
going. A priest comes up and says the Army doesn't want crowds
gathering, and to break it up. We do.

Above, from a helicopter, an upper-class English voice makes
incomprehensible announcements about the so-called curfew.

Back via Armagh. Sherry at the Palace. Portraits (King
William III). The younger American asks where is the portrait of
James II. Laughter.

Six days later I had a look at the Orange procession from
Belfast to Finaghy, which I had watched before in the quieter
atmosphere of 1968:

*12th July:* The walk to Finaghy. More people along the footpaths
than in 1968, and more serious. Music subdued within the inner
city. 'Ye'd think there was no band at all.' Louder on the Lisburn
Road. General air of stolid satisfaction. Had they really feared that
this march might have been cancelled too, and the world ended?
A few people recognize me; not unfriendly. 'Are ye takin' a look?'
Straw-hats with Union Jacks, 'We are British.' No 'Fuck the
Pope' this year, and only the traditional and printable songs.
Girls snake-dancing, wearing Union Jacks, and automatically
picking up nice Protestant boys, in an atmosphere of parental
approval. The breeze bulges the big banners: temperance, ship-
wrights, temperance, dockers, The Secret of England's Greatness,
the Crimson Banner, the Breaking of the Boom, one of George VI
—a modern note—and William, William, William. A bus full of
old ladies, each clutching a Union Jack. A hippie with a Union
Jack. A group dressed exclusively in Union Jacks. The bands
grow louder, drums beat harder as we go on up the Lisburn Road.
A lot of the marchers are clearly not 'regulars'—young men,
bareheaded, in ordinary clothes.

Near the ground there is a narrow bridge crossing the railway
line, just wide enough for the marchers. We join the march, in
step. No objections.

The Field very cinematic. Columns of marchers with banners
continuing to arrive; groups of picnickers on the grass; a couple
necking; a band of young men playing a provocation game,
singing:

'If ye hate Gerry Fitt, clap yer hands,'
'If ye hate Gerry Fitt, clap yer hands.'

How many people, in the back streets, have clapped their

hands, without hating Gerry Fitt? How many have failed to clap and been beaten? The little song says very much what the whole march says.

Eat a king-sized beefburger—Ulster is British—at a stall, and pay for it in the currency of the Republic. No objection.

We don't wait for the speeches, catch the train at Finaghy station. A number of the marchers do the same. Two middle-aged middle-class men on seats near us, pack their collarettes into attache cases. Very hard to get collarettes this year, one of them remarks. Not exactly the Sash their Fathers wore.

*16th July:*Explosion at Northern Bank, in High Street, Belfast. Thirty-one injured, two seriously. R.T.E.[28] announcer refers to the 'daring and dangerous' action. Would it have been 'daring' if it had been in the Falls Road? Recall J.D.'s remark after Falls Road search that, now that 'defensive' methods have been discredited, the offensive will be resorted to. This kind of offensive? Coventry? Battle of Algiers?

The I.R.A. view that the escalation of violence was a response to British aggression is reflected here. This is a complicated question. It is clear that I.R.A. elements (probably in both sections) before 5th–6th July, did sometimes co-operate with British forces in averting violent clashes (see diary entry for 28th June). It is also clear that both I.R.A.'s foresaw an *eventual* clash with British troops (see diary 'Bodenstown' entries for 15th and 21st June). Since I.R.A. influence was directed towards getting the Catholics to see the troops, with whom they had fraternized earlier, as an army of occupation, it necessarily tended towards increased tension, including minor acts of violence— stone-throwing, etc.—by adolescents anxious for the approval of 'the big men'. Any military reprisals for such actions— beating of stone-throwers—were seen as aggression, and invited further reprisals. But bombs in cabs, offices, department stores and pubs cannot be reasonably seen as reprisals against the army. They are part of an offensive against the Protestant population, which regards the army as its defenders.

*18th July:* The Communist Party magazine *Irish Socialist* for July–August. Piece by James Stewart (!) on the North. Backs T.U.

[28] Irish radio-television.

anti-sectarianism *and* hails victories of the Catholic candidates, Devlin, Fitt and McManus. 'The gain of the Fermanagh-South Tyrone seat by the Unity candidate, Mr Frank McManus demonstrates the correctness of the call by the c.p. of Ireland in the Election manifesto for *Unity* Conventions and a united opposition in the face of Unionism.'

It also demonstrates the correctness of the statistic that there are more Catholic than Protestant voters in Fermanagh-South Tyrone.

Why should the c.p. sew itself into the Unity/Catholic bag? Is this a determination 'not to repeat the mistake', the c.p. made in Algeria when it cut itself off from the Moslem population? All the easier 'not to repeat the mistake' in that British c.p.—which would be damaged by a c.p.–i.r.a. *rapprochement*—is small and perhaps expendable, unlike French c.p.

Predictable that, with the c.p.–i.r.a. line-up the c.i.a. will now be working the Provisionals, with predilection for Haughey/Blaney wing. In order to 'control' what may they 'foment'? From their point of view sectarian incitement would have this to commend it:

(a) There is a real market for it, and one which the c.p.–i.r.a. or Provisional *leadership* are 'inhibited from tapping'.

(b) It is an alternative to the anti-imperialist, anti-British Army line, which could be embarrassing for Anglo-American relations, and Tory Government, etc.

(c) It could be used to break 'the Communist grip' in the t.u. movement.

*20th July:* Fergus Pyle[29] to-day suggests a 'third group' to be responsible for the High Street affair (now disclaimed by both i.r.a. and provisionals). This 'third group' said to be 'anti-Protestant and interested only in fomenting civil disturbance'.

The kind of group a quiet American might well be interested in.

Note: The Provisional hand-out on the High Street affair referred to it as 'dastardly', a decenter description than r.t.e.'s 'daring'.

I have no evidence of c.i.a. involvement, and would not attribute any major significance to such a factor. Since the Communists are to some extent involved, it seems certain that the c.i.a. must also be, and that anti-communist patriots must attract its attention.

*23rd July:* Stormont announces ban on parades, including Apprentice Boys, and re-policing of Falls and Bogside.

[29] In *Irish Times.*

In the evening, aggregate meeting. E.E.C., Coalition. Enthusiasm for alliance with Sinn Féin (against Common Market entry). Can we ally ourselves, for one set of purposes, with people whose principal line of policy we are against in so far as it involves the use of violence? Or can we take it that the official I.R.A., politically represented by S.F., is in practice—as distinct from teleology—opposed to violence, and more effective in its opposition than we are? An attractive argument: dangerous also, in so far as it overlooks the hidden pressures of foment/control. Explosives are likely to be one of S.F./I.R.A. arguments against the Common Market. Are we condoning this if we share platforms with S.F.? Don't think so; in any case if we are going to become effective we'll have to put up with quite an amount of 'appearing to condone' in some shape or form.

I read over the last words above with considerable distaste. But it was not until the following summer that I reached a position of *total* rejection of both Sinn Féins and both I.R.A.s. 1971 of course saw the refutation of the theory that the Official I.R.A., as compared with the Provisionals, was an anti-sectarian factor of restraint.

*8th August:* To Armagh with Tom Flanagan.[30] We expect to hear John Montague[31] read 'The Siege of Derry,[32] outside Armagh Jail. Outside Armagh Jail[33] there is a lot of space, no John Montague, and a man outside a pub solemnly beating a Lambeg drum. Inside the pub, insignia of loyalty, and the sound of the drum, very loud. A Neanderthaler at the bar smiles and says: 'I hope Bernie likes it'.

Outside Armagh stopped by a patrol of Ulster Defence Regiment. Training in how to search: 'Break nothing, put everything back'. In Tanderagee we find a Presbyterian publican with whom we had had friendly talk on the Republican side of the border. Sober, but hospitable, stands us two rounds of pints, refuses a drink himself. We all 'deplore the situation', in carefully balanced and non-sectarian terms. The publican's name is MacDonald. He has a brother with him, young, lean, fair, blue-eyed. MacDonald talks about Coalisland, where the *News-Letter* says the I.R.A. have taken over. He shakes his head; it's very hard to know. He volunteers (to console Papists of the well-meaning sort) that 'there are some hard cases in the Shankill Road'. He is

---

[30] American specialist in Anglo-Irish literature, friend of the writer.
[31] Distinguished Ulster poet, quoted, and possibly read, by Mr. Jack Lynch.
[32] Patriotic poem.
[33] Where Miss Bernadette Devlin was then lodging.

called into the other bar. The brother smiles faintly and says his
brother is 'very interested in Irish history'. The smile hangs in the
air. Then, rapidly, nervously: 'Some very bad mistakes have been
made. Like winding up the Specials. I was in the Specials.' I ask
him did he join the U.D.R.[34] 'I did. As a matter of fact we are
expecting an alert any time now. A lot of the older fellows wouldn't
join though.' A pause, a smile, then: 'Maybe they were afraid
they wouldn't pass the medical.'

*9th August:* With Liam Burke[35] to Casement Social Club in
Andersonstown. Provisionals. Arthur Price on Brendan Behan:
'How could he be a homosexual he wasn't even much interested
in women?' Price's idea: a soldier fighting by any means to get a
united thirty-two county Ireland. Not interested in Protestants
and Catholics. Not a Catholic himself. Wouldn't injure Protestant
as Protestant, but prepared to kill loyalists for the sake of united
Ireland. Some Catholics are loyalists: some Irish Catholics are in
the British Army. All these deserve what is coming to them. 'If a
lodger tells me I can't decorate my own house, I get rid of the
lodger.' Others, including (Paddy) Devlin, uncomfortable at this
line and indicate a very feeble and tentative dissent. Fundamentally, I think they all agree. All object to anti-gun-running position.
Argument amicable. L.B: 'A nephew of mine was arrested, I never
thought he was any good at all.' Atrocities: A British Tommy
deliberately smashing a small picture of P. Pearse (Fenian
Bastard!). Tom remarks afterwards that the educational level of
enlisted men in H.M. Forces must have risen sharply. Group a
little subdued by shock of news of Jimmy Steele's[36] death, but
obviously happy and confident. All expecting U.N. Forces. Not
before the Cossacks and the Holy Ghost.

In street outside women make their complaints to P.D.
Obviously genuine. One woman tells how her son and another
boy were beaten by two British soldiers. One soldier says: 'I think
they've had enough.' The other: 'Your one can still stand up.'

L.B. speaking of Tom Clarke and Jimmy Steele has a catch in
his voice. He tells of efforts to stop the stoning of the troops.
Ascribes it to long-haired kids. Describes seeing kids breaking up
head-stones in the Protestant cemetery to throw them at living
Protestants. Almost worse than the desecration at Bodenstown.
Catch again. When he tells about how much education has
improved, I ask him about the stone-throwers. He explains that
these are the ones who drop out, either through poverty or
stupidity, most often stupidity.

[34] Ulster Defence Regiment.
[35] Belfast Republican, member of Wolfe Tone Club.
[36] Provisional I.R.A. leader, then just deceased.

He says that he was glad when the British troops moved in, but warned his children to have nothing to do with them. They'll be fighting us inside two months.

He calls a taxi. The taxi driver is a very nice fellow. A Protestant. Better not to talk politics. In the taxi, L.B. talks about the Ford Cortina. It is nippy in traffic, he says.

On 12th August, in Derry, I had an experience which seems to have discouraged me from continuing to keep a diary. The following account of this experience was written shortly after it:

The 12th of August is the day on which, in Derry, the brotherhood of the Apprentice Boys, (a Protestant brotherhood) annually commemorates the relief of the city by the Protestant forces in 1689.

I went to Derry as an observer on behalf of the Irish Labour Party. My brother-in-law Seamus McEntee, a psychiatrist who practises in England, was with me. We had to stay outside the town as the few hotels in Derry itself were either taken over by the military or by the representatives of the world press. It had been announced that Derry itself would be closed to visitors on that day except for the Apprentice Boys and others who had legitimate business there. We wondered whether our business would be accepted as legitimate.

Our car was checked about half a mile outside Derry by a member of the Royal Ulster Constabulary (formerly an armed force and now disarmed following the events of August last). I stated my business and he gave us an entry permit which we handed up to a police cordon at the entry to the Craigavon Bridge which spans the wide estuary of the Foyle river and links the rest of Northern Ireland to the Derry area, which geographically is an enclave in the Inishowen peninsula. The rest of Inishowen forms part of Donegal and the Republic of Ireland. The bridge itself, like the rest of the city, was strongly held by the British Army. Cars which had been cleared by the police crossed the bridge without further clearance by the military. We went to the City Hotel where we found the press, including a reporter for the London *Daily Express*, whom I had met nine years before in Elisabethville, Katanga. In the streets Apprentice Boys were walking around in twos and threes or standing at the corners. They were wearing bowler hats and crimson collarettes with the names of the local clubs. They could hardly have been taken for Shriners; they were less natty and less cheerful. Considerably less cheerful, for their annual outing of this year had been spoiled. The point of their celebration had always been a triumphal

parade but this year the Government, under British pressure, had
forbidden the parade, to avoid provoking the Catholics into a
re-enactment of the troubles which the Apprentice Boys' march
set off in August last year. Not only was the parade cancelled but
the pubs were closed, also by Government order. Most of the fun
had been taken out of the celebration, as well as most of the pride
and the pomp.

We began the morning by a walk around the city which was
thick with military and police barriers. Inner Derry is a walled
city; the walls have been piously preserved in memory of 1689.
The walls themselves were now completely held by the military
and the gates between the inner city and the Catholic Bogside were
heavily sealed off by military barricades. It was possible, however,
to get from the inner city to Bogside by a roundabout route. In
Bogside people complained about the inconvenience of the
barriers and the behaviour of the military. Boys came up and
asked for my autograph. In the South, and especially the rural
South, I am often suspected of heresy, but in the North my state
of belonging to the Catholic people is never called in question.
This is not always an advantage, as I was to find later.

We returned to the inner city, where Apprentice Boy dignitaries laid a wreath at the War Memorial. The Derry War Memorial
may well be the most bloody-minded in the world; on one side a
huge sailor seems to be hurling a grenade, on the other a huge
soldier is in the act of driving a bayonet down into an invisible
but clearly prostrate foe. The band played 'God Save the Queen',
soldiers and Apprentice Boys standing to attention. A reminder
that soldiers and Apprentice Boys, whatever ill-feeling may arise
between them, share a common ultimate allegiance, not shared
by the people of Bogside, the majority in this city.

Walking away from the War Memorial, down the steep slope
of Shipquay Street, I met a friendly Royal Ulster Constabulary
superintendent who had read some of my books. He had also
read reports of what I had been saying in the Dáil about the
Northern crisis and approved. 'We'll all be one some day,' he
said, 'but things have got to be given time to settle down a bit.'

Further on down Shipquay Street a burly middle-aged
Apprentice Boy brushed past me asking: 'Were ye ever in the
Congo?' I smiled and he wheeled and came back: 'I wanted ye
to know ye've been spotted. It will be safer for you to leave town.'

At the foot of Shipquay Street I met two friends from Dublin,
Jack Dowling and Lelia Doolin: with them was Michael Canavan,
a prominent Derry Nationalist. Canavan recognized two passing
Apprentice Boys as neighbours. He called them over and they
came. (Relations between Catholic and Protestant neighbours in
Derry and most other parts of Northern Ireland are normally
reasonably good except during the seasonal commemorative

cycle of July and August; some traces of neighbourliness often subsist even in these months.) This being the day it was, the manner of the two young Apprentice Boys was correct but cold and forbidding: 'Correct' with a capital K, as someone has said.

One of them was atypical; he wore a beard and was highly articulate in a staccato way: 'You were very keen on civil rights and freedom to march last year, what about *our* civil rights and *our* freedom to march, why are you not protesting now?' I pointed out that the Derry Labour Party—a local leftist group headed by Eamonn McCann and drawing its support from Bogside—had in fact defended the right of the Apprentice Boys to march, and had condemned the Government ban on the march.

This was brushed aside: 'The Derry Labour Party just want anyone to break the law anywhere, any time, for any reason.' He went on about the lawlessness of the Roman Catholic population. Could even Mr. Canavan claim that he obeyed the law? Mr. Canavan said he did. 'Always?' asked the Apprentice Boy with extreme scepticism.

I asked whether he was suggesting that Catholics were the only people who broke the law in Northern Ireland. He agreed that this would not be true, and then went on to say that separate education of the two communities was the root of the trouble. 'Did we believe in integrated education?' he asked. I said 'yes'. Mr. Canavan said 'yes and no'. The Apprentice Boy said that every attempt at an integrated school in Ulster had been broken up by the Roman Catholic priests. He gave examples. He added: 'You don't want the schools for religion. You want them for political indoctrination.'[37]

In the afternoon there was to be an Apprentice Boy rally at St. Columb's Park on the outskirts of Derry across the Foyle and remote from the Bogside. This was a substitute—a highly unsatisfactory one from an Apprentice Boy point of view—for the usual triumphal parade. It was also an important occasion however as it was to be addressed by William Craig, the hard-lining former Minister for Home Affairs, who was then making a bid, supported by the whole Unionist right, to be the next Prime Minister in Northern Ireland. We decided to attend this rally.

This was not quite so imprudent as it might appear. On 13th July in Belfast I had walked with the great Orange March to Finaghy Field, had been recognized several times and without any unpleasantness, but that had been a happy occasion for the Orangemen: they had held their march with full traditional pomp. The Apprentice Boys on the other hand were forced to use

[37] Many Protestants believe that the Catholic hierarchy's insistence on separate education is a major cause of the trouble. Professor Rose's survey gives little support to this view (see *Governing without Consensus*, chapter XI).

maimed rites. No one minds onlookers for triumphs; humiliations are another matter.

Also bad news was spreading. The two (Royal Ulster Constabulary) men who had been seriously injured the day before by a booby-trapped car in the Northern Ireland village of Crossmaglen were now dead. Their murderers were still unknown but all Protestant Ulster assumed them to be 'the I.R.A.' The fact that the murder had occurred within two miles of the border was regarded as the clinching clue to its 'I.R.A.' origin. It was therefore not the best of days for a Southerner to take a walk in Protestant Ulster. We thought it important, however, not to be restricted to the Catholic ghetto, if we could avoid this.

We arrived late at St. Columb's Park. It was dark and rainy, adding to the misery of the day. I was wearing a heavy raincoat. I bought some literature from a stall at the entrance to the grounds: two sets of prison messages from Dr. Paisley, dating from different periods of incarceration, and a booklet with the title, *The Pope is the Devil*. To keep the booklets from the rain I shoved them inside the front of my white trenchcoat. When we reached the fringe of the crowd of about five thousand, Mr. William Craig was speaking. A sign over his head said simply Welcome. At each side of the covered speakers' stand were Union Jacks and the plain crimson flag which is the emblem of the Derry Siege.

Mr. Craig's theme was law and order. The Government had failed to maintain law and order and had betrayed Ulster by disarming the Royal Ulster Constabulary and disbanding the B. Specials. The R.U.C. must be rearmed—whether they wanted to be rearmed or not—and the Specials reconstituted. There would have to be a new government which would do all this and generally restore order by all means necessary, possibly including 'the use of methods that might make me shudder'.

A young man who had been behind me stumbled against me, stood beside me and asked me what was inside my coat that made it bulge. I told him books. He asked to see the books and I produced them. The book on top was *The Pope is the Devil*. He looked puzzled, relaxed a little, smiled and said: 'Sorry. I thought you might be the reporter for the *Derry Journal*—the local Catholic and Irish Nationalist paper.'

Mr Craig reiterated his point about re-forming the B. Specials. Most of the audience clapped but a good many did not. Ulster Protestants are an undemonstrative breed. The young man who had bumped against me asked me why I didn't clap. I said I didn't clap because I didn't agree with a lot the speaker had said (by this time I had a fair idea that I was going to get a beating and on the whole preferred being beaten without having clapped to clapping and then getting beaten as well). The young man

told me I was to clap. I told him—speaking within the context of
the emphasis on law and order—that it was my lawful right to
decide whether to clap or not to clap at a public meeting. This
was an unsatisfactory reply.

The substance of Mr. Craig's remarks was inflammatory, but
his manner and delivery were quiet. He was succeeded by a 'Free
Presbyterian' (Paisleyite) minister who said the same sort of thing,
but in a scream. The temperature went up. The applause became
more frequent and several young men moved in around us
clapping frequently and vigorously and nudging us with their
elbows as they did so. Then they started kicking our legs quite
gently from behind. None of these was an Apprentice Boy.

We moved away from them in order to leave the ground,
slowly. For the moment they did not follow. As we moved away a
big man in Apprentice Boy regalia came up. He suggested we
should leave the grounds immediately. We said we asked for
nothing better and moved away with him. As we were doing so
several of the young men who had been jostling us came up and
struck us. I got a bloody nose and lip; Seamus a lump on the head.
The Apprentice Boy told them to go away and was joined by two
other Apprentice Boys with the same message. They drew back
and we went on with our Apprentice Boys. One of them said it
was foolish of us to come. We could not very well disagree, and he
did not rub the point in. The other said he believed in defending
Ulster but didn't believe in this kind of violence. He pointed out
that our assailants were not Apprentice Boys.

At this point we had got about halfway across a large meadow,
following a route that was intended to take us clear of the crowd
toward the police ranks. (Police were at the exits of the ground,
not on the ground itself.) A large group of young men now came
running toward us from behind. They were more purposeful this
time. An identification had occurred. They wanted 'to get
O'Brien'. They hit me several times and I fell down, then they
started kicking me. An Apprentice Boy said: 'Is it murder ye
want?' After a short while they stopped kicking and went away.
I was shaken and sore but not badly hurt; Seamus—who had
been trying to pull back my main assailants but who had not
been attacked by them this time—said that the long wet grass got
in the way of their boots.

We walked away through the long wet grass with the three
Apprentice Boys for about a quarter of a mile. At the edge of the
meadow we met a Royal Ulster Constabulary man who took us
over to a police car. Our Apprentice Boy guide disappeared at
this point. As we got into the police car a small crowd—it was
near the exit to the grounds and near the end of the meeting—took
notice of us and began to shout. One man said: 'Ye didn't get
half enough.' There was nothing personal in this anger; our

former assailants had not followed and nobody in this crowd recognized me. It was just that I was bleeding from the nose and mouth, I had obviously been beaten up at the Apprentice Boy rally, and was therefore clearly a troublemaker and enemy of Ulster. As the police car drew away the crowd began to hammer with fists and umbrellas on its roof and windows.

The noise brought my mind back to when I had heard that noise before. It was outside the Ulster television studios on Ormeau Road, Belfast, early in May after I had taken part in a televised discussion with the Reverend Ian Paisley. That had been at the time of the crisis in Dublin and that crisis had been the subject matter of the panel. U.T.V. had set up a panel consisting of two parliamentarians from Dublin, two from Stormont considered sympathetic to Dublin, and Paisley. Paisley however analysed the composition differently. After the show had been on the air for a while he walked out, exclaiming: 'Four to one!' That is, four Roman Catholics to one Protestant. Abusive telephone calls started immediately and a small crowd gathered outside the studio.

As Paisley's co-panellists left, under police protection, the crowd had hammered on roof and windows in exactly this way. I remembered, in particular, a nine-year-old boy, his face contorted with hate. Paisley's followers had been bidden to attend the Apprentice Boys rally in substitution for one of their own. I believe that my attackers of St. Columb's Park came from among them and that their particular enthusiasm to 'get' me was derived from the television incidents. Or it may quite simply have been that I was a well-known Southern Catholic.

*Postscript:* The diary entries reflect my impressions at the time, before the opening of the Provisional I.R.A.'s offensive. Now, in 1972, the 'gentleness', which still marks Mr. Ó Brádaigh's deportment, makes a very different impression on me.

# II

## Under the Bony Thumb
## (August 1970 – January 1972)

*'But who is there to argue that*
*Now Pearse is deaf and dumb?*
*And is their logic to outweigh*
*MacDonagh's bony thumb?*
w. b. yeats, *Sixteen Dead Men*

After the fierce flare-up of July and August, the remaining
months of 1970 in Northern Ireland were relatively quiet.
Public opinion in the Republic, always prone to easy op-
timism—and also easily bored with the North as a topic of
conversation—began again to assume that the troubles in
the North were over (except perhaps for seasonal disturbances each year, around the twelfth). In the North itself
people knew that a decisive shift had taken place. A year
before, the Catholics had welcomed the British troops as
their protectors (in Belfast, saviours) and given them cups
of tea, sometimes with a tricolour along, to take the harm
out of the thing. Between the two summers, relations had
slowly worsened, partly through normal Army-civilian
friction, partly as a result of the i.r.a.'s anti-fraternization
policy. Still, few Catholics, outside the Republican minority,
really thought of the British Army as a hostile force. July–
August 1970 changed that. A great many Catholics, probably most, now thought of the Army as hostile, or at the
very best as thoroughly unreliable, and suspect in its role of
protector. This had an important corollary. If the British
Army was now a menace rather than a protection, then the
only protection left was the i.r.a.—a new i.r.a. which had

proved itself by taking on both the Protestants and the British Army in the fighting of June–August 1970. In consequence, the status, importance and authority of the I.R.A.— both sections, but mainly the Provisionals—increased enormously. The I.R.A. now largely controlled the ghettoes. It only remained to be seen what use it would make of this control.

Near the end of 1971 the London *Sunday Times* published a valuable 'Perspective on Ulster'[1]—a history of events there from October 1968 on. The 'Insight' team rightly identify the summer of 1970 as the time of 'the decisive change'. They stress, also rightly, the responsibility of the authorities —the Tory Government, the military command and Stormont—for the disastrous deterioration. The decision to allow provocative parades, followed shortly by arms searches among those provoked, constituted crass and irresponsible handling of an explosive situation. But where, I think, readers of 'Perspective on Ulster' may be misled is in relation to the role of the I.R.A. 'Perspective' shows that, before July (and even afterwards: (below p. 258)), there had been some co-operation between even the Provisional I.R.A. and the British Army in keeping the peace. This is quite true, as I saw myself (above p. 224). But the unwary reader might assume from this that this kind of co-operation need never have given way to hostilities, had it not been for the blunders of the authorities in July 1970 (and again in January 1971: p. 258). In reality, for the I.R.A., just as for Mr. Lynch, the very presence of the British Army was 'unacceptable, certainly in the long term'. But the I.R.A.'s idea of a long term was much shorter than Mr. Lynch's. At Bodenstown (above pp. 221, 223), just *before* the time of the decisive shift, both factions of the I.R.A. had pledged themselves to fight the British Army, and they competed in militancy: the 'Official' statement, coming second, was the stronger. The Provisionals incited minor acts of violence—e.g. stone-throwing—against the troops.[2] When they co-operated with the same troops in

[1] *Sunday Times*, 14th and 21st November 1971. Later expanded into the Penguin Special *Ulster* (1972).
[2] This has sometimes been denied, but I have talked to people who saw the incitement going on, both in Belfast and Derry, and who named the provisionals concerned.

peace-keeping this was purely tactical; to use Mr. Ó Brádaigh's terms they were 'controlling' troubles they themselves had 'fomented'. But in the context of Northern Ireland in 1970, foment/control was necessarily an escalating mechanism. As between the two I.R.A. factions, whoever did the more 'fomenting' would have the more prestige: whoever did too much 'controlling' would be likened to the old irrelevant I.R.A. of 1969. So the Provisionals pressed ahead, and the Officials tried to catch up.

Had the I.R.A. been what the people of the ghettoes had looked for—a defensive militia—then a system of self-policing enclaves might have been worked out, providing relatively peaceful conditions for the carrying-out of the reform programme and the building of new political structures. But the I.R.A. is not simply defensive, and not interested in any meliorist programme. Defence in conditions of foment/control is a very different thing from normal defence. You are acting defensively (within the foment/control system) if you shoot in defence of some Catholic youths, even if you have yourself incited the youths to commit the provocative act for which they are exposed to the retaliation from which you defend them. Both sections saw this as applying to the British troops. These troops had no right to retaliate when people threw stones at them, since they had no right *to be there*. But the Provisionals applied the same thinking also to the Orangemen. A crowd which threw stones at an Orange procession was showing the right spirit. If the Orangemen retaliated and looked like winning you could shoot them.

From the summer of 1969 to 1970, the British Army had maintained a position of something like impartiality, through a kind of balance of unpopularities. Catholics tended to object to its presence in principle, but felt the need for it in practice. Protestants approved its presence in principle but objected to its role in practice, as protecting Catholic 'no-go areas', in which the I.R.A. could build up its strength un-hampered by 'normal policing'. (There was some truth in this view of the British Army's role at this time, and it accounts for the I.R.A.'s intermittent interest in co-operating with the British Army.) But after the Falls Road search, the popularity of the Army among the Protestants naturally shot up. The Army searches on the Shankill in October had provoked a similarly favourable response among Catholics. But there was always something 'unnatural' and therefore brittle in Catholic approval of the British Army, and there was always the Republican influence, devoted to making the Army unpopular again. Among the Protestants, approval of 'our Army' was more natural and proved more stable—once Catholic hostility to the Army became reassuringly plain. For the soldiers, from the summer of 1970 on, Catholic areas were unfriendly, while Protestant areas—barring exceptional incidents—were friendly. So Catholics were clearly bad guys, Protestants (relatively) good guys. Soldiers remaining in this atmosphere for any length of time were likely to begin to 'understand' the Orange point of view, or at least to understand the value of Orange taunts ('Fenian bastard', etc.) as verbal weapons against Catholics. This was a highly satisfactory development, from an i.r.a. point of view. When a lorry-load of British troops went through Catholic territory singing 'The Sash my Father Wore' they were making an essential i.r.a. point far more effectively than the i.r.a. themselves could do. For what the troops were singing, as Catholics heard it, meant: 'As long as we are here, the Orangemen will rule and the Catholics will get it in the neck'.

A Labour Government in Britain, to judge by its record from August 1969 to June 1979, would have tried to check this dangerous trend. The Tory Government at first did nothing to check it. 'Perspective on Ulster' makes a good point about one of the key decisions of July, 1970—that on arms searches in the Falls Road—that it was 'not the result of new Tory pressure but just the reverse—the lack of any political pressure at all'. The same seems to hold good more generally. The natural tendency of the Army from very early on was to take on an increasingly Orange colouration. Instead of discouraging this, the Government seems itself to have become affected by it through 'Impartial Army assessment'. How impartial some of these were might be divined from the 'Sinn Féin oath' distributed by the Army authorities (under the *Labour* government) as part of the briefing for the troops. This was a ferociously *Papist* document[3] and therefore impossible as a Sinn Féin document: such documents are never sectarian in language, however sectarian the feelings of those who compose them may in fact be. The message of this alleged 'Sinn Féin oath' as distributed to the soldiery, was: 'Catholic and I.R.A. mean the same'. There was no doubt what interests this served, and little doubt about the provenance of the document. It diffused a rich odour of *Canard à l'Orange*.

The Catholic ghettoes were growing markedly more anti-British, the Army markedly more anti-Catholic. The death-roll at the end of 1970 was twenty. By the end of the following year it was to reach ten times that figure.

ii

In the last months of 1970, the centre of interest, for politically-minded people in both parts of Ireland, shifted from the North to the Dublin Bridewell, where the trials of Charles J. Haughey and his co-defendants were being held.

The first trial opened on 22nd September, and ended without a verdict on 29th September. The judge, Mr. Aindrias Ó Cuiv—who had earlier declared himself 'reluctant to take this case'—dismissed the jury, after counsel for one of the accused had suggested that the trial was being unfairly conducted. The second trial opened on 6th October and ended on 23rd October, with the acquittal of all the accused. Immediately after the verdict, Mr. Charles J. Haughey told the press that he thought 'those who are responsible for the débâcle have no alternative but to take the course that is open to them'. Mr. Jack Lynch was in New York when the (presumably distasteful) news of the verdict reached him. There was 'no doubt' he said 'of an attempt to smuggle arms and that those dismissed were involved'.

---

[3] Containing references to the Blessed Virgin and the Blessed Rosary as well as the Red Gore of the Saxon Tyrants. Text in Penguin special, *Ulster*.

Far from taking 'the course that was open to him' (resignation) Mr. Lynch sought and obtained a vote of confidence (74 to 67) on 4th November. Among those who voted for him were Mr. Charles J. Haughey, Mr. Neil Blaney and their friends. No one in Fianna Fáil wanted an election in the immediate aftermath of the Arms Trials.

The trials were very fully covered in the Irish newspapers, and many people read very little else during September and October 1970. For a variety of reasons most Irish people, Catholic and Protestant, North and South, disliked the picture which emerged from the trials.

Northern Catholics felt that the trials unnecessarily and irresponsibly increased the dangers to which they were exposed. The revelation, for example, that certain arms, allegedly intended for distribution to Northern Catholics, had been stored 'in a monastery' was not helpful. Above all, the fact that Mr. John Kelly, a Belfast Catholic patriot, could be put on trial in Dublin for trying 'to bring help to our people' in times of danger, seemed both outrageous and incomprehensible. Since the case against Kelly could also be used against him by the Northern Ireland police, Dublin's case ranked as 'felon-setting': helping the English, or their allies, to punish a political offender. And 'felon-setting', with the closely related offence of 'informing', are the deadliest crimes known to the traditional Irish nationalist ethic.

For Northern Protestants, the prosecutions meant that Dublin now admitted there had been a conspiracy against 'Ulster'. The course of the trials showed that this conspiracy was wider than the group of defendants: that it included the Minister for Defence, Mr. James Gibbons, and probably also the Taoiseach himself. Mr. Gibbons himself and his evidence seemed to confirm certain unfavourable Ulster Protestant stereotypes about Catholics (see pp. 250–4). And the monastery arsenal did not go unremarked.

Southern reactions were a blend of hilarity and shame. The trials were *funny*, for which much, in Dublin, is in a way forgiven. Yet it was bitter laughter, for *we* were the butt of the joke. When a ticket collector on the Dublin-Tralee train, talking of the 'intelligence' revelations of the trial said,

'It's like Laurel and Hardy playing James Bond,' there was
indignation as well as mirth in his voice. After all, it was *our*
intelligence service. It was also *our* Prime Minister, *our*
reluctant Judge, *our* elastic Minister for Defence, *our* ex-
Ministers voting 'confidence' in men they were known to
distrust and despise, *our* ambiguous Taoiseach. People were
puzzled, also, as to what the case was really about. Captain
James Kelly, for example, was charged, like the others, with
attempted illegal importation of arms into the Republic.
He admitted the attempt, but claimed that he had been
acting under orders. Both his immediate superior, Colonel
Michael Hefferon, and the Minister for Defence, Mr. James
Gibbons, had known and approved everything he did;
Colonel Hefferon, called *as a prosecution witness* in the first
trial (but not in the second), fully corroborated everything
that Captain Kelly[4] had said. Mr. Gibbons, in his long hours
on the stand, revealed himself as a martyr to amnesia and
ellipsis.

No one in Dublin with whom I discussed the case—and I
discussed it with many people of widely different views—
had any hesitation in believing Captain Kelly and Colonel
Hefferon. This had disturbing implications. If Mr. Gibbons
had known of these things, if they were really contrary to
Government policy, and if he had failed to inform the
Taoiseach about them, then he had been guilty of a grave
breach of trust. But in that case the Taoiseach would presumably have removed him from office. In fact, Mr. Gibbons
remained a member of Mr. Lynch's cabinet, and remains so
at the time of writing. He shared in the Lynch government's
vote of confidence in November 1970, and was the recipient
of a personal vote of confidence almost exactly a year later.
(On both occasions Mr. Charles J. Haughey voted confidence
in Mr. Gibbons; although the judge at the second arms trial
had pointed out that there was a clear conflict between the
sworn testimony of the two men, which could not be accounted
for by failure in recollection.)

[4] Captain Kelly himself in his book *Orders for the Captain?* (Dublin 1971) notes
that the breaking off of the first trial helped the prosecution, allowing them to
get rid of so very inconvenient a 'prosecution witness'.

Mr. Lynch had dismissed Mr. Haughey and Mr. Blaney because he could not bear that even 'a shadow of suspicion' should fall upon one of his Ministers. Presumably, therefore, he was satisfied that no shadow of suspicion rested on Mr. Gibbons. But for anyone who accepted Captain Kelly's evidence—as the jury and the country did—this necessarily implied that *Mr. Lynch knew*, through Mr. Gibbons, of the transactions in which Captain Kelly had engaged, and for which Mr. Lynch's Attorney-General had had Captain Kelly put on trial.

If this was true, Mr. Lynch had connived at a policy of 'arms for our people in the North', until it became the subject of embarrassing publicity (embarrassing to his government's relations with Britain). Then he dropped, and prosecuted, the people most intimately concerned with the operation, thereby ridding himself of his most influential rival in the party, Mr. Charles J. Haughey. Machiavelli would have approved the concept, if not the details of the execution.

The Taoiseach was not called in the Arms Trials, and the man who had to bear the burden of the great anomaly in the Government's case was Mr. Gibbons. Mr. Gibbons did not succeed in convincing the jury or the country that Captain Kelly had acted without his authority; but his evidence did leave a haunting impression of the style in which the Republic was being governed, in this time of crisis. There was, for example, the question of the Derrymen who, on Mr. Gibbons's authority, had been accepted for military training by the Irish Army in Donegal. Counsel for Captain Kelly suggested that military training implied a willingness, on the Government's part, to supply guns.

MR. GIBBONS: 'I would not agree.'
COUNSEL:     'What was the point of training them in the use of guns if they were not going to get guns?'
MR. GIBBONS: 'My chief motivation in this gesture would be to convey to them that their dire straits were perceived by us and were sympathized with by me.'

The key word in this is 'gesture'; it was apparent that a large part, if not the whole, of the Government's concern, in and after August 1969, lay in devising the appropriate gestures. Unfortunately gestures look different from different angles. This particular gesture was dropped after a few days as a result of newspaper publicity.

In the long debate in May, an opposition Deputy, Mr. Richie Ryan, referring to this episode, had said that training had been 'given in at least one military camp to civilians in the use of arms'. Mr. Gibbons had interrupted with the words: 'That is not true'. The nuance Mr. Gibbons had relied on for this crisp intervention was that the men, just before being 'trained', had been sworn into the F.C.A. (Local Defence Force, territorials, militia) and were thus technically not civilians. The Dáil just got the ringing denial; its slender foundation did not appear until the court proceedings:

COUNSEL: 'Does not that mean that this was a device to enable the army to train them for the defence of the Bogside?'

MR. GIBBONS: 'I admit that this was a device to enable Derrymen to joint the F.C.A. and obtain training.'

COUNSEL: 'Do you think then that your reply to Deputy Ryan was not something of a half-truth?'

MR. GIBBONS: 'I am suggesting that what Deputy Ryan said was inaccurate.'

COUNSEL: 'Would you accept that in this instance you had not told the truth but only half the truth?'

MR. GIBBONS: 'This was a Dáil debate.'

COUNSEL: 'Is that your answer, Mr. Gibbons, that one is not bound to tell the truth in a Dail debate?'

MR. GIBBONS: 'This is a Dáil debate in which Deputy Ryan and his colleagues are seeking to demolish the Government and the Government party.'

Then there was the question of the five hundred rifles moved on Mr. Gibbons's orders, at Mr. Blaney's request, to Dundalk near the border in April 1970. Colonel Hefferon had testified that he had recalled Captain Kelly from the continent 'to assist in the distribution of these arms, the five hundred rifles, because he knew the people in Northern Ireland'. Mr. Gibbons would not agree:

COUNSEL: 'What was the purpose of sending five hundred rifles without men attached, even against the dire situation which you really did not believe would break out; what were they going to be used for?'

MR. GIBBONS: 'Rifles! Certainly the function of rifles in our Defence Forces is for defensive purposes.'

COUNSEL: 'Ah, Mr. Gibbons, you understand my question. On 2nd April 1970, to meet a dire situation which might break out, what was the purpose of moving five hundred rifles without men to Dundalk? What were they going to be used for?'

MR. GIBBONS: 'If the Doomsday situation of which we are all afraid . . .'

COUNSEL: 'What would you do with the rifles?'

MR. GIBBONS: '. . . broke upon us, it would be much more logical to have the rifles in Dundalk rather than elsewhere.'

COUNSEL: 'What were you going to do with them?'

MR. GIBBONS: 'We had no immediate plans for their distribution.'

COUNSEL: 'Why not move blankets or anything else, why move rifles?'

MR. GIBBONS: 'Because blankets are a rather inefficient method of defending one's life.'

COUNSEL: 'Isn't the truth of the matter, Mr. Gibbons, that you moved the rifles to Dundalk, while you did not think it was going to arise, against the outside possibility that you would have to distribute arms to the people in Northern Ireland?'

MR. GIBBONS: 'The eventual reason probably was. . . we were dealing with a hypothetical situation which could take many, many forms. It could take the

form of assault on the Nationalist, Catholic
areas. It could take the form of total breakdown
of law and order. It could take the form of the
full occupation of the British security forces in
other areas, with outside areas totally unpro-
tected.'

COUNSEL:    'Yes?'

MR. GIBBONS: 'There were a great many conceivable forms
which this situation might give rise to, anything in the matter of the protection of life.'

COUNSEL:    'Is it not correct to say that the only way five
hundred rifles without five hundred men fitted
into that picture was that they were to be
distributed to civilians in Northern Ireland?'

MR. GIBBONS: 'No, this is not a reasonable deduction at all.'

Mr. Gibbons may have been right in the sense that there
may have been no serious intention to distribute these
particular arms. The move, which the military men naturally saw in military terms, was made by politicians for
political purposes. In general, its purpose could be defined
as Mr. Gibbons had defined his purpose in giving military training to people to whom he did not intend to
supply arms: 'to convey to them that their dire straits
were perceived by us and were sympathized with by me'.
More precisely, the purpose was to convey this message to
people who mattered in the Republic: the members of
Fianna Fáil who sympathized with Mr. Blaney.

Mr. Gibbons in himself is not alarming: he is a chirpy,
bright-eyed little man, with a pleasant sense of humour, and
quirks of speech which in another context might have been
endearing. But his evidence was alarming, especially in the
light of the vote of confidence that followed it. It was as if the
Government said to the people: '*Of course* we fool you any
time we can get away with it, what do you expect us to do?'
Some may perhaps find this attitude refreshing in its frankness (of a sort) and preferable to the spectacle of the British
public in one of its fits of morality. But in fact if there is no
adequate reaction when a politician is found out, the credi-

bility of democratic government is at an end. The Government, by retaining Mr. Gibbons, and the Dáil by voting confidence in the Government that retained him, were accepting the Gibbons technique of communication as acceptable. No Minister henceforward need fear being caught out in any substantial piece of deception, provided he could produce under pressure some technical quibble previously concealed by him. Nor was this cynical slide accompanied in practice by any 'refreshing frankness'. Mr. Lynch is one of the most sanctimonious politicians alive and his sanctimony continued, throughout and after the trials, its bland unbroken flow. As for Mr. Gibbons, he stated in response to criticism that he owed his ethic to 'the penny catechism'. It is not likely that this testimonial did much to enhance the regard in which that document is held among Ulster Protestants.

If the most disturbing thing about the vote of confidence was its implications for the condition of our democracy, the most disturbing thing about the arms trials themselves was their implications about the unfitness of the government of the Republic to cope with the Northern crisis, even in its early stages. It seemed that the government had been content to execute a series of gestures, designed to produce the *appearance of covert intervention* in the North, with as little of the substance as possible but with *some* substance: some men received some training, some guns were moved; it is a reasonable inference, though not brought out in evidence, that some guns, with official approval or collusion, did cross the border. These gestures were always liable to be hurriedly abandoned on becoming too visible in Britain, and eventually the whole involvement was disavowed, through the dismissals and the prosecutions.[5] There are many things about this process which make it hard to take it seriously: its sketchy improvizations, its half-heartedness, the brittleness of its falsities, and a certain dull and petty frivolity of mind underlying it all. Yet the issues themselves were serious. People's lives were in danger in the North, and these proceedings put them in greater danger. Catholics in the North were

[5] Mr. Lynch has never *quite* solved his basic communications problem; that of making a gesture which is visible in Ireland but invisible in Britain (or *vice versa*).

encouraged in the dangerous hope—dangerous *for them*—that 'the Free State' would come to their rescue in the event of serious trouble. The I.R.A. were encouraged, through the same hope, in the direction of creating the trouble in question —'forcing Lynch's hand'.

Another ominous feature of the trials was that the 'politicians'—the elected representatives of the people—came very badly out of it while 'the soldiers', both regular and irregular, came out looking good. One politician, it is true, looked good for a fortnight. This was Mr. Charles J. Haughey who, in the moment of his acquittal and of his challenge to Mr. Lynch, looked to a wide public rather like the Man of Destiny his friends suppose him to be. This glory became tarnished when, on 4th November, Mr. Haughey voted confidence in Mr. Lynch's government, including Mr. James Gibbons.[6] Thus the net combined result of trials and vote was the discredit of all the politicians involved, and of democracy.

The honour of the soldiers, on the other hand, remained intact. The two regular officers, Captain James Kelly and Colonel Hefferon, had clearly been doing what they took to be their duty, and although their evidence was contested it was never shaken. But the real hero of the arms trials, the man whose words seemed to many to shine out against a sordid political background, was the man from Belfast who spoke with the voice of the Provisional I.R.A.: John Kelly. Alone among the defendants, Mr. Kelly made use of the court, in the classic tradition of Irish republicanism, to deliver a 'speech from the dock',[7] an unsworn and highly effective piece of patriotic rhetoric. Mr. Kelly brought to clear and deadly light the fact that the principles on which he had *acted* were the identical principles *professed* by the government which had put him on trial:

[6] Mr. Blaney also voted confidence at this time, but a year later jibbed at a personal vote of confidence in Mr. Gibbons, and was later expelled from the Fianna Fáil party. Mr. Haughey did not jib, and remains, at the time of writing, a member of the party (and elected one of its Vice-Presidents—February 1972).

[7] The judge refused to allow the speech to be so described, but could not stop it being so heard.

. . . And I would not like to think, gentlemen, that this court would try to impute to the Citizens' Defence Committees, a word which first became known from the mouths of the Stormont Government, that this Court should impute to them the tag, 'subversive', or that they would be smeared in an Irish court with this tag. It would be more than injustice, it would be a travesty of truth and something that could only be engaged in for political expediency. But I might recall that this was the situation in Belfast on the 14th, 15th and 16th August and thereafter, and Dr. Hillery, the Minister for External Affairs, had gone to the United Nations and asserted there that the breakdown of law and order in Northern Ireland and the plight of the minority community was due to the partition of Ireland, brought about by an Act of the British Parliament, in which not a single Irish vote had been cast, and I quote what he said next: 'The claim of Ireland, the claim of the Irish nation to control the totality of Ireland has been asserted over the centuries by successive generations of Irishmen and women and it is one which no spokesman for the Irish nation could ever renounce.'

And Taoiseach Lynch, in what has become known as his 'we will not stand idly by' speech, said . . .

JUDGE:      'I am afraid, Mr. Kelly, we cannot have extracts from speeches. You are entitled to say anything you wish to say to the jury which bears on your own defence, within reason.'

MR. KELLY:  'My Lord, this would bear on my own attitude. This is part of the reason why I stand in this court today; these are the reasons why I stand here.'

COUNSEL:    'Let me remind your Lordship, the prisoner is not giving evidence.'

JUDGE:      'It is not normal for people making statements, sworn or unsworn, to quote from political speeches.'

MR. KELLY:  'Specifically, this was the situation in Belfast and what I am coming to is that it was in exactly this situation and in these circumstances that I first met Captain Kelly.'

JUDGE:      'If you would kindly pass on to that.'

MR. KELLY:  'Well, I reluctantly pass on, my Lord, because I think what Taoiseach Lynch said is very, very significant as far as I am concerned, but I will pass on reluctantly.'

JUDGE:      'Please do.'

Though urged to 'pass on' by a judge who seemed more interested in keeping out references to the Taoiseach than he was in eliminating other supposed irrelevancies, Mr. Kelly managed to get in a further allusion to 'speeches by people, political figures of authority in this part of Ireland, speeches which had led the Six County minority to believe sincerely that a new era was dawning in Irish life'.

Mr. Gibbons when asked whether he was 'unaware of any request or requests by representatives of these (defence) committees in the North for arms to be supplied to them by the Irish Government', had replied: 'I have no recollection of the remotest kind. I disbelieve its truth.'

Mr. Kelly, who had been spokesman for the Belfast committee, *did* have a recollection:

We did not ask for blankets or feeding-bottles. We asked for guns and no one from Taoiseach Lynch down refused that request or told us that this was contrary to Government policy. . . .

Mr. Kelly ended with the words:

I think it is, as far as I am concerned, only right that I should point out that throughout the period from August of last year until the first time that I was arrested in Dublin, everything that happened within that time leaves me in no doubt whatsoever but that what was being done was being done with the full knowledge and consent not only of Mr. Gibbons, but of the Government as a whole. And it is my conviction, whether I be right or whether I be wrong, I am only speaking from knowledge that I have, it is my conviction that what Mr. McKenna said at the beginning, that this trial is an exercise in democracy or a case of the people of Ireland versus the accused, and many things have been done in the name of the people of Ireland, it is my conviction that I stand here and those who stand with me, that we are here as a matter of political expediency, and not from any desire that the course of justice be impartially administered.

My Lord, I find it a very sad occasion indeed, that these institutions for which so much was sacrificed, which had been gained by such nobility, should be abused in this manner. There is no victory for anyone in these proceedings, my Lord. There is only an echo of sadness from the graves of the dead generations. I thank you, gentlemen, I thank you, my Lord.

Those who applauded included a member of the jury.

Ordinary democratic politics, respect for parliament, for the law and for the state, were all seriously weakened by the arms trials. Some of the respect lost by this system and these institutions was transferred to the patriotic law-breakers, the 'freedom-fighters in the North': in short, the Provisional I.R.A.

For those committed to democracy there was no consolation in the thought that a democratically elected government had *deserved* to forfeit respect, and that men who acted on principles the government professed *deserved* more respect than a government which only pretended to be guided by these principles. Whatever the relative entitlement to respect, it remained true that our democracy, shabbily as it was working, was still better than anything the noble gunmen were likely actually to deliver. But this truth was hard to defend in Ireland against the mystic force invoked by John Kelly: 'An echo of sadness from the graves of the dead generations.'

> *And is their logic to outweigh*
> *MacDonagh's bony thumb?*

### iii

In early 1971 in Belfast 'foment' won out over 'control'. In the initial heavy rioting in Ballymurphy (10th–17th January), it seems that the Provisionals still made some effort to 'control', or at least to persuade the British Army that that is what they were doing. The 'control' even at this stage was not very effective. A Provisional spokesman explained to British journalists that teenagers who hated the sight of a British uniform outnumbered 'non-rioters' (Provisionals) by twenty to one. 'And we couldn't start beating people around because they disliked the British, could we?' Clearly they could not, especially as they had done so much to foment the 'dislike' in question. It appears from 'Perspective on Ulster' (see above, p. 244) that British Army officers and Provisional leaders were still trying as late as January to work a 'tacit truce', leaving the I.R.A. in effect to police the Catholic ghettoes. It could hardly have lasted very long, partly because of Protestant suspicion and resentment at such arrangements —there was serious rioting in the Shankill on 23rd–24th

January—and partly because the logic of the I.R.A.'s objective would require it to use such bases as springboards for 'the reconquest of occupied Ireland'. They could never accept the role of a kind of Swiss Guard in a system of 'Vatican City' enclaves—and any of them who might be tempted by such a role for other than a very short tactical period would be superseded by others with more enterprising ideas (as in the Provisional/Official competition). Specifically, the I.R.A. was bound to use any such tactical breathing-space in order to build up its armed strength, and the British troops, as the most probable targets of the arms in question, were bound to search for the arms.

Whatever truce there was was broken on 3rd February by British Army arms searches in the Clonard and Ardoyne areas. This action set loose a 'third phase' of violent disturbances, more intense and more prolonged than either the first main phase (August 1969) or the second (June–August 1970). This third phase lasted until the moment when the introduction of internment without trial (in August 1971) opened a fourth phase, still more violent than the previous three.

What was most ominous about the third phase was that it opened in February. Violence was ceasing to be a seasonal affair. By the end of February 180 people had been arrested: before mid-March fifty people had been killed, since August 1969. Violence took multiple forms: Protestant and Catholic inter-rioting and riotous attacks by Catholics and Protestants (but now usually by Catholics) on police and army: shooting by I.R.A. at the army and at I.R.A. (and suspected I.R.A.) by the army: some shooting—in March—between the Provisional and Official factions of the I.R.A.; some shooting and bombing of uncertain 'fringe' or merely criminal provenance: killings and maimings of unarmed civilians, as a result of I.R.A.-Army crossfire, 'mistakes', and speculative bombing. Five civilians were killed in a land-mine explosion on Brougher mountain, Co. Tyrone, on 9th February. On 10th March three unarmed British soldiers were taken or decoyed from a pub at Ligoniel on the outskirts of Belfast and shot in the back of the head.

Protestant indignation at the I.R.A. revival, and the failure of the security forces to cope with it, led to the fall of the Chichester-Clark government and the coming to power at last of Mr. Brian Faulkner, on 25th March. In terms of the Ulster Unionist tradition, Mr. Faulkner was an exotic leader, almost a Disraeli. He did not belong to the landed gentry, and he had no military rank. He was brisk, astute, educated in the South (at a Protestant school of course, but all the same . . .) and he made an articulate leader for a notably non-verbal community. Protestant Ulster wanted a man who could convince the British of the need to restore the essentials of the old Stormont system. O'Neill had betrayed them; Chichester-Clark had been ineffective. Perhaps, just perhaps, a clever wee man like Brian would do the trick. Both the strength and the weakness of Mr. Faulkner's position lay in the widespread belief that he was the last of his line: that if he fell Stormont was finished, and would be replaced by direct rule from Westminster (possibly followed by betrayal into the hands of the Republic) or by U.D.I. For the Unionist Party, though not for U.D.I.-minded Protestants, this implied the wisdom of sticking to Faulkner, for fear of worse. But for Catholics, whose unarmed and armed activities had brought down Mr. Faulkner's predecessors, the thought of Stormont's vulnerability through 'the last Prime Minister' was a stimulus to further turbulence: one more good shove and the whole structure would come down. The Provisional I.R.A., whose aggressive tactics had brought down Chichester-Clark, could hope that through more of the same they could bring down not merely Faulkner but Stormont with him. Beyond that, it was not expedient for the moment to look.

iv

Still, in those early months of 1971, contemporary events in the North registered only faintly in the Republic. At the Irish Labour Party Conference at the end of February, for example, the North was not a major issue (although sectarianism in the Republic was). Next year, at the Wexford conference of February 1972, 'Northern policy', and my own role as party spokesman on the subject, were at the centre of controversy. In February 1971 they seemed less significant than the policy towards the E.E.C., towards contraception and towards the expulsion of a member of the parliamentary party who had made anti-semitic remarks. In the Dáil also, in the spring and summer of 1971, contemporary Northern happenings were little noted. The Government directed most of its externally-available energy to pushing through an apparently anachronistic and futile measure, the Forcible Entry Bill. This was directed against protest-by-squatting, and the encouragement of such protest: directed, that is, against tactics favoured by the *Official* Sinn Féin-I.R.A., under its left-wing leadership, especially in the period before August 1969. Squatting, by mid-1971, was hardly the most urgent of the threats to the Irish State and people, and the measure itself—through the calculated looseness of the word 'encourage'—seemed to threaten freedom of the press and of comment. The Bill was almost universally condemned by the press and vigorously resisted, to the verge of filibuster, by the opposition: I devoted several hours myself in the Dáil (with the aid of the big O.E.D.) to an analysis of the range of meanings and sub-meanings of the word 'encourage', and this analysis was still far from complete when it was cut short by the guillotine. At first sight, this unpopular and unnecessary law seems merely pig-headed. Yet it carried a message, which was that the Government was not prepared to take even the smallest amount of nonsense from the official I.R.A., within the territory of the Republic. In this domain the government's passion for law and order was intense. But this very intensity, combined with apathy and myopia in a related area, carried a supplementary message and a more important one: so long as the I.R.A. refrained from coat-trailing within the territory of the Republic, and confined itself to planning and organizing activities in the North, it would not be asked too many questions. Thus the Bill conveyed a warning to the *official* I.R.A., and at the same time a tacit reassurance to the *Provisional* I.R.A. The warning helped to refurbish the Government's 'law and order' image, somewhat dilapidated by the arms trial. The reassurance on the other hand was what kept the government in power, by holding the governing party together. The Lynch government, holding office by the votes of eleven or more deputies who sympathized with the Provisionals, was thereby constrained to a kind of collusion with the Provisionals. Despite the fall of Messrs. Haughey and Blaney, and despite Mr. Lynch's peaceful orations, the orientation of the Government's 'northern policy' remained much as it had been in 1969–70. There was still an ambiguous and precarious involvement with 'the defenders of our people'. The main difference was that the defenders had now gone over to the offensive.

Contact with the Republic, with Britain and with the North in this period produced a peculiar, multiple uneasiness. In the North, two mutually unintelligible communities, each locked in its exclusive historical myth, and yet acutely conscious of one another as threat and as grievance, were held apart by an Army which basically neither understood nor cared for either community, but was tilted by the pressure of events in favour of one and against the other. In Britain, all the ancient difficulties of Anglo-Irish communication came into play. There was the problem of *scale*: Ireland—and all the more, Northern Ireland—was simply too small to engage the sustained, continuous attention of British politicians or opinion-formers. There was the problem of violence; violence was highly effective as a means of gaining the intermittent attention of the British public, but the combination of violence and 'intermittent attention' only worsened the crisis—since if the minority looked like getting its way through violence, the majority would be sure to try the same method. And there was also the problem of the kind of 'understanding' that comes from intermittent attention. This understanding often takes the form of a progress from a dim perception of some obvious truth—as that Protestants and Catholics in Northern Ireland are not on the best of terms—to something more profound but more misleading, as that 'religion is really irrelevant'. Those who progressed in this way sometimes ended up by promoting the folk-lore of one side or the other, like that *New Statesman* writer who assured his public that Protestants might well be responsible for the geligniting of Protestant pubs, and that 'it is said that Protestants are notoriously nervous with gelly'.[8] Those who acquired this kind of easy familiarity with the Ulster scene were more likely to have been conned by Catholics than by Protestants, because Catholics—in common probably with most underdogs—are more given to ingenious explanations, things-are-not-what-they-seem theory and all those forms of 'inside dope' that best deserve that description. It has been said that where intelligence falls below a certain level, as unhappily it so often does, Protestants are more likely to be *stupid*, Catholics *silly*. Stupidity is tongue-tied and friendless, but silliness diffuses universally its own ineffable charm. The Catholic cause might be thought to benefit by this, and so it does—in terms of the media. But in fact the community that stands in the greater danger from the worsening of the crisis is the minority community—the Catholics—and its short-term propaganda victories worsen its danger and increase its tribulations.

In the Republic, people often referred, patronizingly or angrily, to the incapacity, or wilful refusal, of Englishmen to understand the realities of Northern Ireland. But in fact few citizens of the Republic know much about Northern Ireland either, and in some respects their relation to it resembled that of Englishmen. Like the English, they have paid only intermittent attention to it, and like the English it is to violence they have paid attention. During the famous 'fifty years of neglect' the indifference of the English did not in practice greatly exceed that of the average citizen of the Republic· Yet this general and routine indifference was combined with an equally general, theoretical commitment to the propositions that Northern Ireland was ours by right, cut off from us by British interference and to be recovered some day by negotiation or by force. The habit of asserting this commitment included a habit of ignoring the existence of Ulster Protestants, or of minimizing or distorting the significance of what they represented.

[8] Article, 'Ulster: the other Terror', by James Fenton, in *The New Statesman*, 8th November 1971.

Among the minority in the North the existence of the Southern commitment had a triple implication. It meant first that the minority was not a minority at all, but part of a majority in the whole country. This in turn implied that since the democratic right of the majority to rule was denied, the use of force to change this situation was morally justified. And finally the Southern commitment meant that, in the last resort, the Republic would have to intervene. So the Northern minority thought.

To some people, including myself, this conjecture began to look peculiarly sinister and ominous when the Provisional offensive of 1971 succeeded the Arms Trials of 1970.

It was at this period that I came to feel that the relation of us all—citizens and especially publicists and politicians of the Republic—to the Provisionals in the North, uncomfortably resembled the relation of Mr. Jack Lynch and Mr. James Gibbons to Mr. John Kelly, as revealed in the Arms Trials (above, pp. 247–58).

Our words and habitual assumptions, combined with our silences and evasions, encouraged young men to acts of violence, which then we deplored and disavowed. I had long been aware of this relation,[9] but not of the full terrible potentialities with which it now seemed fraught. It now looked as if the Catholic minority in the North might be impelled—as some of them had actually already been impelled—in the direction of a hopeless rising, in which they would look for help from the South, which would not be effectively forthcoming, and which if it were forthcoming at all—even in token form—would only speed on the destruction of the outnumbered and outgunned Catholics of Belfast.

v

From 8th to 11th June, the Irish Transport and General Workers' Union held its annual conference in Galway. As a

[9] See for example the article 'The Embers of Easter' in the collection: *1916: The Easter Rising* (ed Owen Dudley Edwards and Fergus Pyle: London 1968). There are things in this article—written in 1966—with which I am no longer in sympathy, but the relation of 'official Ireland' to the I.R.A. is I think correctly analysed in it.

member of the Union and of the Dáil I attended the conference. The Northern question did not dominate the proceedings, but there was one significant resolution calling for
the release of all political prisoners. What this meant was
well understood by all. A resolution in support of the I.R.A.
could not be carried at a meeting of this kind. The respectable
middle-aged fathers of families who made up the bulk of the
delegates generally disliked violence and, like most citizens
of the Republic, had been on the whole repelled and puzzled
by the ferocity of the Provisionals' campaign. But 'release the
prisoners' was calculated to touch a reflex formed by Irish
history. The boys might be mistaken, but they were ours,
and brave, and resembled the patriots of the past, and the
least you could do for them was to call for their release.
Republicans, influential in the Union hierarchy, could therefore confidently expect that a resolution of this kind would
be carried unanimously by conference, without question and
without discussion. The passage of the resolution could
afterwards be invoked as proof that the organized working
class was behind the Republican movement, of which the
advancing edge was the Provisional offensive in the North.

Having been brought up in a 'release-the-prisoners' culture
—of which my Aunt Hanna had been a pillar, along with
Madame MacBride and Madame Despard—I did not need
to have any of this explained to me. I also understood that
with a release-the-prisoners resolution the thing to do, if
you could not actually support it, was to shut up, and preferably keep out of the way altogether. Republicans will
tolerate general condemnations of violence, specific condemnations of particular acts of violence, and even verbal attacks
on the I.R.A. People who talked like that were soft and
wishy-washy but not necessarily bad at heart; they were
inferior to Republicans, but still they were Irishmen of a
sort. But to question 'release the prisoners' was to refuse the
*minimum* Republicans expected of *all* Irishmen, and thus to
risk exclusion from the Irish nation, in one way or another.

The previous winter I had been a speaker at a meeting
convened to call for the release of Miss Bernadette Devlin.
As a result of skilful Republican floor-management the

meeting had been converted to one calling for the release of all 'political prisoners'. I had protested about this to the Chairman, but had not made my protest public. I was in politics, and I knew very well what bad politics such a public protest would be.

By June 1971, it was still bad politics, but bad politics into which I felt constrained to plunge. Thinking about the implications of the Provisionals' offensive it seemed to me that failure to question 'release the prisoners' now would be a kind of combined connivance and betrayal, rather closely analogous to the policy pursued by Mr. Lynch, in relation to 'the defence of our people'.

The resolution was formally proposed and seconded, without speeches, on the morning of 11th June. I then got up and asked, what was a political prisoner? If, for example, a man booby-trapped a car, putting children's lives at risk and killing innocent civilians—if that man were tried, sentenced and imprisoned could he then become one of the political prisoners for whose release we were asked to call?

One press report of the conference said I was 'shouted down'; another that I was 'roundly condemned by conference'. Neither of these things happened. My short and almost entirely interrogative speech was heard in complete silence, and applauded at the end by most delegates. Then a series of Republican speakers, mostly ex-prisoners or internees, took the stand and made the air ring with the names of the patriot dead. None of the speeches answered my questions. All of them denounced me for asking them. All of them were also applauded by most delegates, and very loudly indeed by a minority. My party leader, Mr. Brendan Corish, and the President of the Union, Senator Fintan Kennedy, defended my right to speak and question. They also were applauded. The resolution was then put and carried by an overwhelming majority. On the agendas distributed to delegates it had been marked with a tick, presumably indicating that the union leadership wanted it carried. A handful of delegates none the less voted against, presumably because they were dissatisfied that the questions raised had not been answered. Several delegates, most of whom had voted for the resolution, told me afterwards they were glad I had raised the questions. Most delegates clearly did not care one way or the other. My removal as Labour Party spokesman on the North became, from Galway on, an objective of Sinn Féin-i.r.a. policy. I was not particularly important, but it was important for Sinn Féin-i.r.a. to have at least the passive support, and where possible the tactical alliance and 'cover' of the Labour movement and party.

The Republicans of course 'won' at Galway, but their victory was something of a sham. Watching the proceedings on television people were impressed by the thunderheads of patriotic emotion, but failed to observe the yawning abyss of apathy below. In particular, Provisionals who watched Galway from afar must have been pleased: those who saw it close up can hardly have been encouraged by the quality of their support.

And a number of ordinary people, who had been uneasily half formulating certain questions for themselves, were relieved that these had come to the surface of public life.

The commemorative summer unfurled itself once more. On 12th June, an Orange march at Dungiven was broken up by British troops. On the following day the Provisional i.r.a. commemorated Wolfe Tone at Bodenstown: 10,000 people are said to have attended, an impressive display of support for what was more and more becoming *the* Republican movement. The other Republicans, Fianna Fáil and the Official i.r.a., plus the regular Army, were at Bodenstown the following Sunday, 20th June, in separate and rather anti-climactic ceremonies. On 25th June still another Republican Party, *Aontacht Éireann* was launched, too late for Bodenstown.

Wolfe Tone apart, 1971 was a major commemorative year. It was in fact the last year of the commemorative cycle that opened in 1966, with the ceremonies for 1916. It contained the last historical event which all Irishmen, claiming descent from 1916, could celebrate together. This event was the Truce, which came into operation between the Irish insurgents and the British forces on 11th July 1921. On 11th July 1971, accordingly, Mr. Jack Lynch betook himself to the Garden of Remembrance and made a speech. On the previous 11th July—which had no commemorative significance, except for being the day before the Twelfth—Mr. Lynch had said: 'This whole unhappy situation is an Irish quarrel. I admit that others come into it either because they misunderstand it or because they misuse it—but they are not an essential part of it. We must settle this quarrel among us ... Let us not appeal to past gods as if past generations had said the last word about Ireland.'

Those were sensible words, and it is possible that Mr. Lynch believed them. But they were not quite appropriate to the fiftieth anniversary of the Truce, or to the setting of the Garden of Remembrance. On 11th July 1971 Mr. Lynch could hardly avoid appealing to past gods and past generations. 'We have fulfilled', he thought, 'many of the hopes and aims of those who fought for our freedom and maintained our separate identity through centuries.' It was in this context that he now had to situate the idea of 'settling this quarrel': 'Let us today rededicate ourselves to reconciliation among Irishmen . . . This is how we can best honour those whom we commemorate. This is what they would demand mostly of us.'

In the Garden of Remembrance the 'whole unhappy situation', which had been 'an Irish quarrel' exactly a year before, now became primarily an Anglo-Irish one. Mr. Lynch quoted a statement Mr. de Valera had made fifty years before: 'We cannot admit the right of the British Government to mutilate our country, either in its own interest or at the call of any section of our population; we do not contemplate the use of force. If your Government stands aside, we [sic] can effect a complete reconciliation.'[10]

The phrase 'we do not contemplate the use of force' is not quite as reassuring as it may sound. In Mr. de Valera's large and well-thumbed lexicon, 'we do not contemplate' does not mean 'we exclude'. Mr. de Valera sometimes held that the use of force by the majority in Ireland against the

[10] Text as from 'Speeches and Statements: Irish Unity/Northern Ireland/Anglo-Irish Relations: August 1969–October 1971': Dublin, Government Information Bureau, 1972.

secessionist minority would be as justified, in the last resort, as Abraham Lincoln's use of force against the Confederacy.

Mr. Lynch continued, even in the Garden of Remembrance, to condemn acts of violence, and even to be generous, in his insinuating feline way, to the Northern Protestants:

Perhaps the national majority need to examine their consciences in relation to the national minority. Have our political concepts been sufficiently wide to include them? Have we been considerate enough about the things they believe in as passionately as we might believe otherwise? Do we agree that as John Hewitt writes, they 'have rights drawn from the soil and sky' which are as good as any title held by any previous migration into Ireland?

If we can answer these questions to their benefit, then we are entitled to suggest that the constitutional predilections of the Northern majority should take second place to their being Irish. I believe that the notion of being Irish is not the prerogative of sectional interests; it is not a private possession. To make it so is further to divide.

'If *we* can answer these questions to *their* benefit . . .' In theory Mr. Lynch spoke for the Irish nation of which the Protestants were a part. In practice, as his pronouns revealed, he spoke as chieftain of the Catholics.

At any time, the Garden of Remembrance in Dublin would have seemed to most Ulster Protestants an unpropitious place from which to launch an appeal for 'reconciliation among Irishmen'. But there were reasons why the fiftieth anniversary of the 1921 Truce made such an appeal, from such a place, peculiarly inauspicious. 'On the 11th July, 1921', according to Mr. Lynch, 'Britain had finally been brought to agree to recognize the Irish nation.' What had brought about this recognition? Inescapably, within the historical perspective of the Garden, the courage and the arms of those therein remembered: the Irish Republican Army. And did not this imply, in terms of 1971, the need for a new Truce with the new I.R.A.: a new recognition, this time full and final, of the Irish nation? Mr. Lynch—whose speech was about as moderate as was possible for a Fianna Fáil Taoiseach—in that setting and time—would certainly have resisted the drawing of this or any precise conclusion from his remarks. But, irrespective of what Mr. Lynch might have wanted to say, what the Garden and the Truce said, in part through him, was what the Provisionals and their friends wanted to hear.

And the day after the fiftieth anniversary of the Truce in Dublin came in Belfast the two-hundred-and-eighty-first anniversary of the Battle of the Boyne.

We all seemed to be like sleep-walkers, locked in some eternal ritual re-enactment, muttering senselessly as we collided with one another, wrestling in the dark.

Very shortly after this, on 2nd July, I decided personally to opt out of the commemorative culture. I did so by refusing to attend an Erskine Childers commemoration in my home village of Howth, and by stating my reasons for refusing:

In the present time, with its steadily increasing tempo of political violence, commemorations of this kind are liable to be exploited for purposes disruptive of peace in this country. . . . Under these conditions there is an implicit threat and provocation in any public commemoration, however well meant, of past military exploits in this island. It is one of the most painful of historical ironies that the annual ceremonies at Bodenstown, intended to honour a man who sought to unite Irishmen—not just the territory of Ireland—has degenerated into a sort of Catholic answer to the 12th of July.

Let us have a truce on commemorations until we can find something which Irishmen of both the main political and religious groupings can commemorate in peace together.[11]

I now seemed to be committed to the use of logic against the bony thumb. I was aware that the odds were heavily in favour of the thumb.

### vi

On 9th August 1971 internment without trial was introduced in Northern Ireland. In both the Republic and Northern Ireland, statutes conferring the power to intern without trial exist, and may be put into force by the Government at any time. The Government of the Republic had threatened, in

[11] Letter of 22nd July 1971 to the Childers Commemoration Committee.

the previous December, to apply internment without trial. Their ground for doing so was that they had knowledge of a plot for the kidnapping of prominent people, including the Minister for Justice. They gave no details of the plot, and their threat evoked considerable public protest, including protest in the Dáil, for which several deputies, including myself, were suspended. The government did not proceed at that time with its internment plans, although it did construct buildings suitable for internment, and did notify the Council of Europe that it might be obliged to intern and so derogate from the European Council on Human Rights.

Although the government of the Republic had shown itself willing to intern without trial in conditions of far less pressing danger than those which prevailed in Northern Ireland, this did not prevent Mr. Lynch from instantly appearing to condemn internment without trial when it was introduced in Northern Ireland. 'The introduction of internment without trial in the North this morning,' he said on 9th August, 'is deplorable evidence of the folly of the policies which have been pursued there for some time and which I condemned publicly last week.'

Ill-placed though Mr. Lynch was to preach in this way, it remained true that the introduction of internment without trial marked a further steep drop in the downward Northern spiral. Both its timing and its selective application were such as to consummate the alienation of the Catholic community, and to seal its internal secession within Northern Ireland.

As regards timing, internment came at a moment when the Catholic community in both Derry and Belfast, and to a somewhat less extent throughout Northern Ireland, were already at an exceptionally high pitch of excitement and resentment. Early in July, two Catholics had been shot dead by British troops in Derry. The Army claimed they were armed, the Catholics of Derry were convinced that they were not, although they, or one of them, might have been throwing stones. The refusal of an enquiry into the incident precipitated the withdrawal from Stormont of the Social Democratic and Labour Party—that is of most of the elected representatives of the Catholic community. This had dashed hopes aroused in the previous month by the positive response of the s.d.l.p. to an initiative of Mr. Brian Faulkner's, for giving the opposition a role in government through the use of a committee system, and an expanded Senate. Mr. Faulkner had had to balance this overture by hurried obeisances to his own particular 'past gods', at a meeting of the Royal Black Preceptory in Lurgan. This of course made it harder to defend, in the Catholic community, anything that might look like a deal with Faulkner. The killing of the two men, and the refusal of an inquiry, built the pressure to the point where the dramatic gesture of withdrawal, repudiating any possibility of a deal, seemed the best solution, if the elected representatives were to hold the confidence of the Catholic community. So the s.d.l.p. withdrew, but the door was not yet shut and barred behind them.

On 7th August, in Belfast, a van driver, who happened to be a Catholic, was shot dead by British troops. Whatever about the two Derry men, there could be no doubt at all of the entire innocence of the van driver, Harry Thornton. He was shot because his van had backfired passing a barracks. His terrified companion had then been taken into the barracks and brutally beaten, presumably to get him to say something that would justify the killing of Thornton.

It naturally was, and is, the practice of Sinn Féin-i.r.a. to build up any instance of bad behaviour by a British soldier into as big an atrocity as possible. In this case, however, such an effort would have been superfluous. The news of Thornton's death, accompanied by the picture of his companion's battered face, and the story of who battered it, when and why, threw the already exasperated Catholic community into a state of fury.

Two days after this, the government introduced internment without trial, and in applying it proceeded to arrest people on the Catholic side only.

Superficially, the timing of this act might seem like utter folly on Mr. Faulkner's part. Internment would have been resented at any time by the Catholic community, but the resentment would have been less explosive if it had been introduced immediately after an i.r.a. atrocity involving civilians,[12] instead of after a British Army atrocity involving civilians. But the timing was set not by Brian Faulkner as an automonous decision-maker, but by Brian Faulkner under pressure not only from Mr. Ted Heath, but from a rather dilatory seventeenth century general named Percy Kirk who finally decided to break the siege of Derry on a particular date in 1689.

The question of whether the Apprentice Boys' parade would be banned again in 1971 as it had been in 1970 (see above, Chapter 10) had been hanging over the politics of all Ireland that summer. I had referred to it on the adjournment debate, as the Dáil went into recess on 6th August.

'As the clock ticks on, and the calendar runs out, we move to the fateful day of 12th August. Any of us concerned about this—as we all should be—are thinking of Derry and what may happen there on that day now that the parade almost certainly will take place. We cannot help feeling a sickening apprehension as that time comes on. It can mean tragedy there, irrespective of what is said or done in this House'.[13]

What I failed to foresee was that the cancellation of the parade, and the manner of compensating for that cancellation, could also lead to tragedy.

The British Army command knew that, in the mood of Catholic Derry after the July shootings, the Apprentice Boys' parade, if held, would involve very serious disturbances. It seems that the British Government, on Army advice, decided that the parade should be cancelled. But Mr. Faulkner knew that Protestant resentment at the cancellation of that parade had been among the reasons for the downfall of his predecessor, Major Chichester-Clark. So Mr. Faulkner needed—as the S.D.L.P. leadership had needed in corresponding circumstances—a dramatic gesture. He had always wanted intern-

[12] A British soldier was killed by a sniper in Ardoyne on 8th August. This ranked as an atrocity in Protestant eyes; but for most Catholics ranked as an act of war, like the killing of an admittedly armed I.R.A. man by British soldiers.
[13] Dáil Debates vol. 255 no. 20 column 3836, 6th August 1971. Mr. Lynch was more confident about the future. He wound up the debate by telling opposition deputies: 'They can be perfectly assured, as I said this time last year, that the country is in the very best of hands.' (Ibid column 3878.) In this context, 'the country' has to be the twenty-six counties.

ment—and had been trying to get it ever since he took office in March—but now he needed it urgently. The Army had been reluctant to agree to internment but the expanding I.R.A. campaign—and in particular the spectacular blowing up of the *Daily Mirror* plant in Belfast on 17th July—wore down their objections. The Army must have known that internment would provoke at least as much trouble as the holding of the parade but internment *might* pay security dividends, whereas the Apprentice Boys' parade was just a tiresome piece of Irish nonsense. So Mr. Faulkner got internment, in the nick of time, for him.

The Apprentice Boys' parade was a kind of ritual acting out of the military crushing of the Papists. The only thing that could adequately compensate, in Protestant eyes, for the non-performance of the ritual, was the recurrence of the reality. To a great extent, the application of internment without trial, and the manner in which it was applied, satisfied this Protestant need. For this was internment of Catholics only. If people thought to endanger the peace were to be interned without trial, it seems reasonable to assume that people like the screaming Free Presbyterian I heard in Derry might have been put on the list. If they had been, the Catholic reaction against internment would certainly have been less. But Mr. Faulkner, naturally—in this a mirror image of Mr. Lynch—was far more concerned with *Protestant* reaction, on which his political survival depended, than with the comparatively exotic and speculative subject of Catholic sensibilities. For him to lock up *loyal Ulstermen* together with Papist murderers would mean an even quicker political death than cancellation-without-internment would have brought. The Army had no adequate incentive to insist on internment of Protestant extremists. After all, the gunmen who were killing British soldiers were the gunmen of the Catholics. The British Government in its intermittent Irish cogitations, guided by the highly plausible and articulate Brian Faulkner, and by officers whose soldiers were being shot at by Catholics, seems to have grossly underestimated the extent, intensity and duration of Catholic resentment at the introduction of internment of Catholics without trial, on 9th August 1971.

vii

The decision to introduce internment in this manner and at this time was disastrous both in its immediate and long-term effects.

Immediately, it produced by far the worst explosion of violence the North had yet known. Twelve people were killed and more than 150 houses burned out on internment day itself. By 12th August, twenty-three people had been killed in four days of internment—as compared with twenty killed in the whole of 1970. One of the dead was Father Mullen, shot in Derry by a British soldier while administering the last rites of the Church to a wounded Catholic. The soldier apparently thought the priest was kneeling to take aim, but many Catholics saw the act as deliberate sacrilegious murder of a priest holding the sacrament—'like in the Penal time' of the seventeenth and eighteenth centuries—part of a systematic war on the Catholic people and its faith. In this context the several hundred arrests under internment seemed also part of such a war, stripping the Catholic people of those who —granted the current dispositions of both police and army —seemed like their only defenders. In shock and panic, Catholics rioted throughout Northern Ireland.

The long-term effects of the introduction of internment were even more serious. Violence remained at a higher level until, by the end of the year, the death-roll had reached two hundred. The sharply increased use of gelignite bombing against civilian, and mainly Protestant, targets frightened and infuriated the Protestant people until, by the end of the year, Catholic-Protestant relations were worse than at any time in living memory.

Politically, the post-internment crisis resulted in a complete and sustained breakdown of all overt relations between the elected representatives of the two communities. The representatives of the Catholics had indeed walked out *before* internment, but they had not made this irrevocable. Now they were impelled to declare that they would never return to Stormont, and that they would not even engage in talks about a successor system to Stormont unless—as a precondition—internment without trial was ended, and all internees released. Until then a campaign of civil disobedience, including non-payment of rent and rates, would be kept up.

All this seemed the minimum that the mood of the Catholic community demanded. It also proved to be a formula for political deadlock and continuing violence. No government responsive to the feelings of the *Protestant* community would end internment willingly so long as bombing of civilians and shootings of police and reservists continued. Thus the Provisional I.R.A., by simply continuing these activities, could prevent the elected representatives of the Catholics from playing any 'constitutional' or mediatory role, and could confine them to roles seen by the Provisionals as ancillary to their own activities: the organization and promotion of civil disobedience and anti-internment protest.

The Provisionals thus acquired a veto over all meaningful political initiative and dialogue within Northern Ireland. At the time of writing they still hold and exercise this veto. An effort to break the deadlock, through talks between the three Prime Ministers, at Chequers on 27th and 28th September, proved a complete failure. Mr. Lynch, indeed, claimed that the very fact of his being invited to talks with the British and Northern Ireland premiers about Northern Ireland represented a historic break-through. To the extent that this claim was accepted, it raised the prestige of the Provisional I.R.A. which was able to assert credibly that the historic break-through in question was due to its own exertions, not those of Mr. Lynch. In any case the Chequers talks fizzled out ignominiously, with an agreement which, in effect, reported the existence of a common problem rather than any progress towards an agreed solution:

We are at one in condemning any form of violence as an instrument of political pressure; and it is our common purpose to seek to bring violence and internment and all other emergency measures to an end without delay.

The word-order was significant. The order 'bring violence and internment . . . to an end' represented a small but significant victory for Mr. Faulkner, who could now claim that even Mr. Lynch by implication acknowledged that the end of internment depended on the end of violence. Mr. Faulkner's little victory is understandable. Of the three protagonists at Chequers he was the only one who knew anything about Northern Ireland.

In October, the representatives who had seceded from Stormont met in a new 'alternative assembly' in Dungiven. As well as a Protestant parliament for a Protestant people, Northern Ireland now had a Catholic parliament for its Catholic people. It was a logical outcome, and it faithfully reflected the state of latent—and partly actual—civil war into which the province had sunk.

The civil war seemed to show increasing signs of drawing in the Republic. The introduction of internment, and the desperate reaction to it of Northern Catholics, made a greater impact on Southern opinion than any news from the North since Bogside in 1969. In some respects indeed it made a greater impact even than Bogside. Bogside had been a flare-up, but the post-internment crisis was as prolonged as it was bitter. There were no dead on Bogside (though there were some in Belfast the same week); the post-internment crisis was the most bloody any part of Ireland had known for fifty years. Finally, at Bogside, the British troops had appeared only in the paradoxical—and indeed almost incomprehensible—role of deliverers. Now they were back in their old only too well understood role—booted, imperious, bullying the Catholics, hurting them, humiliating them, sometimes killing them. The i.r.a., by contrast, often appeared as dashing and resourceful, carrying out brilliant escapes, holding television and press conferences almost under the noses of the clumsy British who were pursuing them. Certain official British acts, such as the publication of the Compton Report on 10th November, increased the antipathy to the British army, and sympathy with the i.r.a. The Compton Report was a characteristic 'British official' mixture of integrity and hypocrisy: integrity in admitting the use of cruel and intimidating interrogation practices—'hooding', the wall treatment, etc.—and hypocrisy in defining these as falling short of not only torture but even brutality, and coming under the classification of 'ill-treatment'.

In these propitious conditions, the I.R.A. established itself more securely, and flaunted its presence more often, on the soil of the Republic. Juries and magistrates were often unwilling to convict or penalize Republicans for possession of arms or explosives, where it appeared that these were intended solely for use in the North. In some border towns the I.R.A. were potentially a stronger agent of law enforcement—their own law—than the unarmed Gardai (police). The Government's attitude remained equivocal. On the one hand Mr. Lynch had reason to fear the I.R.A. build-up both in itself and for its repercussions on relations with Britain. On the other hand he also had reason to fear that any real, determined action against the I.R.A. might bring him down, through the defection of his own 'dissident supporters' who sympathized with the Provisionals. This hesitation of the Government had a kind of crazy, shaky, sideways momentum of its own. Neither judges, nor the police, nor the army, nor the ordinary citizens who make up juries knew quite where they were expected to stand on this question—and for anyone who did not know, the most prudent and convenient thing was not to annoy the I.R.A.

Yet the mood of Southern Catholics remained remote enough—far too remote in the view of Sinn Féin-I.R.A.—from that of Northern Catholics. In the border districts of the Republic, the Northern mood did communicate itself partly spontaneously, and partly because of a stupid British Army decision to 'crater' the many small 'unapproved' roads which run across the border. As the border generally runs through homogeneously Catholic territory—having been drawn at a time of maximum Protestant influence—the cratering was equally resented on both sides of the border, both because of its practical inconvenience, and because of a more basic biological feeling about a relationship to the soil: the foreigner was deliberately inflicting wounds on our land.[14] The filling in of the craters thus became at once a sacred duty, a restoration of everyday convenience, a socially approved activity and of course a pleasure. It also provided

[14] This is not a fanciful inference, but a feeling expressed in public and private discussion at this time.

a form of activity, and a frame of mind, which gave the
Provisional I.R.A. an opportunity for spreading its influence
and preparing for future border incidents. Here, as often, the
British Army, under the intermittently attentive guidance of
the Tory Government, and the unremitting politically-
oriented pressure of Mr. Faulkner, provided far better I.R.A.
propaganda material than the I.R.A. could ever have thought
of.

Outside the border areas, the fire spread slowly. Those of
us who were trying to check what we saw as a drift to civil
war were not entirely discouraged by the response to our
efforts, even in the post-internment period. I had several
opportunities of testing this response. In late August, before
my local Constituency Council, I attacked both wings of
the I.R.A.—challenging a view, attractive to the left in the
Republic, that, whereas the Provisionals might be a bad lot,
the Officials had the right idea. I followed this up with an
open letter to a friend, Mr. Paul O'Dwyer, asking him not to
help the Provisional I.R.A. leader, Mr. Joe Cahill, to proceed
on a fund-raising tour in the United States. Mr. Cahill, on
his return to Ireland denounced me, at a public meeting in
O'Connell Street, for my 'lousy audacity' in writing such a
letter. On 23rd October, in a public debate with Mr.
Tomás Mac Giolla, President of Sinn Féin (Gardiner Place—
'Official') I renewed my critique[15] of the entire I.R.A. position.

Although these statements, all of them well-publicized,
gave great offence to Sinn Féin-I.R.A., they were quite well
received by ordinary people, immediately at any rate. Most
people, while resentful of the British Army seemed still to
shrink from the ferocity of the I.R.A., and were shocked by
certain actions: the explosions in offices, pubs and streets:
the tarring and feathering of girls who went out with British
soldiers; the murder, in December, of Senator Barnhill.
People were also repelled by the cold-bloodedness of the
explanations of such acts: by the easy references to the
inevitability of civilian casualties and by such claims as that
made by the Official I.R.A. in justifying the killing of Senator
Barnhill—that, as the Senator resisted the 'active service unit'

[15] Reproduced in Appendix I.

which came to blow up his house, the members of the unit only acted in self-defence when they shot him dead.

Mainly, by early 1972, the people were puzzled, disturbed and looking for a lead. There was only one person who could give an effective lead, and that was the Taoiseach, Mr. Jack Lynch. Mr. Lynch condemned violence, indeed he did. He also said that 'violence is a by-product of the division of the country'.[16] This seemed to imply that violence would go on as long as partition did, and that those who were responsible for the violence, which Mr. Lynch so unfailingly condemned, were those who maintained that partition. Did this imply that the I.R.A., though a little hot-headed perhaps, were by and large right? If it did not imply that, why were the I.R.A. —in both forms, both illegal organizations—permitted to display with impunity so wide a range of political, propagandist and para-military activity within the area of Mr. Lynch's effective jurisdiction?

This whole process—governmental hesitation, certain political collusions, prudences of the law and the citizens, an undercurrent of sympathy and hero-worship—encouraged the I.R.A. to go still further, emerging ever more clearly as the army of the Catholic people, operating from a safe base in Catholic territory, against the British fastness in Protestant Ulster.

This was the background of the incident at Dungooley, on the South Armagh border on the 27th January 1972, when a party of Provisional I.R.A., firing from a house inside the territory of the Republic, engaged in a two-hour skirmish with Scots Dragoons in Northern Ireland. At the end of the engagement, Gardai took the names of the men. The Irish Army, from nearby Dundalk, did not arrive until the episode was over.

Dungooley seemed to mark a turning-point, after which the Government would either have to act against the Provisional I.R.A., or abdicate before it. Either way, it seemed likely that the Republic was about to experience its share of the violence which had been so far restricted—with a few sporadic exceptions—to Northern Ireland.

[16] In the Dáil, 20th October 1971.

## 12

# The Water and the Fish

*'Had I known is always in the end.'*
GHANAIAN PROVERB

i

The previous chapters were written at various times from
the summer of 1969 to late January 1972[1]—the last chapter
was finished on 29th January 1972, the day before Derry's
'Bloody Sunday'. This chapter is being written in early June
1972. I have not made any attempt to recast the earlier
chapters in the light of hindsight. If I had done so I should
have recast them more drastically in February than I now
feel inclined to do in June. I am painfully conscious that
the months of July and August—the baneful triumphal
months—may bring back the pressure and the mood, the
insights and the blindness, of Bloody Sunday's aftermath.

On Sunday, 30th January, when an illegal 'anti-internment' rally was held in Derry, British paratroops, taking aim
and firing, shot dead thirteen young Derrymen, all Catholics.

I wasn't in Derry that day and I don't know 'exactly what
happened'. Even if I had been there I should only know a
small part of it. Nor did I expect to learn what happened
from the official report—the Widgery Report—published
in mid-April. However good the intentions of the Lord Chief
Justice of England, who conducted the enquiry, the material
with which he had to deal, and the pressures upon him, were
such as to induce scepticism about his conclusions. As
regards the material, the French have the expression 'to

[1] The phrase 'at the time of writing' used in the later of these chapters means
literally what it says, and therefore varies somewhat from chapter to chapter.

lie like an eyewitness'; the English the expression 'to lie like a trooper'. As regards the pressures, an English judge, confronted with the testimony of an Irish eyewitness and a British trooper, may well prefer the testimony of the trooper. And the introduction to the Report reflects the fact that a report unacceptable to the Army would have been extremely inconvenient.

I shared therefore in the scepticism with which the Catholics of Ireland, plus category two,[2] received the Widgery report, largely exonerating the paratroops.

But scepticism, accompanied by a mild degree of resentment at 'British hypocrisy', was in April, after Widgery. What swept the country (consisting of the above) at the end of January and in early February was a great wave of emotion, compounded of grief, shock, and a sort of astonished incredulous rage against an England which seemed to be acting in the way we often accused her of acting but of which we had not, for decades, really believed modern England capable. The scenario seemed to have slipped back to 1921, or even earlier. For a few days, people talked and wrote of a national change of mood, like that which had set in after the executions of 1916. A Dublin periodical came out with Yeats' words 'a terrible beauty' on its front cover. The 'thirteen dead men', it seemed, would do what the 'sixteen dead men' had done. The bony thumb sharply increased its pressure. Mr. Lynch withdrew our Ambassador from London. And the Sinn-Féin I.R.A., and its friends in the press and media, set themselves both to exploit this mood and to convert it into one of settled hatred, appropriate to a war of Ireland against England.[3]

I shared, and still share, the belief that what happened in Derry was murder, in the sense that the troops deliberately shot dead young men who had probably been baiting them in various ways, but who were not endangering their lives. This was what seemed to emerge from the reports of the

[2] See above, Chapter 3.
[3] They are still trying. Even now (2 June) they still have a permanent exhibit outside the G.P.O. Dublin exhorting passers-by to 'remember the 13'—as they understand 'remembrance'. But at this point in time this seems forlorn rather than formidable.

more reliable correspondents present (such as Mr. Simon Winchester of *The Guardian*). About this, I shared most of the feelings of those around me. But I also feared, more than most, the exploitation of these killings in order to justify other killings, and in order to involve the territory and people of the Republic also in widening, intensifying violence.

I spent the three days after Bloody Sunday in London, where I saw Mr. Harold Wilson, Mr. Jeremy Thorpe, and the Home Secretary, Mr. Reginald Maudling. I went to report to them on the mood of the people in the Republic, but it seems to me now in retrospect that I was not so much an authority on that mood as an example of it. When I saw Mr. Maudling I was running a high temperature and was not making a great deal of sense. It is possible that this was fortunate; I may have made more impact than if I had made more sense, more impact as an exhibit than as an analyst. He knew that I had been saying, both in Ireland and in the international press, that if the British troops were withdrawn under prevailing conditions sectarian civil war would follow. What I had now to say was that I still believed that to be true, but that the continued presence of the troops, after Derry, had also a disaster potential. Not merely would any repetition of Bloody Sunday be likely to involve cross-border retaliation—and inhibit a Dublin Government from checking such retaliation—but the actual presence of British troops would act on the Catholic population, after Derry, as a standing justification for the I.R.A., strengthening their hold on the ghettoes. I therefore urged, not the immediate withdrawal of the troops, but the setting of a date for eventual withdrawal.

When, shortly afterwards, I made public this view, in London and in New York, Mr. Erskine Holmes, Chairman of the Northern Ireland Labour Party, reproached me with practising, or yielding to, what he called 'the politics of the last atrocity'. There is substance in this reproach. To a considerable extent I was responding to the prevailing mood of my own community to the point of losing sight of the reactions of the other community, whose sense of being abandoned, on the setting of a date for the departure of the troops, might well be at least as dangerous as the feelings of the Catholic community about the continued presence of the troops. To that extent, I was over-reacting. Yet what I said was true, in so far as it concerned the relation of the troops to the Catholic community.[4] It is also true that you cannot work for better relations between the two communities in Ireland while remaining completely impervious to the feelings of one's own community. I am sometimes accused of being impervious to these feelings but I am not, as any Unionist reader of this book will readily recognise.

The day I saw Mr. Maudling (Wednesday, 2nd February) was the day of the funerals of the thirteen in Derry. That evening in Dublin members of the I.R.A., acting under cover of a large, but mainly peaceful, mass demonstration, burned down the British Embassy in Merrion Square. That night, from London, I rang my wife, in Dublin. Maire, having been educated almost entirely among Catholics, is usually closer to 'the mood of the people' than I am: not the mood the press and media depict, or the mood Republicans declare to exist, but the way (Catholic) people generally are in fact responding. She warned me not to exaggerate the post-Derry response. It wasn't a '1916' swing: no 'terrible beauty' was in fact being born. The grief and shock were genuine, so had the resentment against England been, especially at the time I left (Monday), but by now the I.R.A. had over-reached themselves in their exploitation of these feelings. In particular the burning of the Embassy had been a mistake from an I.R.A. point of view. People were afraid of lawless violence 'coming down here'. They didn't want any kind of war with England, even an economic war, from which Ireland would suffer more than England. They knew the burning of the Embassy would have to be paid for, in terms of jobs and trade and tourists, and they were not in any such mood of exaltation as would induce them to accept sacrifices.

This was a remarkably accurate analysis. 2nd February represented in fact the peak, at least so far, of popular anti-British feeling. Since then up to now (early June) the pressure of the bony thumb has been endured with steadily decreasing resignation, with increasingly clear expressions of discomfort

[4] Later in this chapter I consider the question of how to cope with this problem.

and disgust, and even with a few faint signs that 'logic' may someday begin to do some 'outweighing'.

The thumb itself continued its savage gouging.[5]

The official i.r.a. claimed credit for an explosion outside a canteen at Aldershot on 22nd February which cost the lives of six civilians, mostly women cleaners, and a Catholic Army chaplain. This was a 'retaliation' for Derry. Other 'retaliations', 'executions' and 'warnings' followed. On 25th February, a Stormont Minister, John Taylor, was shot several times, though not fatally. On 4th March, an explosion in the Abercorn restaurant, Belfast, killed two people, and injured 136, some of whom were horribly mutilated. On 20th March a bomb killed six people in Lower Donegall Street, Belfast. Lesser, or less conspicuous, atrocities were of everyday occurrence.

In the Republic anti-i.r.a. feeling hardened—considering Derry—remarkably quickly. The Fianna Fáil Ard-Fheis (Conference) in mid-February showed approval for anti-violence and 'law and order' sentiments and, considering what had happened in Derry so short a time before, was well below normal Fianna Fáil standards in proclamations of patriotic dedication. The Labour Party's Annual Conference took place in Wexford on 26th February. This was after Aldershot, and after the attempt on John Taylor's life, but before the Abercorn restaurant; it was also less than a month after Bloody Sunday in Derry. There is always some pro-Sinn Féin sentiment in Labour Party Conferences, and Sinn Féin officers had predicted that this would be vindicated at Wexford by my own repudiation as Party spokesman on the North. Nothing of the sort happened. It was clear to all observers that the 'peace' forces outnumbered the pro-Sinn Féin people by about five to one and in the end even the minority joined with the others in what one disgruntled observer called 'the Labour Party love-in'—all concerned 'uniting' on a policy announced by the Party Leader, Brendan Corish, repudiating unequivocally both wings of

---

[5] I do not of course imply that the mind of the chivalrous Thomas MacDonagh would have approved what the present 'heirs of 1916' are doing. But his mind is no longer around; only his thumb.

the I.R.A., and all uses of violence for political purposes. My own position as Party spokesman was thereby strengthened; in other parties also those who—like Mr. Garrett Fitzgerald and Mr. Declan Costello—had overtly condemned the I.R.A. were encouraged by what our Conference showed. So were many others, ordinary people, who had been overawed by the greatly amplified rumblings of a supposed Republican bandwagon.

On 10th March, the Provisional I.R.A., conscious of the trend of public opinion, announced a three-day 'truce'. On 13th March, towards the end of this truce, Mr. Harold Wilson arrived in Dublin. During this visit Mr. Wilson saw, among others, representatives of the three democratic parties. Brendan Corish, Brendan Halligan and I saw him, at Leinster House, fraternally—that is, on behalf of his party's little Irish brother. I shall not here divulge any confidences of Mr. Wilson's; indeed I am not sure he did any confiding. He made some pleasant references to a Doctorate (honorary, of letters) which he had conferred on me the previous summer, in his capacity as Chancellor of the University of Bradford. He also told me, as he usually does when he meets any elected Irish representative, that he, in Huyton, represents more Irish voters than I do, which I am sure is true. For the rest, he patiently performed a pipe-filling ritual, so exquisitely long-drawn-out and so charged with implications of wise negotiation, that I am sure, at any Red Indian pow-wow, it would bring down the wig-wam. We, having heard some disquieting rumours, said how unwise it would be to negotiate with the I.R.A., under present conditions. It would encourage them in the view that they were winning and that they were the true heirs of 1921. This was a highly misleading and dangerous parallel. In the Northern Ireland situation if Catholic gunmen were seen to shoot and bomb their way to the negotiation table, Protestant gunmen would not be slow to emulate their performance, and the trend to civil war would acquire increased momentum.

Mr. Wilson did not dissent. He continued to play with, or on, his pipe. We learned from the papers the following day that he went that evening to see Provisional I.R.A. (alias Sinn

Féin) leaders, with whom he is reported to have spent several hours, in a house in Inchicore, Dublin. Mr. Wilson, clearly, is not a man to push candour to the verge of indiscretion.

The I.R.A. leaders did not grant Mr. Wilson the 'truce' extension he sought from them—the Donegall Street explosion took place within a week of his departure—but they did exploit his visit for the propaganda effect which is part of their military campaign, and of which, in a wider sense, their military campaign is part. His visit, they contended, proved his recognition that *they* were the really important people in the country, and showed his contempt for 'the Leinster House establishment'—that is, for parliamentary democracy in Ireland.

It must be conceeded that here the I.R.A. had a point. Mr. Wilson, like many another British statesman before him, was helping the argument of those in Ireland who hold that power must come from the barrel of a gun. And he did so, at a moment when that power was beginning to wilt from that which alone can cause it to wilt—the disapproval of the people of whom the gunmen are part. In other words—that is, using another metaphor of Chairman Mao's—this untoward visit came at a moment when 'the water' was just beginning to turn a little unhealthy for 'the fish' of the guerrilla. The 'Inchicore summit' put a little sparkle back into the water again, which was certainly as far from the intentions of Mr. Wilson—and of my colleague Dr. John O'Connell who acted as intermediary on this occasion—as it was near to the intentions of the killers with whom Mr. Wilson talked.

On 24th March the Heath Government announced its long-awaited 'initiatives'. A Minister for Northern Ireland, Mr. William Whitelaw, was announced. Hope was held out for the ending of internment without trial. But the towering centre-piece of the initiatives was what was popularly called 'the abolition of Stormont'. Stormont was in fact 'prorogued' for one year but it was universally accepted that it was never likely to meet again, in any form at all closely resembling its old self. Essentially what now came into being in Northern Ireland was direct rule from Britain, through a governor with executive powers.

If the I.R.A.—especially the Provisional I.R.A.—had, at this point, announced, and kept, an unconditional cease-fire, they would undoubtedly have placed themselves in a favourable political position, possibly a commanding one. They would have appeared, to the Catholics of Northern Ireland —as well as to the Protestants, but with different connotations—and to the Republic, as 'the men who brought down Stormont'. This would have been deceptive, but plausible. Deceptive, because it was the Civil Rights movement, and Stormont's own clumsy and brutal over-reaction to it, which had 'brought down Stormont'—in the sense of depriving it of its most essential power, control over law-enforcement— in August 1969 when I.R.A. armed activity was insignificant. Once Stormont had lost that power, and once British responsibility for law-enforcement was established, the most hopeful, and probably also the speediest, way of winning the civil rights demands was by continuing political pressure, including non-violent agitation, whenever 'normal' politics got stuck. The only things the I.R.A. certainly achieved by itself were hundreds of dead people, thousands of injured ones and a vast accretion to the legacy of hatred, fear and suspicion between the two communities. All the same the I.R.A. claim to victory, made in the context of a cease-fire, would have seemed highly plausible. August 1969 was long ago and half forgotten, and now the Unionists themselves were proclaiming at the tops of their voices that the Heath initiatives were 'a surrender to the I.R.A.'

The trouble was that the I.R.A. itself refused to accept it as a surrender. The 'Officials', it is true, did say that henceforward they would confine themselves to 'defence and retaliation'. As in the past, however, the official concept of 'defence' had covered the murder of the elderly Senator Barnhill[6] and 'retaliation' the blowing up of cleaning women, there was little comfort to be derived from this assurance. For the Provisionals Mr. Seán Mac Stíofáin announced, from Navan, Co. Meath, within an hour of the publication of the initiatives, that the war would go on and so it did.

It is now clear that the Provisionals here made a great

[6] Above pp. 279–80

mistake, which may eventually prove fatal to their movement. Even before the initiatives, most people in the ghettoes
and in the Republic had been against the violence, but it had
often been a case of 'against violence but . . .'. The 'but'
meant that Stormont and the British were, or might be, more
to blame for the violence than the i.r.a. were. Now Stormont
was gone and the manner of its going—and the way in which
Protestants took its going—seemed to imply that the British
now meant to ensure that Catholics in Northern Ireland
would get a better deal from now on. What stood, and what
was seen to stand, between the Catholics and that better
deal was now the i.r.a. 'war'. The s.d.l.p. leaders, in
welcoming the initiatives and calling for an end to violence,
were fully in tune with the mood of those who elected them.
With every new i.r.a. atrocity, and especially with every
new *pronunciamento* from Navan 'in the Free State', the 'water'
became a little more unhealthy for the 'fish'. And in the
wider reservoir of the Republic it became more unhealthy
too, even for the Provisional fish, which had hitherto swum
there so freely.

Why did they not stop when the stopping was good?
Partly no doubt for ideological reasons. Since the real enemy
was England, direct rule from England was, if anything,
even less acceptable than Stormont. This is a reason against
peace, but not against a 'tactical' cease-fire. The reason
given against a cease-fire is usually that if they stopped it
would be hard to start again. The mental scenario is that of
1921. Then there was a Truce, reflecting war-weariness,
followed by that 'act of national apostasy'—approved by the
living but never ratified by the dead—the Treaty of 1921.
But really this would be worse. Collins and Griffith did at
least have a prestigious prelude to their act of apostasy: they
sat down at the negotiating table with members of the
British Cabinet. No Englishman of political importance had
yet sat down with the Provisional leaders except Mr. Harold
Wilson, and Ballyfermot is a far cry from Downing Street.
Still, what the Leader of Her Majesty's Loyal Opposition
does today the Leader of her Majesty's Government may do
tomorrow, the Provisionals reason. In order to get to that

point it is obviously worth while to kill and maim any number of people: 'civilian casualties' unavoidable en route to the table. It is true that a certain haze still surrounds that table. Did the Provisionals really expect that the British Government would do something which Lloyd George did *not* do in 1921—that is, negotiate a political settlement with people who were *simultaneously* carrying on a campaign of violence, including the killing of British troops? And if they did not expect this, were they not necessarily looking for a negotiated truce like that which had such lamentable effects (as the I.R.A. saw them) in 1921? And if a new truce were followed by new negotiations, could they really expect these negotiations to lead to Britain's acceptance of an all-Ireland Republic, imposed on a million unwilling Protestants? And if they did not expect that, what could negotiations produce except another 'act of national apostasy'? From a process of logical reduction it would appear that what the Provisional leaders—or at least the more intelligent among them—were looking for was the opportunity to commit an act of national apostasy and win the power that followed such acts in the past.[7]

That opportunity seems remote, at the time of writing. But the Provisionals are not finished. They could be rehabilitated in the ghettoes if there were major Protestant attacks on these, if British troops failed to contain the attacks, and if the Provisionals were thereby enabled to emerge again in the only role in which the ghettoes ever fancied them: that of 'defenders of the people'. It looks as if the Provisionals have been trying to provoke precisely such a situation. At least it is difficult to imagine what other motive there could be in such actions as the planting of bombs in Courtland's polyester plant in Carrickfergus (2nd May) or in the Co-op. in York Street, Belfast (11th May). On 17th May a sniper opened fire on Protestant workers leaving Mackie's works in Belfast, but this particular act was disavowed by the Provisional leaders. 'The ordinary volunteer', as a writer in a

---

[7] From a Republican point of view the first act of national apostasy by former Republicans was the Treaty of 1921 ; the second was the taking of the Oath by Eamon de Valera and his followers in 1927.

Dublin periodical sympathetic to Sinn-Féin-i.r.a. explained, 'is quite happy to strike at Protestant institutions simply because they are Protestant'.[8] Presumably the sniper outside Mackie's was an 'ordinary volunteer'.

The Protestant response to all this has been a wavering one. The Tory 'betrayal' of 24th March had a stunning impact, and Protestant leaders have been divided as to what to do. Mr. William Craig dangles his 'ideas of a u.d.i. nature'. Mr. Brian Faulkner wants the restoration of Stormont. Mr. Ian Paisley, the best reader of the signs, has called for full integration into the United Kingdom. I believe myself that it is round Mr. Paisley's idea that Protestant feeling will eventually consolidate—in much the same way as Orangemen, having protested against the Union in 1800, soon became such fervent Unionists that they forgot they had ever been anything else. But for the moment it is Mr. Craig, the least intelligent of the three Protestant leaders, who is to the fore. His para-military Ulster Defence Association, hooded and masked, marched in formidable strength in Belfast on 28th May. Meanwhile some Protestant 'ordinary volunteers' seemed quite happy to strike at Catholics simply because they were Catholics. On the day when the sniper opened fire on Mackie's workers, a Catholic was found shot dead at Belfast war memorial, in what looked like a kind of ritual murder. Cars began to drive down Catholic streets, opening fire at random.

'You notice there's a sectarian civil war on,' said a Protestant sourly, 'when the Protestants start shooting back.'

In the Catholic ghettoes people still saw the i.r.a. as necessary for their defence, but at the same time came out more openly for a cessation of i.r.a. violence. On 17th May, when a British soldier shot dead a young Derry Catholic, Marcus Deery, the official i.r.a. made the mistake of 'executing' another young Derry Catholic who happened to be a British soldier. The reaction of Derry women was so angry that it led to a cease-fire by the Officials a week later. They were ceasing fire they said because they say the danger

[8] Michael McKeown in *Hibernia*, 26th May 1972.

of a sectarian civil war. What had really happened was that their own sect had repudiated their war. The Provisionals, better established and more highly regarded, kept on their war but under increasing pressure to stop.

Meanwhile Mr. Whitelaw was continuing to make a favourable impression on Catholics by releasing internees, by what was apparently his restraining influence over the Army, by his conciliatory tone and affable personality and —not least—by his unpopularity with Protestants.

In the Republic the news from the North encouraged an anti-I.R.A. swing of opinion of such proportions that Mr. Lynch's government was moved to take some action against the Provisionals.

The swing became evident during the campaign on the referendum to decide the issue of whether Ireland should, or should not, enter the Common Market. Fiannal Fail and Fine Gael were for 'Yes'. The Labour Party was for 'No'. So were both wings of Sinn-Féin I.R.A. I followed my Party's line without exaggerated enthusiasm. The Party's policy was a long-established one, and Party spokesmen presented a rational case, on economic and social grounds, against entry. But as for me I felt, and probably looked, like a dog being washed. I am not temperamentally 'anti-European', and dislike anti-foreign exercises of all descriptions, however rationally they may seem to be grounded. And I disliked our 'allies' more than I disliked even either set of our adversaries. Nor did I much care for the memory that less than two years before I had myself thought such an alliance such a good political idea that I had stifled moralistic misgivings about it. Now I devoted much of my time to explaining that Labour's case was entirely separate and distinct from that of the rather strange-looking people who seemed to be uttering the same monosyllable.

On 10th May the Irish electorate put me, and a few more like me, out of our misery by voting 'Yes' by more than five to one. The total 'No' vote was slightly less than the Labour proportion of the vote at the 1969 general election. Areas where Sinn Féin was supposed to be strong, such as the border counties, voted 'Yes' overwhelmingly.

There were of course many reasons for voting 'Yes'—principally the opinion, expressed by many ordinary people, that once Britain went in Ireland could hardly stay out. But most observers also thought that the activity of both wings of Sinn Féin, vehemently urging a 'No' vote, actually increased the 'Yes' majority. There were quite a few people who, in their hearts, were frightened at the idea of being locked up alone in the cold, clammy dark, with Cathleen ní Houlihan and her memories of the dead. Outwardly such people might be civil and even deferential to Sinn Féin—much as a villager might be civil and even deferential to a reputed witch—but in the secrecy of the ballot-box nothing could prevent them from affirming their real feeling, rejecting romantic nationalism and the cult of the dead.

For professional politicians the Referendum result meant that Sinn Féin I.R.A. (including both factions) was a paper-tiger electorally speaking. Provisional prisoners in Mountjoy Jail therefore picked a bad moment when, just a week after the Referendum result was announced, they staged so serious a riot that the Army had to be called in to quell it. After this, the Government introduced a Prisons' Bill empowering the Minister for Justice, Mr. Desmond O'Malley, to transfer certain prisoners to military custody. The Labour Party had a free vote on this issue and I was among those who voted in favour when the Bill was carried by a very large majority. The Government also announced the setting up of Special Courts—not military courts but judges sitting without a jury. The reason for this was, of course, the danger—and in my view the already existing reality—of intimidation of juries. That the intimidation of witnesses would also be a factor was starkly illustrated in the next month when a County Louth farmer, who had declared his willingness to testify against 'Republicans' who had beaten him up, was found on the other (Northern) side of the Border—stripped, tarred and feathered and shot through both legs. Organizations whose members did this sort of thing were of course loud in protest against the 'violation of civil rights' implied by the setting up of Special Courts. So were those Americans who, while proclaiming their 'friendship to Ireland', manifest this sentiment by helping the I.R.A. to tear the place apart.

The Official I.R.A., feeling the cold breeze of public opinion north and south, announced—on 29th May—a cease-fire. Henceforward, they said, they would act only in a defensive role (dropping 'retaliation'). As an undertaking this meant little except that any killings they carried out would henceforward be described by them as defensive. But, as a reflection of the mood of the country, the Official decision was significant.

The Provisionals however kept right on with the killing. At the end of May, the Government acted against the Provisional leaders. Ruairí O Brádaigh, President of Sinn Fién, was arrested on 31st May, and so was one of the more conspicuous Provisional chiefs, Joe Cahill. Seán Mac Stíofáin went on the run. Ruairí O Brádaigh, who had been in a television debate with me the night before his arrest, blamed me for inciting the Government to this course. His successor as Acting President of Sinn Féin, Mr. Dáithí O Conaill, developed this charge:

The British government can be well pleased with the action of Lynch and O'Malley. Their[9] official mouthpiece in Ireland and abroad, Conor Cruise O'Brien, has long agitated for a policy of violence against Sinn Féin. Violence is nothing new of O'Brien; his legacy to the Irish people is a mass grave of young Irish soldiers in Glasnevin Cemetery and a denigration of the character of one of the world's greatest diplomats—Dag Hammersjkold.

O'Brien's pathological hatred of Republicanism found an outlet in personal vicious attacks on Joe Cahill.[10] It is ironic that Joe Cahill should have been arrested while making arrangements to meet the Evangelist, Mr. Billy Graham, who requested a meeting with Republican leaders for Wednesday night. No doubt, Mr. Cruise O'Brien is now pleased that Joe Cahill did not meet Billy Graham. It shocked O'Brien last March that Harold Wilson would express pleasure at meeting any of Ireland's most dedicated sons.[11]

[9] 'Their' appears to refer to the British Government, not to Messrs. Lynch and O'Malley.
[10] Any criticism of a Republican is a personal vicious attack.
[11] *Sunday Press*, Dublin, 4th June 1972.

The Ireland of the living was at this point heartily sick of 'Ireland's most dedicated sons'. It remained to be seen whether the Ireland of the living people, through its elected representatives, with all their faults and miseries, could prevail over 'the most dedicated sons' of Cathleen ní Houlihan.[12]

At the end of May the chances looked a little brighter than they had looked for some time.

## ii

In the early summer of 1972 it was officially revealed to the general public for the first time that Eamon de Valera, at the time of the Treaty debates more than fifty years before, had not merely repudiated any attempt to impose the will of an Irish majority on Ulster Protestants, but had equated any such attempt with England's effort to impose its will on those Irish who rejected English rule:

*An t Uachtarán* (The President, Eamon de Valera) . . . They (i.e. Dáil Eireann) had not the power, and some of them had not the inclination to use force with Ulster. He did not think that policy would be successful. *They would be making the same mistake with that section as England had made with Ireland.* (Author's italics.) He would not be responsible for such a policy. . . . For his part, if the Republic were recognised, he would be in favour of giving each county power to vote itself out of the Republic if it so wished.[13]

These words of Eamon de Valera contain the key to peace in Ireland. Unfortunately for fifty years it was a lost key. The words were spoken *in private session* of the Dáil. Nobody is recorded as expressing indignation—though two

[12] It doesn't seem to have occurred to the earlier audiences of Yeats's *Cathleen ní Houlihan* that there might be something unhealthy about a mother who shuffles round promising her sons that 'they shall be remembered for ever', provided they get themselves killed for mother's sake.

[13] *Private Sessions of Second Dáil*: published by Stationery Office, Dublin. The volume bears no date of publication, but was released to Dáil deputies in May 1972. The extract quoted is from the minutes of proceedings for 22nd August 1921.

Deputies said they 'disagreed'—and it is clear that their substance was acceptable to a large majority of the Dáil at that time: neither in the private nor the public sessions did 'the question of Ulster' play any significant part. But under the pressure of subsequent events, and especially of competition between different factions of Republicans, 'Ulster' came again to loom as large, and as distorted, as it had when Sinn Féin used it to discredit and smash the old Irish Party. Mr. de Valera's own Constitution in 1937 enshrined the myth of what one of his closest collaborators called 'the indivisible island'.[14] To murmur that it was not merely divisible, but actually divided, by the conflicting wills of sections of its inhabitants, became a suspect activity. When I suggested in the Dáil in 1971 that the claim that Ireland *must* be united, whether Ulster Protestants wanted it or not, was essentially a *colonial* claim, this assertion was deemed offensive to pious ears, and I was accused of national heresy, apostasy, blasphemy and the Lord knows what.[15] Yet what I was saying was of course in substance precisely what the eventual author of the Constitution had said in August 1921, in private among consenting Republicans.

The future solution of the problem depends largely on whether Irish Catholics generally come to accept the truth recognised by Mr. de Valera in 1921, and subsequently lost sight of. As long as Catholics generally think of unity as 'the solution', 'the only solution', 'the only thinkable solution', so long will groups like the Provisional I.R.A. draw from this general vague conviction their mandate and license. So long also will Ulster Protestants generally feel that the slightest concession to Catholics opens the way to Catholic power over Protestants, and so long will some Protestants feel that Protestant murder-gangs are the only answer to Catholic murder-gangs. So long, in fact, will we have all the conditions of sectarian civil war.

I believe that at this moment none of the main sections of

---

[14] Title of an officially sponsored book by the late Frank Gallagher. See also the statements by Mr. de Valera quoted as epigraphs to Chapter 9.
[15] For the overlap of nationalist and religious vocabulary see below, pp. 307–10. It is fair to add that these particular accusations were not made in the Dáil.

the population of Ireland actually wants unity. Ulster Protestants obviously do not. Ulster Catholics are interested in
equality—especially in relation to jobs—rather than in unity,
although their concept of equality does include the right to
wave tricolour whenever a Protestant waves a Union Jack.
The population of the Republic has been accustomed to as-
senting to a theory of unity, but in practice when we say 'this
country' we usually mean the twenty-six county state,[16]
and most of us are less than inconsolable about the rest of
the island, though we are uncomfortable and uncertain about
it, when we happen to think about it at all. The events of the
last few years have caused us to think about it much more,
and with far greater inward discomfort, than at any time in
previous history. But I do not believe that the results of this
thinking, and this discomfort, have increased the demand for
unity. Rather the contrary is the case. Forced for the first
time to have a serious look at the problem, if only as it
appears on the television screens, the people of the Republic
have begun to have second thoughts, rather clearer than the
first, about incorporating the North.[17] In theory these
strange, fierce people are all one and the same as our easy-
going selves: in practice they seem to be a bit different. The
Protestants seem more determined, more numerous and
much more unassimilable than we had thought them, in the
days when we only thought we were thinking about them.
And these Northern Catholics too look a tough lot. They
should, indeed, get a fairer deal, so they should. Up there.

In short what has been coming across to ordinary people is
that our problem is *not* 'how to get unity' but how to share
an island in conditions of peace and reasonable fairness, and
that such conditions *preclude* unity as long as the Ulster
Protestants reject that. In this, ordinary people are, as often,
well ahead of 'public opinion' as expressed by Dublin edit-

[16] For a notable example of this usage see p. 273 *n.* 13. But even that most fiercely
intransigent of Republicans, Miss Mary Mac Swiney could say: 'There is no
man, woman or child in *the country, the south of Ireland* (my italics) who will turn
down the men who fight for Ireland.' (*Private Sessions of Dáil Eireann,* 17th
December 1921).
[17] 'Northern Ireland,' said a woman in my constituency, 'I wish someone would
saw that place off.'

orial writers, merchants of 'inevitable unity' almost to a man. The reason for this, I think, is that the ordinary man or woman is prepared to change his or her opinions with devastating abruptness when conditions appear that make the previous ones inappropriate or inconvenient.[18] The editorial writer on the other hand is stuck with what he said before, even when it begins to look inappropriate. I have yet to read an editorial beginning: 'What we have said before on this subject has been a load of codswallop.'

### iii

The main alternative models for the future of this problem that now seem possible are these:

### A   *The 'benign' model:*

The offensive of the Provisional I.R.A. will falter and fail as a result of the increasingly hostile mood of the Catholic people; the 'water' poisoning the 'fish'. The internees will be released and internment without trial will be ended. Protestant demonstrations against this will be containable (because of the cessation of the Provisional offensive). The end of internment will permit the Catholic elected representatives to enter into serious discussion with the British Minister (Mr. Whitelaw or his successor). The end of I.R.A. hostilities will permit the Protestant elected representatives to enter into similar discussions. This process will lead to discussions between the elected representatives of the two communities, with the British representative in essentially an arbitral role. Out of these discussions will emerge new structures with which both communities can live. These will include a thorough reform of local government, leaving any sizeable block composed of either community in charge of its own

[18] It may be said that I, as an odd kind of chap and an intellectual to boot, have no right to speak for 'ordinary people'. The fact is that some thousands of these have appointed me to speak for them. As an empirical way of finding out whether I am right in assessing their mood I would accept the test of whether I hold my seat at the next election. I have no doubt I shall hold it (barring accidents in the meantime).

local affairs. Local affairs will include local police. A central police authority, responsible to a joint commission, will see to the recruitment, training and payment of the local forces, and will also dispose of a central police reserve, adequate to prevent one 'ghetto' being used as a base for attack on another. The British Army will be withdrawn from all responsibility for policing. As security begins to return, the British Government will invest in a massive reconstruction programme, involving major public works projects in the high unemployment (principally Catholic and Western) areas. Dublin will be invited, and will agree, to contribute to such a programme and will invite the friends of Ireland in America to do likewise. Religious discrimination in job appointments will be progressively eliminated (immediately in relation to new jobs created). Catholics will be convinced that their major grievances are being disposed of; Protestants convinced that the ending of these practices does not entail the end of the world, i.e. Catholic power over Protestants. The Dublin government will affirm its willingness to co-operate without reservation with a Northern Ireland so reconstructed and—while not abandoning an aspiration to eventual unity by free consent—will drop all 'we must have unity' propaganda.

The above is not a 'blueprint'; simply a rough sketch of the *kind* of benign evolution that could take place if the Provisional offensive definitely stopped

If . . .

### B  *The malignant model:*
The Provisional offensive will continue (possibly with a limited 'tactical' interruption) and even escalate. It will provoke an escalating Protestant counter-offensive including the murder of prominent Catholics, followed by retaliatory murders of Protestants. This will be followed by massed Protestant assaults on Catholic ghettoes. Some of these will be contained by the Army, some will break through. Where breakthroughs occur, the only defence the Catholics will have will be the I.R.A. In these conditions the I.R.A. regains control

over the ghettoes in question and can continue its activities indefinitely. The British Army comes under armed attack from both communities. With increasing casualties and no solution in sight, the British public clearly favours a policy of withdrawal. A British Government announces its agreement to the unity of Ireland, for which it receives many telegrams of congratulation from America, and urgent private messages of alarm from Dublin. The British Government, indicating that the policing of a united Ireland is a matter for the Irish Government, terminates its peace-keeping role and begins a withdrawal of its troops. Mass meetings of loyalists in Belfast acclaim 'no surrender'. An official mission from Dublin to negotiate a 'federal solution' is unable to move outside the Catholic areas of Belfast.[19] Armed Loyalists move *en masse* into these ghettoes to get rid of the I.R.A. once and for all, to lynch the Dublin emissaries, and to punish the Catholics generally. Thousands of Catholics are killed and scores of thousands fly south in terror: thus the water and the fish go down the drain together, from the eastern part of Northern Ireland. In the western and southern parts, Catholics start killing Protestants, and Protestants fly north and east. With or without orders from the Dublin government, the Irish army takes over in Newry, Derry and Strabane, and surrounding Catholic areas. Its efforts to penetrate the Protestant hinterland are held off, or beaten back. The Taoiseach appeals to the United Nations for technical assistance in the form of military aid. The Security Council is unable to agree.

As United Nations intervention bringing about the final unity of Ireland is one of the many illusions which bedevils this situation it may be well to dispose of it here. Why should the Security Council *not* agree to such a request from Ireland —since its accession to an identical request from the Government of the Congo in 1960 is a strict precedent, though not an altogether reassuring one? The reasons are many but the basic one is that Britain is a permanent member of the Security Council, with right of 'veto', and that no conceivable British government—least of all one that was having to face

[19] Into which it would have to move by helicopter.

the predictable consequences of such a withdrawal—could agree to a form of United Nations assistance which would necessarily entail 'the armed coercion of Britishers by foreigners'. The Soviet Union and China would loudly urge compliance with the Dublin government's appeal: this would probably tilt the other two permanent members, the United States[20] and France in favour of the British view. In these conditions—i.e. as long as the coercion of Protestant Ulster was a possibility in view—the Security Council would certainly stall: that is, it would call for a cease-fire, send a team of observers and adjourn. Later, perhaps not much later, when the two sides, dead-locked, agreed to a cease-fire, agreement could be found for a United Nations force to patrol the cease-fire line: the new border.

Ireland would be left, once more, with two States, but of even more virulent shades of green and orange than before. The Orange State would be smaller than before—probably about four counties—but would be homogeneously Protestant, without the tiniest Catholic crack or crevice for a new I.R.A. to take root in. The Green State with its massive ingestion of embittered and displaced Ulster Catholics, would be an uncongenial environment for Protestants, most of whom would probably leave. A tiny minority would probably remain in order to proclaim from time to time how well treated they were and how non-sectarian everything was compared with the terrible conditions prevailing to the North.

Both states would be under right-wing governments, scruffily militarist and xenophobe in character. The principal cultural activities would be funerals, triumphal parades, commemorations, national days of mourning, and ceremonies of rededication to the memory of those who died for Ireland/ for Ulster.[21]

The only check on these orgies would be the urgent need,

[20] The ethnic vote would elicit from the U.S. Government expressions of sympathy with Ireland, but no action. See the analysis of how the Eisenhower Government used the U.N. in the Hungarian crisis (1956) in the present writer's *United Nations: Sacred Drama*.
[21] Both states would also be highly 'religious' in the sense discussed in the Epilogue.

felt in both states, to refurbish their connections with England equally necessary for both of them.

Under Model A the water succeeds in eliminating the fish. Under Model B the fish bring on the destruction of the water.

If Model B is described in more detail than A, the reason is that B is so vividly present in my mind, with a vividness increasing over the past two years, that I find it hard not to think of it as inevitable. It is *not* inevitable: A remains possible, and at the moment of writing even looks fairly likely. What does seem certain is that it is in *the general direction* indicated by one or other of these two model/scenarios that things must move. Neither scenario of course is likely to be fully realized and the course of events may often seem to oscillate between them. But in time the substance of one or other will have to prevail.

In short either the division of the island in our time will be accepted and worked reasonably—that is, with justice to minorities—or it will be forcefully denied and the attempt to annul it will perpetuate it in a more vicious form, including the destruction of minorities.

I am not 'against unity'. I should like to see it if it were possible, but there is no meaningful sense in which it is possible now. While two communities are as bitterly antagonistic as are Catholics and Protestants now it is not merely futile but actually mischievous, to talk about uniting Ireland. Mr. Jack Lynch's formula 'Violence is a by-product of the division of the country' is both untrue in itself—since violence preceded and accompanied the division—and is also a formula legitimizing an indefinitely protracted sectarian guerrilla. That is no doubt not what Mr. Lynch intended but in this instance, as in so many others, the Puss-in-boots Provisionalism of Mr. Lynch and his associates has provided a soft and furry cover for the deadly reality of the Provisional 'by-product' itself. It seems at the time of writing that that cover is being withdrawn. If that withdrawal is permanent the chances of model A will be greatly improved.

In fact, what Ireland needs at this time is not 'unity' but a greater flexibility in division. The 'unity of Ireland' is a dangerous illusion but 'the unity of Northern Ireland' is also a dangerous illusion. There is no perfect way of sorting out the hostile and intertwined communities, but autonomy within direct rule offers the best hope: this is the core of Model A.

Cathleen ní Houlihan of course says 'No', opting unerringly for Model B, especially since it offers the enticing prospect of the sacrifice of further sons in future generations. 'The only pleasure in freedom is fighting for it.'[22]

I sometimes fear that Model A may seem to prevail for a time, that peace may return, and that later a new outbreak of intensified violence may precipitate the coming of Model B.

As Albert Camus wrote, at the end of *La Peste*, the bacillus of the plague can be dormant for years 'in furniture and linen' and may again one day 'waken its rats and send them to die in a happy city'.

I refuse to end on that note. The plague is a metaphor for conditions created by men and women, and men and women who have quarrelled can learn through suffering how to live together and apart, as France and Germany have learned. People can wake up in the morning and find an imprisoning myth no longer imprisoning but just plain silly. Cathleen ní Houlihan and King Billy are not necessarily immortal.

[22] Comdt Eoin O'Duffy, 17th December 1921: *Private Sessions of Second Dáil*, p. 241. Commandant, later General, O'Duffy was the founder of the Blueshirts and headed the Irish Brigade of Volunteers for Franco. He would have made a good Provisional.

# Epilogue

*And idle God and cursing priest*
*Shall plague us from Moy Slaught no more.*
SAMUEL FERGUSON

## i

I come back to a question asked at the beginning: is it a *religious* quarrel?

I believe the answer is 'Yes', but with significant qualifications.

To define it as a *national* quarrel has arguments in its favour, but will not quite serve. What would the 'two nations' be? Irish Catholics do not, formally and consciously at least, think in terms of an Irish Catholic nation, but of an Irish nation including both Catholics and Protestants. Ulster Protestants do not—usually—regard themselves as not being Irish, but as Ulster folk, Irish but British as well, as the Scots and the Welsh are British. They regard Irish Catholics as fellow-Irishmen, but without this relationship in itself implying any cordiality:[1] the Catholics are seen as disloyal fellow-Irishmen who refuse the common British bond uniting the rest of the people of the two islands, and who wish to impose a foreign status on people who intend to remain loyal. Nor is it tenable to assert, as most Provisionals seem to do, that it is a national quarrel *between Ireland and England*, with the mass of Protestants in the role of 'England's garrison'. Ulster Protestants form a community with a will of its own. The idea that contemporary England is manipulating the Protestants in order to 'keep its grip on Ireland' is part of the sick world of fantasy in which Sinn Féin lives.

[1] In all this I am using generalization about collective views. There are many personal exceptions, mostly partial, a few total.

Starting from that analysis, it would be tempting to isolate *allegiance* as the criterion. But in fact 'allegiance' takes us straight back to 'religion'. The Boyne was a victory, not of an English king over an Irish one, but of a Protestant king over a Catholic one. Irish Catholics were enthusiastically loyal to the English king, while he was the Catholic James II. Ulster Protestants rebelled against the same English king, preferring to him a Dutch Protestant, as they would have preferred a Protestant of any nationality. The apparent fixation on commemorating the Battle of the Boyne symbolizes not some vague 'loyalty to England' but loyalty to the Protestant succession and the triumph of the Protestant cause.

Nor, despite the frantic efforts of various green Catholic Marxists, can the struggle plausibly be made out to be one of *class*. The fissure in Northern Ireland can be seen as a vertical one, involving horizontal overlaps, more or less like this:

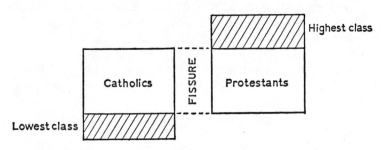

Even this is a little deceptive. As Professor Rose reminds us, 'there are more poor Protestants than there are poor Catholics'. But the very poorest are likely to be Catholics, the very richest Protestants; more Protestants are skilled workers and more Catholics unskilled and so on. That there is class *differentiation*, that Protestants have the edge over Catholics is true, relevant and important. But it is not true that what is happening is a class *conflict*. In politics, in loyalty, in their reaction to different categories of violence, the Protestants, of all social classes, react as one community; the Catholics, of all social classes, as another.[2] The 'revolutionary

[2] Anyone who doubts this should study Professor Rose's book: above, p. 156.

solidarity of Catholic and Protestant workers' is a myth. *Industrial* solidarity was not altogether a myth—there are Catholic shop-stewards chosen by Protestant workers, etc.— and it could become a factor of positive importance, if the future turns towards Model A. But this kind of growth in solidarity requires, precisely the rejection of the notion of *revolution*, which has become a sectarian notion. On a visit to Belfast towards the end of 1971, one Belfast shop-steward, a Communist, told me that after years of trying to bring politics (i.e. left-wing politics) *into* the works, he was now devoting the same energy to keeping politics *out*, because politics inevitably meant sectarian conflict. He also described how management and shop-stewards in this major plant were actually in a kind of collusion to engineer confrontations between 'management and workers', in order to take the men's minds off 'the real conflict' which was capable of blowing the works apart, ruining men and management together. The 'real conflict', which the carefully contrived 'class struggle' ballot sought to avert, was that between Protestants and Catholics. Reality here stood classical Marxist theory on its head: the 'false consciousness' fabricated here was *class* consciousness.

To say that it is a conflict of *settlers and natives* is to tell an important part of the truth, but only a part. It was a Reformation settlement in Counter-reformation territory. What kept alive the difference over the centuries, over a major change of language (among the Catholics), and over the vast changes brought about by the industrial revolution —taking so many 'settlers' and 'natives' alike from the land they had fought over—was the factor of religion, inseparably intertwined with political allegiance. Where settlers adopted the religion of the natives, as in parts of the south and midlands, their descendants became indistinguishable from the native population, into which they merged.

So we are brought back, inescapably, to what so many people seek to deny: the rather obvious fact of a conflict between groups defined by *religion*. This does not mean it is a theological war. It would not even be exact to say that it is a conflict between Catholics and Protestants. It is a conflict *between IRISH Catholics and ULSTER Protestants.* More immediately, of course, it is a conflict between *Ulster* Catholics and *Ulster* Protestants and, as we have seen, southern Irish Catholics are not involved in it in the same way. But the fact that the southern Irish are Catholics and identify, even though rather inconsequently and distantly, with Ulster Catholics makes it an Irish Catholic affair. Above all, the Ulster Protestant's response is proportioned to his concept of a siege conducted by a majority in the island.

The actual *religions*—the systems of beliefs and of feelings about those beliefs—cherished by Ulster Protestants and by Irish Catholics are distinct, in reality though not formally, from the religions of the same name as practised elsewhere.[3]

In both cases the actual, as distinct from the formal, religion is an amalgam of the strictly ecclesiastical body of doctrines and practices, and of other doctrines and practices derived from the past history of Irish Catholics and Ulster Protestants. A cult of the ancestors enters into both, and is acted out in the annual commemorative rites at Bodenstown, Finaghy and elsewhere.

In theory the religion is a separate and distinct matter from the political heritage, but in practice things are not so easily compartmentalized. Two witticisms make this point rather pithily:

The first is a venerable anecdote. An old man is asked by a youth (or a foreigner): 'Who was King Billy?' His reply is: 'Away man, and read your Bible.'

The second is a more modern quip: 'Elsewhere', wrote Mr. Terence de Vere White recently, 'Easter is celebrated as the Feast of the Resurrection. In Dublin it is celebrated as the Feast of the Insurrection.'

These are rather more than just jokes. An ikon of the Bible, in its aspect of 'The Secret of England's Greatness', is hauled in annual Orange processions along with King Billy and Queen Victoria as a sort of tribal talisman and charaismatic source of power. And in Patrick Pearse's mind, and those of some other notable Irish patriots, the sufferings

---

[3] 'Elsewhere' has of course countless sub-varieties and amalgams but I am not concerned with these here.

of Christ and those of the Irish (Catholic) people were in a particular sense one: the sacrifice of Irish patriots was analogous to the sacrifice of Christ; and the resurgence of the national spirit that such a sacrifice could set in motion was analogous to the resurrection of Christ. The timing of the Rising for Easter was no coincidence.

The intrusion of such elements would no doubt be reprobated by theologians, though I have never seen any sign that Irish theologians are much interested in the matter. But in fact it is not surprising that Biblical Christianity can be given such a twist. The Bible is the story of a Chosen People, and the various sets of people who have laid claim to it have habitually regarded *themselves* as chosen. The fundamentalist Old Testament character of Ulster Protestantism is well known. But in Gaelic poetry also there is an identification with the people of the Old Testament:

> *Clann Israel uair san Éigipt*
> *Fá an-bhruid nirt námhad Dé*

'The children of Israel in Egypt under the oppression of the power of the enemies of God.' The Gaels were the children of Israel and of course 'the enemies of God' were the Protestants, who were themselves the children of Israel in their own eyes.

One could say that Ireland was inhabited, not really by Protestants and Catholics but by two sets of imaginary Jews.

In theory Irish Catholics and Ulster Protestants shared a religion of love. But they shared also a belief in a God of love, who is ready to torture throughout eternity anyone who seriously offends Him. In these conditions 'love' becomes something of a technical term. You were supposed to love your neighbour, even of the 'opposite' religion, but as his beliefs and behaviour were obviously so offensive as to mark him out for hell-fire it didn't seem to matter if you knocked him about a bit in this life, if only to prepare him for what was coming to him in the next. It didn't mean you didn't 'love' him, as God 'loved' the sinner to whom he handed out eternal torment.

Crude perversions of Christian belief no doubt, yet they, and generations of Christian clergy propounding something very like them have helped to shape the present scene, extending local tribal ill-feelings to cosmic dimensions.

Since the rise of the oecumenical movement many Christian clergymen, and laymen and women, have been trying valiantly to undo the results of this past and to make the relationship a genuinely loving one. If we reach Model A they may have time for this. But the past drives towards Model B.

ii

Mary Holland has written of the extraordinary nature of the Catholic community in Derry, 'the tightly knit loyalties built around chapels and schools, the fact that the whole identity of the community, its tribal senses, centre on being Catholic'.[4]

This is certainly true, and true also of other communities, both Catholic and Protestant, in Ireland. It gives in a nutshell the reason why the division between the two communities can never be defined in purely political terms, and why it is ridiculous to dismiss religion as 'irrelevant'. But when Mary Holland, in the same article, implies that a major clash between the Official I.R.A. and the Church may be building up, and that this will be a good thing if it leads to the overthrow of clerical authority by the Officials, I must differ with her strongly on both points. In the first place this somewhat phantom clash between the Church and the Fenians (I.R.A., I.R.B., Sinn Féin, Republican Movement) is more than a hundred years old. The Fenians can neither subvert the Church (nor do most of them wish to) nor can the Church quell the Fenians. When the Church condemns patriotic violence the Church becomes inaudible,[5] without losing its authority in other spheres, such as sex. The fact is that the Fenians and the Church never really meet head on.

[4] Article 'The Church and the I.R.A.', *New Statesman*, 2nd June 1972.
[5] Unless the people, for other reasons, want to listen as in 1922. Hopefully this may apply now.

This is because they are involved in different sections of the 'Irish Catholic religion', as broadly defined above. The Church are concerned with the *Catholic* end of Irish Catholicism: the Fenians, belonging to the *Irish* end, are felt to fall outside the Church's sphere of jurisdiction, in respect of their Irish patriotic activities. So when a Bishop condemns the I.R.A., and an I.R.A. man replies 'mind your own business', Irish Catholics generally listen to this traditional exchange with monumental placidity. (Something similar clearly happens when a Church of Ireland Bishop tries to reprimand 'Loyalists'.)

As Péguy's Joan of Arc remarks in a similar context: 'Even if God did want that, it's none of his business.'[6]

In thinking of Official influence replacing clerical influence as involving some kind of liberation, Mary Holland presumably is thinking of the vaguely internationalist and progressive rhetoric used by the left-wing of the Republican movement. But language used to claim credit for what they would do if they had power is surely less significant than the use they have made of the power they actually have—the power that grows out of the barrel of a gun. As compared with those men who ordered—and claimed credit for—Aldershot, and the Barnhill and Best murders, among others. I have no hesitation in preferring the Bishop of Derry and Cardinal Conway any day of the week including Sunday.

I recently asked a colleague noted for his anti-clerical views:

'If you had to choose between Holy Mother Church and Cathleen ní Houlihan who would you vote for?'

It seemed a hard choice but he had no hesitation:

'Holy Mother Church every time.'

Me too.

Not that there hasn't been a dangerous amount of collusion between the two. I am not thinking here of those priests who have given various forms of support to the Provisional I.R.A.; I think these are more a sample of their community than representative of the Church, and in any case they are more than balanced by the many clergy, from Cardinal

[6] *Et quand Dieu le voudrait ce n'est pas son affaire.* Péguy was a bit of a proto-Provo.

Conway down, who have condemned I.R.A. violence more unequivocally than the Dublin Government has done. It is not their fault if their voices hardly seem to penetrate the sound barrier.[7]

What I have in mind is something more general: the role of the Churches is encouraging, exalting and extending the kind of tribal-sectarian self-righteousness which forms a culture in which violence so easily multiplies.

This is more obvious on the Protestant side. The Catholic tradition has nothing exactly corresponding to the line of demagogic Pope-baiting divines from Hanna to McKea, and including to some extent also the more complex and formidable figure of Ian Paisley. On the Catholic side the thing is subtler, or slyer, as one might expect,[8] but no less effective in inculcating the conviction that 'we' are morally superior to 'them'. The 'need' insisted on by the Hierarchy for separate schools is part of this, but really only the tip of the iceberg. Over generations the Irish Catholic clergy systematically fostered, not a militant, overt anti-Protestantism, but a well-enforced avoidance of social contact with Protestants, a sort of creeping freeze-out. The laity happily co-operated: the boycott had a sectarian edge, favouring Catholic shop-keepers as against Protestants (Loyalists).

'Irish society, both Catholic and Protestant, is not a secular society; it is a deeply religious one', said Cardinal Conway on the radio on 4th June 1972. This sounds a rather oecumenical and conciliatory sentiment but in its context this was not the case. The Cardinal was rejecting any idea of a secular Constitution since this would not reflect 'the basic values' of Irish society. These basic values, as interpreted by the Cardinal, required the continued prohibition of divorce, in all circumstances, as part of the Constitution. Many Protestant spokesmen—and a number of Catholics, including some priests—object to this provision. But it is the Cardinal who determines what a deeply religious position is. Protestants who object to the legalization of divorce in any circumstances —and there are supposed to be many of these—are 'deeply

[7] Above p. 311.
[8] Above pp. 192–4.

religious', since they adhere to the Catholic point of view laid down by the Cardinal. Protestants (or Catholics) who find that the possibility of legal divorce in certain circumstances is quite compatible with their concept of the 'moral law' do not count as being 'deeply religious'. In the last resort it is the Cardinal who decides not merely what the proper outlook is for Catholics but also *which Protestants are religious and which are not*. In practice there is little reality in the appearance of esteem for 'deeply religious' Protestants, since it is well known that these Protestants who are most strongly opposed to the so-called 'permissive society' are most apt to include Papists in the category of what ought not to be permitted. The two varieties of intolerance, different as they are in tone and presentation, in fact feed on one another and feed their cruel children, ultra-nationalism and sectarianism, Cathleen and King Billy.[9]

'Irish society, both Catholic and Protestant, is not a secular society; it is a deeply religious one.'

Considering how parts of that 'deeply religious' society were behaving all around him in that summer of 1972, the Cardinal might have asked himself whether a secular society might not be preferable to the deeply religious one, as exemplified in Belfast and Derry. There were indeed some genuinely deeply religious people, both clerical and lay, committed to Christianity as a religion of love, and acting on their commitment. But there were others, more conspicuously active that summer, who combined formal devotion with callous brutality.

I think of a girl of fifteen beaten, tarred and tied to a lamppost by the I.R.A. near a Belfast Catholic church, in order to be seen by the congregation coming out of early Mass. It does not appear, from reports, that the deeply religious congregation found anything particularly shocking in the

---

[9] The Cardinal's statement was shattering to certain moderate Protestants —Dick Ferguson, Barry White and others who had been cautiously exploring the idea of a 'New Ireland' in which both communities could meet on a basis of genuine equality of rights. They now found that the version of equality fulsomely pressed on them apparently rested on the assumption that they were, or were prepared to be, 'deeply religious', on terms laid down by the Catholic Primate.

spectacle. It would have been different, and offensive to the 'basic values', if the girl had had no clothes on.

Mr. Jack Dowling, on reading the above passage, offered some valuable comments, from which I quote the following:

'What I would want you to consider is how far the "religion of love" *did* get across. Most Protestants, I would rashly claim, have shown a positively heroic Christian fortitude and restraint, an exemplary respect for the law of non-retaliation and a real concern for civilized values which came to them from their faith. "Most" is a big claim. I think that most Catholics were (and are) outraged by civilian bomb-mutilations, murders, ghetto-bullying and contempt for girls' human dignity. I would go so far as to say that if these had not had religious convictions and habits of judgment, the tide of events in Northern Ireland would have been nearer to Pakistan than Naseby.'

Mr. Dowling's point is a valid one, within certain limits. It still seems to me, however, that a society in which such crimes as those listed are of daily occurrence, and are to some extent condoned, should preferably not be described as 'a deeply religious society', of which a secular constitution would be unworthy.

### iii

On the day I am finishing this epilogue and this book—Monday, 12th June 1972—the *Irish Times* front page headlines: 'Four shot dead in Northern Ireland: Gun Battles: Troops, Protestants and Catholics clash in Belfast'; 'Big Crowd at Grave of Wolfe Tone: Coaches stoned in Belfast'. On inside facing pages are spread out pictures of a Loyalist rally in Banbridge, and of the crowd at Bodenstown. At Bodenstown the Provisionals pledged themselves to 'continue the struggle until our country is free'. At Banbridge the word was 'no-one shall destroy Ulster's traditions and Ulster's way of life'. At Cregagh, Belfast, a Minister warned: 'Let there be no doubt that a conflagration of unbelievable horror awaits us if our people (Protestants) fail to keep their heads.'

At Bodenstown one speaker, Sean Keenan of Derry, said that: 'To-day most Republicans were Catholics by mere accident of birth'[10] (*sic*). This kind of thing—and various 'liberal', 'socialist' or (in the case of the Officials) Marxist phraseology associated with it—serves the purpose of camouflaging the reality of the civil war that imminently threatens between Irish Catholics and Ulster Protestants.

## iv

This book is neither impartial nor detached. It was written in the course of events with which it deals, and while the writer was being shaken and changed by these events. Not that the writer played any part in the course of events inside Northern Ireland: of these he was only a marginal observer. But he *was* involved in the politics of the Republic, and especially in the controversy concerning what attitude the people of the Republic should take towards the events in the North. That his part in that controversy has not been entirely insignificant, leaders of both wings of Sinn Féin-I.R.A. have acknowledged after their fashion.

*States of Ireland* is written from the Catholic, specifically Southern Catholic, side of the fence.[11] I have tried to understand some of the feelings shared by most Ulster Protestants and to communicate some notion of these feelings to Catholics in the Republic; as a result of which I have been accused of being hyper-sensitive about the Protestants, and caring little about the Catholics. In fact the reverse accusation would contain more truth. It is to the Irish Catholic community that I belong. That is my 'little platoon', to love which, according to Edmund Burke (whose family were in that same platoon), 'is the first, the germ, as it were, of publick affections'. I am motivated by affection for that platoon,

[10] He also referred unfavourably to 'agnostics like Conor Cruise O'Brien' (Boos and groans). He might have referred with equal truth and greater relevance to 'agnostics like Wolfe Tone': the ironic inhabitant of what the speaker called 'the holiest spot in Ireland'.

[11] I am interested here in a socio-political fence, not a primarily theological one. Above, *passim*.

identification with it, and fear that it may destroy itself, including me, through infatuation with its own mythology.

I fear primarily for the Northern Catholics, for what can happen to them, if the Provisionals or some similar future organization succeed in precipitating the advent of Model B. But in a more intimate sense I fear for the people of the South, for *us*, if Model B becomes a reality, or even if there is a major oscillation in that direction. If the worst happened, everything and everyone I like in Ireland would go under, while a sort of Irish equivalent of the Greece of the Colonels took over. In these conditions the people who could get out would be the lucky ones. That may seem a remote nightmare. Unfortunately it seems less remote as I write than it did when it first came to me, two years ago.

May it seem more remote by the time this book appears.

# Appendix

Statement by Conor Cruise O'Brien in public debate with Tomás Mac Giolla, President of Sinn Féin (Official) at Newman House, Dublin on 23rd October 1971.

Mr. Tomás Mac Giolla is President of Sinn Féin. But what does it mean, to be President of Sinn Féin? It would be impossible, I believe, in any other country in Western Europe to find a parallel for what it means.

Sinn Féin is the open, civilian legal expression of a secret and illegal army.

Mr. Mac Giolla appears as head of an organization, but he is not really head of it. The real head is Mr. Cathal Goulding, Chief of Staff of the Official I.R.A.

Many of you in this hall, I have no doubt, are clear about that relation. I would ask the rest of you to keep it firmly in mind, because it is essential to an understanding of the true meaning of this debate.

I speak here for a Party which accepts normal democratic process. That acceptance includes recognition of the legitimate authority of an elected government which one does not like, and which one seeks to replace by democratic process. We wish Mr. Jack Lynch were not Taoiseach, but we recognise that he is Taoiseach because the people of this State—living, breathing Irish people, making marks on pieces of paper—decided in 1969 that in terms of Dáil Deputies elected it was Mr. Lynch they wanted.

Mr. Mac Giolla, on the other hand, speaks for a movement which recognizes no validity in that transaction.

For that movement true, legitimate authority is derived only from the generations of the dead who died for Ireland,

and is properly wielded in the present by the organization of men and women prepared to repeat the blood sacrifice.

To some people, and certainly to a significant minority in this country, that idea—of the authority of the dead and those who volunteer to die—will seem more noble than democracy. I would even agree. It is more noble. Being noble is what it is all about.

To belong to a military elite is noble—in the strictest, earliest meaning of the word—and the authority of a military elite is the real present-day meaning of this movement. The dead can only validate: real power is wielded by the living military elite. They decide who is to die and when, and they possess the prestige which the power to decide that confers.

Unpretentious though they may sometimes be in dress and manner, they are in fact aristocrats, Samurai, no ordinary people, and subject to no common measure. Mr. Mac Giolla is the spokesman here for that military elite, and for nothing else.

Democracy, on the other hand, is not noble, and not compatible with the ideals of a military elite. Under democracy, civilians, not soldiers, have supreme power. And literally all sorts of people join in the choice of those civilians. The man who likes greyhound racing and reads the *Daily Mirror* has the same vote as a dedicated patriot who reads the *United Irishman*. People who value peace above national unification have votes. The military elite for which Mr. Mac Giolla speaks decides that these votes don't count. For us, who accept democracy, all the votes count, and the dead don't vote.

Now this division, between those who accept democracy and those who don't accept it, is fundamental. If people disagree about that, their verbal agreement on other political matters is utterly deceptive.

There are, apparently, many common elements in the Labour Party programme, and the Sinn Féin programme. Some people in both organizations imagined that it would be possible to build a common effort of the two parties on those common elements. That is an illusion, because the Labour Party and Sinn Féin are radically different entities, divided on this fundamental issue of democracy.

For us, socialism is not only something to be striven for

through democratic process; it is also itself an extension of democratic process, the placing of the essential resources and skills of a country—and eventually of the world—under public control, responsible to the people as a whole. Sinn Féin might agree with much of that, verbally. But they would not mean the same things we mean. By 'the people' we mean something precise, measurable, even hum-drum.

Here and now, we mean all the men and women on the electoral register of this State. Sinn Féin may occasionally condescend to address itself to that electorate, but it recognizes nothing conclusive in its verdict. It does not recognize, for example, the right of the living people, through its elected parliament and government, to control the armed forces of the State, and to suppress private armies. It cannot recognize that right, because it is itself the political extension of a private army.

Sinn Féin in fact reserves to itself—or rather to the army which it serves—the right to set aside as invalid any decisions of the people, or its elected representatives, which the private army does not like. Such decisions are not, in Sinn Féin's view, decisions of the people at all, because Sinn Féin is itself the expression of the will of the people, irrespective of the ballot.

'The people' in Sinn Féin's vocabulary becomes a term of art, a tricky term carrying any specific meaning which it suits Sinn Féin to ascribe to it from time to time, but carrying always the general overtones of a mystic and irrational concept: an imprescriptible and inalienable quality, inherent in Irish nationhood, of which the guardians, guarantors and executants are the I.R.A., whether the actual living Irish people, in any given generation, like it or not.

We, on the other hand, are for the living people. We reject Sinn Féin's mystical concept of the people. We reject it on behalf of living people whom we represent, and who do not want it.

We reject it on behalf of a socialist tradition, concerned with living realities, and recognizing always that mystical politics, the language of sacred soil and the cult of the dead, are part of the apparatus of the enemy.

And we reject it above all as rational beings, intent on using our minds to understand and change society, and utterly
denying the right of the dead, or of their living servants, to
put a veto on our thinking, on our speech or on our power of
decision.

I accept that Mr. Tomás Mac Giolla is sincere in his
adherence to his concept of socialism, and in his abhorrence
of Fascism. I understand that Mr. Cathal Goulding shares
these views and feelings. Unfortunately the subjective aspirations and intentions of individual leaders have little
importance in comparison with the objective momentum of
the private army, the logic of the gun.

You may be as benevolent as you like in your ultimate
intentions, the society to which you aspire may be just,
socialist and democratic and altogether more admirable
than the society in which we actually live.

But if you set out to bring the society you want into
existence, through denying the validity of democratic process
in the society you actually have; if you set out to win it
through a private army, withdrawn from democratic control;
if you set out to win it by exploiting the latent forces of
romantic nationalism and hatred of foreigners, and if you
hope to control these forces by authoritarian methods in
your Republic within a Republic—if you set out in this way,
then I say to you that the forces you hope to use and control
will use and control *you*.

Your movement will *not* move in the direction of socialism,
not if we accept the idea that socialism must have a democratic base and content. In certain conditions, a movement
like yours could perhaps move in the direction of authoritarian State socialism, a kind of Stalinism. But in a country
like ours, with its great weight of social conservatism and
profound distrust of Communism, it is not in that direction
either that your movement can hope to succeed. It is not in
the direction of any kind of socialism, even authoritarian
socialism, that your movement will go. Where it is going is
towards Fascism.

It is going in that direction because Fascism is the natural
destination of an anti-democratic, militarist, authoritarian,

ultra-nationalist movement, whose ultimate appeal is a mystique inaccessible to reason. These elements are in fact among the principal distinguishing marks of Fascism, and all of them are abundantly present already in your movement.

This is not speculation. We know what has *already* happened to your movement. We know that, before August 1969, some of you tried to take the emphasis off the gun and the bomb, although you never finally disavowed these. You tried, to your credit, to put the emphasis on social objectives. The emphasis is now back on the gun and the bomb. There is nothing surprising about that, because the gun and the bomb are what your movement is about.

The I.R.A. is now waging sectarian civil war in Northern Ireland. Not us, you tell us—the Provisionals. Maybe so. What difference does it make? Have not the Provisionals as good a right to call themselves the I.R.A. as you have? Is not their right to take life just as good or as bad as yours? We deny that right to both of you, not just to them.

You tell us that you were in the majority, they in a minority at a certain meeting. Majority! Minority! How can *you* talk to us of majorities and minorities, those democratic concepts for which the whole history of your movement shows such a sovereign contempt? You have been defying majority rule ever since the Treaty.

Ah, but, you may tell us, the pro-Treaty majority in the country, and all the various majorities since then, were made up of simple people, who were led astray by bad Irishmen, traitors to the nation. A majority at a Sinn Féin Ard-Fheis, attended only by enlightened and patriotic people, is something else again.

But this does not hold water. The Dáil which approved the Treaty was itself a Sinn Féin assembly, and the minority then decided the majority did not count. Why should not the Provisionals decide likewise? Why should *they* not exercise the right you *all* arrogated to yourselves—that of deciding who is a good Irishman and who a bad one, whose vote should count and whose should not? They have decided *your* votes don't count. What right have *you* to complain?

Once you reject democratic process, and set the example

of the private army, there is nothing to prevent any determined group which can get its hands on guns and bombs,
from setting up as the true heirs of the national tradition.
There is, indeed, a way of deciding between such forces. It is
not the democratic way, for you are living—all of you—
outside the democratic rules. It is the arbitrament of force,
the ecology of the gun.

The closer your movement approaches to success, if it
does approach success, the more it will be a movement
dominated by the most efficient and ruthless gunmen.
Whether they call themselves Provisionals or Officials does
not matter very much. What does matter is that these will
not be people who were drawn to your movement by socialist
idealism.

They will be people who were attracted to you by the
fascination of the gun and the bomb and the power these
represent. There are also wealthy men, and ambitious
politicians, who are interested in the potential of such gunmen. Alliance between that kind of wealth, that kind of
politics, and that kind of gunman is not only possible: it
already exists.

This alliance may not succeed. But if any kind of politics
based on the use of private armies *does* succeed, that is the
kind of politics that it will be; not the socialism of Mr. Mac
Giolla but the Right-wing nationalism of a Blaney, or a
Haughey or a Boland. If it triumphs here—as it might if
things get bad enough in the North—then our State will be
like the Greece of the Colonels. What else can be expected if
we allow private armies to destroy a working democracy?

Many people who dislike i.r.a. operations in the Twenty-
six Counties approve its operations in the North. 'They are
defending our people.' But who *are* 'our people'? Do they
include the Ulster Protestants, or don't they? If they do, it
would be hard to convince Ulster Protestants that they are
being defended by the i.r.a. In fact i.r.a. elements are using
random terror methods against the Protestant population.

These are *Provisional* tactics, you will tell me. No doubt,
but it doesn't matter much to Protestants who are killed or
injured, or to their friends, which particular Catholic private

army did which particular job. In fact the process whereby, after each new horror, each private army issues its solemn claim to the deed, or its repudiation, or even condemnation —this process has become nauseatingly familiar, as a kind of bureaucratic aftermath of murder.

To the Protestant population—almost without exception —i.r.a., in *all* its varieties, it seen both as a cruel and deadly enemy, and as the expression of the hostility of the Catholic community towards Protestants. That is what your latter-day Republicans have succeeded in doing with Wolfe Tone's ideal of the common name of Irishman.

I am not defending or extenuating British Army brutalities, nor the violence of Protestant extremists, nor am I saying that the i.r.a. has a monopoly of violence.

But i.r.a. violence must concern us here, not only because this debate is with the President of Sinn Fein, but because this is the form of violence now on the offensive and because it is a form of violence which derives its emotional sustenance from the community to which most of us here belong—the Irish Catholic community—and therefore something with which our responsibility is especially engaged. I am here to deny that it has a mandate for what it is doing, and to deny also that any good can come from its activities.

The claim of the i.r.a. to be the defenders of the minority —the Catholics—is unfounded. When that minority was in serious danger at the hands of Protestant extremists, in August 1969, the i.r.a. was not much in evidence. It became a significant force only *after* the British Army had been deployed to protect the minority.

And what the i.r.a. set itself to do was to break the fraternization which then existed between the Catholic people and the British troops and which was unacceptable in terms of i.r.a. doctrine. So the i.r.a. encouraged provocations against the troops, and then 'defended' the Catholics from the troops who had been provoked.

The defence involved the killing of troops, and turned the army altogether against the Catholics. The combinations of killings of soldiers and killings of Protestants have brought about a situation whereby, in Belfast, a Catholic minority is being protected by British forces which detest it, and which it detests, against the elemental wrath of a Protestant majority which would wipe out the Catholics, and the I.R.A. along with them, if the troops were withdrawn.

That is the situation which the Catholics of Belfast owe to the I.R.A. and its methods of defence. All this is being done, of course, not only for the defence of the Catholics, but for the unity of Ireland—and indeed the confusion between these two quite separate concepts is responsible for much of the hideous mess which has been created.

It is crazy to believe that unity could be won by these methods, or that if it could be won it would be anything but a terrible and burdensome irony for the survivors.

Here the Northern Catholic bishops have asked the appropriate question: 'Who in their sane senses wants to bomb a million Protestants into a United Ireland?' Who wants to— and also, who in their sane senses thinks they can do it? The attempt can not result in unity. It could if it is persisted in result in U.D.I. in the North, in civil war, in the liquidation of the Catholic minority in the Belfast region, in a new border and in two Fascist States, Orange and Green.

That is the maximum extent of the kind of 'success' which this movement, and this campaign, can achieve. And to achieve even that would cost tens of thousands of lives. The campaign has only recently entered its second hundred.

I would ask those of you who entered this movement because it sounded radical and progressive to think again, and begin to think your way out of it. I know it is not easy to do. They have offered you what looked like a brilliant short-cut to a brighter future, an Ireland transformed as well as united.

We, who are committed to the democratic process, cannot pretend we have any short-cut. It is a long haul, even until Labour is as strong here as it is in the rest of Western Europe. There are many reasons for that. One of them is the appeal of romantic nationalism, and the cult of the dead—forces ably exploited by Fianna Fáil, but gripping many others, including members of Sinn Féin.

We are trying to substitute for that a politics of the living, the struggle for better conditions in the here and now, without brilliant short-cuts, without blood, without the heady wine of the Apocalypse: a politics in which both reason and compassion will be vital components.

Those who had the idea of drawing Sinn-Féin-minded people into the Labour movement and Labour Party were right, in the sense that Labour needs people with that kind of energy and dedication.

We need them, that is, provided they are prepared to abandon the short-cut, to make a clear and final break with the politics of the secret army, and commit themselves unreservedly to working for socialism by democratic means and those alone.

We have in our ranks already a certain number of people who have passed through these fires, who have made that painful and courageous break, and entered into that unreserved commitment. It is no exaggeration to say that on such choices, now being weighed in many minds, the future of our country, and the survival of democracy among us, now depend.

# Index